Classics and Contemporary Thought,
edited by Thomas Habinek

I. Catullan Provocations: Lyric Poetry and the Drama of Position, by William Fitzgerald

II. Reading Sappho: Contemporary Approaches, edited by Ellen Greene

III. Re-reading Sappho: Reception and Transmission, edited by Ellen Greene

IV. Tragedy and Enlightenment: Athenian Political Thought and the Dilemmas of Modernity, by Christopher Rocco

V. Warriors into Traders: The Power of the Market in Early Greece, by David W. Tandy

Tragedy and Enlightenment

Tragedy and Enlightenment

Athenian Political Thought and the Dilemmas of Modernity

Christopher Rocco

UNIVERSITY OF CALIFORNIA PRESS
Berkeley · Los Angeles · London

University of California Press
Berkeley and Los Angeles, California

University of California Press, Ltd.
London, England

Library of Congress Cataloging-in-Publication Data

Rocco, Christopher, 1958–
Tragedy and enlightenment : Athenian political thought and the dilemmas of modernity / Christopher Rocco.
p. cm. — (Classics and contemporary thought ; 4)
Includes bibliographical references and index.
ISBN 0-520-20494-8 (alk. paper)
1. Greek drama (Tragedy)—History and criticism—Theory, etc. 2. Greek drama (Tragedy)—History and criticism. 3. Civilization, Western—Greek influences. 4. Philosophy, Ancient. 5. Philosophy, Modern. 6. Enlightenment. 7. Plato. I. Title. II. Series.
PA3131.R57 1997 96-11600
882′.0109—dc20 CIP

Printed in the United States of America
9 8 7 6 5 4 3 2 1

The paper used in this publication meets the minimum requirements of American National Standard for Information Sciences—Permanence of Paper for Printed Library Materials, ANSI Z39.48-1984.

The splinter in your eye is the best magnifying glass.

Theodor Adorno, *Minima Moralia*

To my parents, Haidee and Frank Rocco,
and to the memory of Elizabeth Suzanne

Contents

Acknowledgements

This book has had many sources of inspiration over the years, and I have looked forward with pleasure to this moment of public acknowledgement. I first conceived (albeit most dimly) of the improbable, although profound, relationship between Athenian political thought (especially Socratic-Platonic philosophy) and various strands of contemporary theory as an earnest but ignorant student in the classroom of Manfred Henningsen while an undergraduate at the University of Hawaii. Manfred simultaneously introduced me to Greek thought, the critical theory of the Frankfurt School, and French poststructuralism. It is no exaggeration to say that the present volume is the result of my attempt to make sense of that first meeting. To him I owe a lifelong intellectual debt: he kindled in me the wonder at the world that, according to Aristotle, is the beginning of philosophy. Although it has been hard to convince parents, friends, subsequent teachers, and present colleagues that I did more than surf during my years in paradise, the political science department at UH provided then, and continues to provide, an exemplary program in political theory. Manfred Henningsen, Michael Shapiro, Henry Kariel, and (now) Kathy Ferguson can all attest to the fact that thinking and surfing are not mutually exclusive activities. As long as I am mentioning formative intellectual debts, I also wish to thank Adrian Kuzminski, who at the time taught European intellectual history, did not believe in political theory at all, yet humored me anyway. He was then, and continues now to be, a good friend.

Graduate study did little to dampen my enthusiasm for exploring the improbable connection between ancient Athenian thought and contemporary social and political theory. As an undergraduate I had been fortunate enough to have negotiated the theory/science wars of the time by assiduously avoiding political science, while avidly devouring every political theory and philosophy course I could. That fortune stayed with me as a graduate student: political science at UC San Diego had marginalized theory in a department that was fast gaining fame for its program in comparative politics. I was left free to pursue my idea, and my theory teacher there, Tracy Strong, encouraged my endeavors. He also did two other things: he suggested that if I was serious about the Greeks, I ought to learn their language, and then he introduced me to Peter Euben. I spent the next year studying Greek with Elliot Wirshbo and the following quarter (thanks to Strong and Euben) studying Athenian thought (and much more) at UC Santa Cruz. I eventually left San Diego for Santa Cruz, and it was there, through the generosity of Euben, his colleague John Schaar, and the Board of Studies in Politics, that I continued to study both classical and contemporary thought. Seminars with Euben and Schaar in political theory, as well as with David Hoy in philosophy, remain foundational experiences for my present thinking. They also remain the most satisfying and pleasurable intellectual experiences in my memory. These were times and locations where I could freely pursue what was becoming an obviously interdisciplinary project, one that drew on classical studies, political theory, structural anthropology, hermeneutics, critical theory, feminism, and poststructuralism. Fellow and sister graduate students Mark Nechodom, Mark Reinhardt, Rick Zinman, Paige Baty, Steve Rugare, Karen Davis, Mary John, Bruce Bauman, Avram Davis, and Suzanne Reading constituted a vibrant intellectual community throughout my stay at Santa Cruz. These were political *thinkers* all, not one of them familiar with the methodological niceties and instrumental subtleties of a "data sack" (*sic*).

At UCSC I continued to read in Greek, with Seth Schein, Gary Miles, and John Lynch, largely dividing my time between Cowell and Kresge Colleges, between Mary Kay Gamel's fine productions of Greek tragedies and the ultra postmodern performances of Hayden White, Donna Haraway, Jim Clifford, and Teresa de Lauretis. I had found the perfect place either to become schizophrenic or continue work on my project. My "phrens" relatively intact, I eventually did complete a dissertation that vaguely resembled what this book was finally to become. For both of these achievements I wish to thank UC Santa Cruz and Peter Euben. Peter not only convinced me of the importance of Greek tragedy but was an unparallelled intellectual mentor and friend. He remains exemplary for me to this day. I should also thank Peter for indulging my addiction to large quantities of food and drink: never did a more generous host frequent the numerous and excellent restaurants and bars of Santa Cruz. Both Peter and Olga Euben deserve credit for sustaining me intellectually as well as physically during my five years there as a graduate student.

I then took a job in the political science department at the University of Connecticut. Everyone who knows me also knows the extent of my debt to that institution. My colleagues in political theory, Rich Hiskes and Ernie Zirakzadeh, have done more than I shall probably ever know to facilitate my work. They have also provided me with unconditional support. Tom Giolas, director of the University of Connecticut Research Foundation, materially sustained this project from its very beginnings with numerous grants, among them a Junior Faculty Summer Fellowship, which relieved me from teaching at a crucial time during the book's writing. I am also grateful to Robert Vrecenak, director of the Interlibrary Loan Department, his assistant Lynn Sweet, and all their staff for their tireless and unfailing efforts to procure for me an endless stream of books, articles, and other research materials from around the country. This book would not have been completed without their assistance.

It was in Connecticut that this book took its present form, the last stage in a long metamorphosis that had begun with an inchoate idea, more felt than known, many years previously. I would like to thank Charles Hedrick (whom I did not have the pleasure of knowing at UCSC, since his arrival and my departure coincided) and Thomas Habinek (the editor of Classics and Contemporary Thought, the series in which this book appears), as well as an anonymous reviewer for the University of California Press, for their comments on, and commitment to, the manuscript. Special thanks go to Mark Reinhardt of Williams College, who, since our time together at Santa Cruz, has remained an important intellectual companion and colleague. Much of what is good in this book resulted from lengthy telephone conversations with him. He also read large portions of the manuscript, and the book has benefited immensely because his keen eye saw what was needed when my own vision failed. Most of all, though, I owe a tremendous debt to Joel Schwartz, who read every version of the manuscript with unflagging patience and good cheer. It was his faith in the project that kept it (and me) alive during the desperately cold intellectual winters that regularly traverse northeastern Connecticut. Without his vision, faith and patience, this book would not be in print. Mary Lamprech of the University of California Press deserves abundant praise for her work on this project. She too saw its promise and encouraged me through the most trying stages of revision. She has been everything one can hope for in an editor. I also wish to thank Peter Dreyer, whose expert copyediting saved me from mistakes I was unaware I had committed. A number of graduate students at the University of Connecticut have suffered through the writing of this book as I tested my ideas on them in seminars. Thanks to Catherine Flavin, Steve McDonald, Julie Walsh, John Burns, Amanda Ross, Dave Johnson, Jane O'Neill, Yvonne Davis, Jessica Kulynych, and Carole Steen for stimulating discussions that forced me to be clear and precise.

Throughout the entire writing of this book, my family has provided unfailing love and support. Suzanne Reading has been with me since its beginning, and it is largely on her shoulders that this book has been written. It is customary to acknowledge the support of one's spouse, "without whom . . . ," as the saying goes. I have seen no acknowledgments that would do her justice. Suffice it to say that this book was completed because Suzanne Reading agreed to move across a continent (leaving family and friends behind), thereby delaying her own career for the past five years. It is no exaggeration to say that my career has flourished at her expense. This book explores the dynamics of constructing masculine civic space literally on the bodies of women. As material and intellectual object, the book exists because gender inequality and the exploitative wages of university instructors have yet to be righted in a society that insufficiently values women. This situation has produced a debt I doubtless cannot repay in my lifetime. Let us work to repay it in the lifetime of our children. I also owe a debt to our oldest daughter, Rashelle, for having the endless patience to endure with forbearance and even good humor a two-academic family. I can only apologize for the boring dinner conversations over the years (as well as for no television). Sophia, our youngest daughter (and appropriately named), has provided unrelenting relief and inspiration over the past four years. She has taught me firsthand the most important insights of the tragic theater: vulnerability, fragility, the irruption of the unexpected, the contradictoriness of experience, and the irreducible complexity of human life. Gabriella, who is not yet here, but whom we have anticipated for a long time and with great joy, has constantly reminded me of the mysteries of life. I know she will be ready for the world. I can only hope that the world will be ready for her.

I dedicate this book to my parents, Haidee and Frank Rocco, who, in the face of my father's fight with cancer, have shown remarkable faith, courage, love, and hope. That my father has lived to see the publication of this book is truly the triumph of a heroic spirit. I also dedicate this book to the memory of our daughter Elizabeth Suzanne, who was never destined to see the faces of a mother and father who had so much love to give her. Her untimely death taught us that suffering can, and often does, bring wisdom.

Introduction

The Persistence of the Past

I do not know what meaning classical studies could have for our time if they were not untimely—that is to say, acting counter to our time and thereby acting on our time and, let us hope, for the benefit of a time to come.

—Friedrich Nietzsche, "The Use and Abuse of History for Life," in *Untimely Meditations*

We are much less Greeks than we believe. We are neither in the amphitheater nor on the stage, but in the panoptic machine.

—Michel Foucault, *Discipline and Punish*

TAKING LEAVE OF ANTIQUITY?

We are much more Greeks than we care to admit.

I say this in full knowledge that current academic fashion tends to ignore, debunk, or otherwise dismiss classical Athens. Social scientists reject the idea(l) of Athenian democracy as more fantasy than fact, while deeming the moral claims made by Plato and Aristotle on behalf of the polis and its politics radically incommensurable with the realities of the large, structurally differentiated, functionally interdependent, modern nation-state. Social historians carefully reconstruct the practices of everyday life in order to debunk the "glory that was Greece" by reminding us, rightly of the cruel and objectionable practices and institutions upon which the ancient ideal of civic freedom rested: slavery, the subjugation of women, and acute xenophobia. Feminist critics reveal the deep structures of Greek literature and philosophy as irredeemably misogynist, while one recent investigation of classical Athens has endeavored to unmask the popular view of the Greeks as a construction of nineteenth-century racist historiography.[1]

But fashion changes. While Nietzsche's observation that the value of classical studies lies in their untimeliness remains as appropriate as ever, recent developments make possible a new appropriation of the literary and philosophical works of classical Athens. A sea change similar to the one that recently reconfigured the global political map has begun to transform the study of classical Greece. While a conventional division of labor still holds sway at the core of the field, some rebellious scholars have breached disciplinary walls. In an intellectual disturbance remarkable for its innovation and daring, classicists have increasingly come to adopt historical, philosophical, and poststructuralist literary methods in their analyses of ancient texts. Conversely, scholars from such diverse fields as philosophy, comparative literature, historical sociology, and political science now move on terrain that was once the exclusive property of classical philologists.[2] These deliberate trespasses against the conventions of scholarly rectitude yield surprising results: epic and tragic poetry suddenly contribute to our understanding of concepts such as agency, responsibility, autonomy, and freedom, which are usually associated with the philosophical tradition; instead of being consigned to the "primitive" stage of archaic thought, Greek tragedy is now recognized as playing a constitutive role in the emergence of clas-

1. On the devaluation of classical political thought by the behavioral revolution, see Sheldon Wolin, "Political Theory as a Vocation," *American Political Science Review* [hereafter cited as *APSR*] 63, 4 (Dec. 1969). For a dismissal of the moral and political claims of the ancient polis, see Robert Dahl, *Democracy and Its Critics* (New Haven, Conn.: Yale University Press, 1989), as well as Stephen T. Holmes, "Aristippus in and out of Athens," *APSR* 73, 1 (Mar. 1979): 113–27. For recent social history, see Orlando Patterson, *Freedom*, vol. 1: *Freedom in the Making of the Western World* (New York: Basic Books, 1991). A few feminist examples are Kate Millett, *Sexual Politics* (Garden City, N.Y.: Doubleday, 1971); Susan Okin, *Women in Western Political Thought* (Princeton, N.J.: Princeton University Press, 1979); Jean Bethke Elshtain, *Public Man, Private Woman* (Princeton, N.J.: Princeton University Press, 1981); Nancy Hartsock, *Money, Sex and Power: Toward a Feminist Historical Materialism* (New York: Longman, 1983), and Mary O'Brien, *The Politics of Reproduction* (Boston: Routledge & Kegan Paul, 1981). On the construction of Greece by German classicists, see Martin Bernal, *Black Athena: The Afroasiatic Roots of Classical Civilization*, vol. 1 (New Brunswick, N.J.: Rutgers University Press, 1987)

2. A few examples among classicists are Charles Segal, J.-P. Vernant, Pierre Vidal-Naquet, Simon Goldhill, John J. Winkler, Froma Zeitlin, and Josiah Ober. See also John Peradotto, *Man in the Middle Voice: Name and Narration in the Odyssey* (Princeton, N.J.: Princeton University Press, 1990), ch. 1, for an account of the influence of poststructuralism on classical scholarship. On the invasion of classics by nonspecialists, see *Athenian Political Thought and the Reconstruction of American Democracy*, ed. J. Peter Euben, Josiah Ober, and John Wallach (Ithaca, N.Y.: Cornell University Press, 1994), introduction.

sical political theory and as informing the "tradition" of Western political thought. Meanwhile, the central moral and ethical claims of classical philosophy have been cast in a new light, and are now being studied with reference to Greek literature's preoccupation with moral deliberation and choice.[3]

As traditional academic disciplines continue to redraw their boundaries, Greek poetry and philosophy find themselves at the center of some of the most important philosophical, political, and ethical debates of the present day (consider, for instance, the controversy over a multicultural curriculum and the relevance of "canonical" texts to education). This newfound immediacy requires as a condition for successful interpretation that scholars bring the past close enough to make the Greeks intelligible and yet keep them sufficiently distant to preserve their otherness. As a result, the barriers between the ancient and modern world have become more permeable, the archaic past has become a more frequent interlocutor of the modern (or postmodern) present, and the present less sure about "progress" and its own position of moral, political, and cultural hegemony over the past. Given such historical and cultural decentering, "later" no longer inevitably means better. These deliberate trangressions of both culturally and temporally constituted boundaries facilitate an appropriation of the classical past in ways that require it to speak to the most pressing problems of the present moment *and* avoid nostalgia for a world that perhaps never was. Such are the tasks of historical and cultural translation that take us from the modern (or postmodern) to the ancient world and back again. And although this labor is both difficult and necessarily always incomplete, it tells us that, by better understanding the Greeks, we can perhaps begin better to understand ourselves. I intend this book as a modest contribution to the search for political and theoretical self-understanding that motivates this most recent "classical turn."

In the absence of a more finely detailed and richly textured survey of a rapidly changing field, my account of the recent (anti)disciplinary disturbances in classical scholarship necessarily remains incomplete. Yet the transformations sketched briefly here undoubtedly suggest alternative paths to the past: the drawing of fresh maps proclaims old territory

3. See Bernard Williams, *Shame and Necessity* (Berkeley: University of California Press, 1993); J. Peter Euben, *The Tragedy of Political Theory: The Road Not Taken* (Princeton, N.J.: Princeton University Press, 1990); Martha Nussbaum, *The Fragility of Goodness: Luck and Ethics in Greek Literature and Philosophy* (Cambridge: University of Cambridge Press, 1986).

now open for renewed exploration. These disturbances thus make possible an imaginative and critical reappropriation of ancient Athenian thought. A growing number of contemporary social and literary theorists, none of whom harbor sympathetic attitudes toward the classical past, have in fact already begun this work. Thoroughly modern (or postmodern) in their concerns and methods, these theorists nonetheless remain engaged, in some way or on some level, with the Greeks: Michel Foucault with the Sophists, Jacques Derrida with Plato's *Phaedrus,* Jean-François Lyotard with Aristotle's *Rhetoric,* and Jürgen Habermas with the classical conceptions of dialogue and deliberation.[4] Moreover, contemporary democratic theorists, interested in what they variously call the "public sphere," the "public realm," or simply the "political," find themselves turning more and more to the central categories of Athenian political thought. Although the most current disputes over the constitution of political space, the public sphere, and the politics of identity and difference have been inspired by Habermas and Foucault, these discussions inevitably return (via Nietzsche and Hannah Arendt) to the deliberative and performative aspects of classical Greek politics. Feminists, who once excoriated those unredeemed (and presumably unredeemable) heroic aspects of the masculine polis, have now begun to theorize an "agonistic feminism." Postmoderns still committed to democratic institutions and practices—yet who otherwise suspect as bad nostalgia a politics of place monumentalized in the memory of the "democratic" Greek polis—are tentatively formulating a concept of "agonistic democracy." Even those moderns who defend rational discursive content against performative practice acknowledge the force and appeal of Athenian-inspired virtuosity and theatricality in politics.[5]

4. See Foucault's essay "Nietzsche, Genealogy, History," in *The Foucault Reader,* ed. Paul Rabinow (New York: Pantheon Books, 1984); Jacques Derrida, "Plato's Pharmacy," in *Dissemination,* trans. Barbara Johnson (Chicago: University of Chicago Press, 1981); Jean-François Lyotard and Jean-Loup Thébaud, *Just Gaming,* trans. Wlad Godzich (Minneapolis: University of Minnesota Press, 1985); and Jürgen Habermas, *Theory and Practice,* trans. John Viertel (Boston: Beacon Press, 1973), and *The Theory of Communicative Action: Reason and the Rationalization of Society,* trans. Thomas McCarthy (Boston: Beacon Press, 1984, 1987).

5. See, e.g., Dana Villa, "Postmodernism and the Public Sphere," *APSR* 86, 3 (Sept. 1992): 712–21; Bonnie Honig, "Arendt, Identity and Difference," *Political Theory* 16, 1 (Feb. 1988): 77–98; Chantal Mouffe, ed., *Dimensions of Radical Democracy* (New York: Verso, 1992), and id., "Democratic Citizenship and the Political Community," in *Feminists Theorize the Political,* ed. Judith Butler and Joan Scott, pp. 369–84 (New York: Routledge, 1992). For feminist criticisms of Arendt, see, e.g., Patricia Springborg, "Hannah Arendt and the Classical Republican Tradition," in *Thinking, Judging, Freedom,* ed. G. T. Kaplan and C. S. Kessler (Sydney: G. Allen & Unwin, 1989), pp. 9–17;

Whether we want to fashion a postmodern agonistic subjectivity that disrupts the regulative ideal of rational consensus or to redeem the enlightenment promise of a society comprised of deliberating citizens, ancient Athens has ironically become a site of contest for thinking about the most current problems in theory and politics, especially for those most likely to resist its claims and reject its authority.

These struggles—fought on and over the theoretical and political topography of the ancient city-state—represent neither a petty war over academic turf of dubious value nor merely a passing fancy for things antique. They indicate, rather, the continued presence of a deep and abiding conflict. The present dispute over who shall control the meaning of the classical polis provokes some of the most important issues challenging us today. For encoded in the contest over how that past is to be interpreted, represented, and subsequently appropriated—as stable origin for a culturally hegemonic reason or as shifting site for a disturbing sophistic (ant)agonism—is a struggle over the legacy of the Enlightenment, and so over the very character and identity of modernity. Obviously, these disputes over the classical polis are as much, if not more, about who we are now, how we ought to live, and what forms our intellectual, social, and political institutions shall take as they are about

Wendy L. Brown, *Manhood and Politics: A Feminist Reading in Political Theory* (Totowa, N.J.: Rowman & Littlefield, 1988). On the concept of agonistic feminism, see Bonnie Honig, "Toward an Agonistic Feminism," in *Feminists Theorize,* pp. 215–35. But see now also her recent book *Political Theory and the Displacement of Politics* (Ithaca, N.Y.: Cornell University Press, 1993). Exceptions to this are Hanna Pitkin's attempt, in "Justice: On Relating Public and Private," *Political Theory* 9, 3 (Aug. 1981): 303–26, to rescue Arendt, not via Foucault, Nietzsche, and the politics of agonistic subjectivity, but via an appeal to justice and the Aristotelian category of deliberation, as well as Ann M. Lane and Warren J. Lane's appropriation of the Aristotelian categories of praxis and phronesis for feminist thought. See their essay "Athenian Political Thought and the Feminist Politics of Poiesis and Praxis," in *Athenian Political Thought and the Reconstruction of American Democracy,* ed. J. Peter Euben, Josiah Ober, and John Wallach, pp. 265–88 (Ithaca, N.Y.: Cornell University Press, 1994). On the concept of "agonistic democracy," see William Connolly, *Identity/Difference* (Ithaca, N.Y.: Cornell University Press, 1991), x. *The Phantom Public Sphere,* ed. Bruce Robbins (Minneapolis: University of Minnesota Press, 1993), is another postmodern attempt to theorize the "public sphere" that relies, implicitly and explicitly, on the classical categories of republican virtue, public and private, and the agora (the public as a phantasmagoria, or phantom agora), if mostly by way of critique and in opposition. For a modernist acknowledgement of the Greeks, see Seyla Benhabib, "Models of Public Space: Hannah Arendt, the Liberal Tradition and Jürgen Habermas," in *Habermas and the Public Sphere,* ed. Craig Calhoun (Cambridge, Mass.: MIT Press, 1992), pp. 73–98. Also see Nancy Fraser, "Rethinking the Public Sphere: A Contribution to the Critique of Actually Existing Democracy," *Social Text* 8, 9 (1990), who tends to confuse discursive reason with theatrical space, most notably on p. 57.

the Greeks. Not so obvious is how these disputes are to be settled when the once seemingly immobile and solid soil of modernity has revealed its rifts, instabilities, and fissures—when that ground begins to shift under our feet. It is to this shifting terrain that contemporary theory responds, for what ultimately provokes this ironic turn to Athens—as paradigmatic precursor of rational deliberation or as instructive exemplar in agonistic virtuosity—are the profound social and political transformations wrought by modernity.

POSTMODERN SHIFTS

At the close of the twentieth century and on the edge of postmodernity, we are witnessing transformations as rapid as they are radical. The emergence of new and pervasive configurations of power, the contraction, systematic distortion, and inexorable displacement of public speech and space, the rise of politics as spectacle with the advent of mass-mediated publics, the increasing permeability of national "sovereignty" to the global movement and metabolism of capital, people, goods, information, images, and viruses, both biological and digital, together with the appearance of increasingly heterogeneous identities, practices, and forms of life—these are but a few of the most widely visible structural transformations currently reconfiguring the terrain of contemporary politics.[6] Such transformations have posed a fundamen-

6. On such transformations in the power of the state and economy, see, e.g., Sheldon Wolin, "Democracy in the Discourse of Postmodernism," *Social Research* 57, 1 (1990): 5–30, and "Democracy and the Welfare State: Theoretical Connections between *Staatsräson* and *Wohlfahrtstaatsräson*," in *The Presence of the Past: Essays on the State and the Constitution* (Baltimore: Johns Hopkins University Press, 1989): 151–79; William Connolly, *Politics and Ambiguity* (Madison: University of Wisconson Press, 1987); Scott Lash and John Urry, *The End of Organized Capitalism* (Madison: University of Wisconsin Press, 1987); Michel Foucault, *Power/Knowledge: Selected Interviews and Other Writings, 1972–77*, ed. Colin Gordon (New York: Pantheon Books, 1980); Jürgen Habermas, *Toward a Rational Society*, trans. Jeremy Shapiro (Boston: Beacon Press, 1970), and *Theory of Communicative Action*. On politics as spectacle and the general destabilization of once-settled categories, see Jean Baudrillard, *In the Shadow of the Silent Majority* (New York: Semiotext(e), 1983), and "The Precession of Simulacra," in *Simulations* (New York: Semiotext(e), 1983), pp. 1–79, esp. pp. 3, 11–12, and 83, as well as Umberto Eco, *Travels in Hyperreality: Essays* (London: Picador, 1986). A more concrete treatment of politics as spectacle is Michael Warner, "The Mass Public and the Mass Subject," in *The Phantom Public Sphere*, ed. Bruce Robbins (Minneapolis: University of Minnesota Press, 1993). On the reconfiguration of political space and the increasing irrelevance of the democratic, territorial nation-state, see William Connolly, "Tocqueville, Territory and Violence," *Theory, Culture and Society* 11, 1 (Winter 1994): 19–41, which fruitfully explores the tension between those elements adumbrated in his title. In a more radical vein, see Paul Virilio's *The Lost Dimension* (New York: Semiotext(e), 1991), who

tal challenge to the conceptual categories and political vocabularies of the modern enlightenment. As a result, the terms of debate have begun to shift away from "politics as usual" as new concerns are raised and new demands are issued that remained inarticulate within the confines of an older practice and discourse. Recent years have witnessed the emergence of a "new politics of protest" in the liberal democracies of the West that is both sign and symptom of modernity's unstable foundations. Unchartable by means of the traditional coordinates of class, group, or self-interest, largely indifferent to the material goods distributed by the welfare state, suspicious of (or opposed to) electoral success and the official systems of party and parliament, the new politics challenges the very foundations of enlightened modernity and continues to provoke a fundamental rethinking of its grounds, goals, and practices.

Although the issues, scenes, and groupings transform themselves daily, these diverse challenges to enlightenment hegemony are obvious to even the most casual ethnographer of contemporary North American politics. In past decades, the peace, antinuclear, and environmental movements have actively resisted both the material affluence of consumer culture and the destructive potential of an administrative state and a global system of transnational capitalism locked into the logic of technical control, mastery, and domination. More recently, a politics of identity and difference has begun to assert itself against a hegemonic European cultural tradition advertised as universal history. For today's cheeky consumers of culture, the West has lost its universal appeal precisely at a time when it can no longer appeal to universals. In a society increasingly fragmented by centrifugal displacements of once-centered authority and community, fierce struggles over local identities, although they hardly approach the violent intensity of the resurgent nationalisms that have recently swept the Balkans, pose a new and unruly challenge to the current politics of cultural hegemony. These radical dispersals continue to engender a rapid proliferation of new social codes, which are just as rapidly transformed into a micropolitics of difference based on supressed, submerged, or otherwise ignored narratives of ethnicity,

seems to conclude that political space as we know it has been irretrievably lost. From a postcolonial perspective, see Arjun Appadurai, "Disjuncture and Difference in the Global Cultural Economy," in *Phantom Public Sphere,* ed. Robbins, pp. 269–95. On the African diaspora as challenge to Enlightenment cultural hegemony, see Paul Gilroy, *The Black Atlantic: Modernity and Double Consciousness* (Cambridge, Mass.: Harvard University Press, 1993) and *Small Acts: Thoughts on the Politics of Black Cultures* (London: Serpent's Tail Press, 1993).

gender, race, religion, sexuality, class, and other cultural (and subcultural) affiliations. Such affiliations range from the now highly differentiated women's movement to queer politics, from the hardcore urban scene, with its punks, gangsters, crack, and guns, to the more innocuous suburban landscape of shopping malls, MTV, designer drugs, television talk shows, late night movies, and alternative music scene.[7]

Whatever the social code or subcultural milieu, the new politics of difference presently asserts itself against the falsely universalized projection of a unitary European history, culture, and identity. In myriad locations and in strikingly inventive ways, resistant and rebellious selves continue to struggle against current enlightenment assumptions that define the "subjects" of politics. Through agonal acts of resistance to contemporary cultural hegemony, new subjects, selves, identities, and practices are presently being fashioned and refashioned. These most recent challenges to enlightenment hegemony endeavor to open up political spaces for contesting present forms of cultural exclusion, domination, and hierarchy.

In the academy, the current struggles against politics as usual have inspired (and been explained by) that loose alliance of feminists, multiculturalists, and poststructuralists suspicious of the universal categories that are the Enlightenment's legacy. What this diverse group of critics threatens to uncover and unsettle are the founding fictions of the Enlightenment itself, its pretensions to, and promises of, truth, reason, and individual liberty, packaged as universal moral progress. Whether the issue is the recovery and deployment of suppressed and heterogeneous subject positions, the unmasking of universal concepts as differential markers of race, class, or gender, the deployment of rhetorical figurations as "governing representations" in contemporary politics, or the current struggles against newly intensified forms of discipline and the subsequent refashioning of resistant selves and alternative (political) spaces from the cultural materials at hand, these critics demonstrate that our fundamental enlightenment categories have been conjured from the acts of exclusion, subjugation, and repression that attended their origin. Attempts to unsettle these constructions reveal that the shifting terrain of postmodernity owes much of its instability to the

7. See Fredric Jameson, "Postmodernism, or, The Cultural Logic of Late Capitalism," *New Left Review* 146 (July/Aug. 1984): 53–92, and Dick Hebdige, *Subculture: The Meaning of Style* (London: Methuen, 1979).

already-present fault lines that traverse its enlightenment foundations.[8] The current contests are fought in and along these seams as attempts to disperse a singular origin, resist homogenizing categories, expose settled vocabularies, practices, and institutions as strategic deployments of power, and reveal the modern subject of enlightened reason as discursively and historically constructed, as the effect of a struggle over meanings as much as the author of those meanings.

Such struggles continue to redefine the contours of the present political moment, and they have provoked lively, often acrimonious, debates in recent years (and across a wide range of academic disciplines) about the meaning, status, and fate of modernity and the Enlightenment. Much of this controversy has been articulated through the juxtaposition of temporal categories, in terms of succeeding—and embattled—periods or eras: postindustrialism, postphilosophy, poststructuralism, post-Marxism, and *posthistoire* confront and attempt to replace their prefixless affiliates. But the central terms of this contest, around which the greatest controversy turns, are the categories *modern* and *postmodern,* and the crucial figures in that debate are Jürgen Habermas and the late Michel Foucault.

In articulating the dilemmas, disappointments, and aspirations of our time, Habermas and Foucault have largely defined the controversy over the origins, meaning, and future of postmodernity. Virtually every current theoretical reflection on politics takes its bearings from their co-

8. On the recovery of plural, counterhegemonic, and subaltern experiences in the construction of "the" Western "public," recent revisionist historiography is particularly telling: in revolutionary France, the masculine public sphere constituted itself through the exclusion of women's publicity as republican *vir*tuosity; in England and Germany, "the public" represented itself as a universal category, conveniently concealing the particular class origins of its universality; while in the nineteenth-century United States, competing public spheres and counterpublics comprised of women provided a variety of alternative and competing routes to public life. During Reconstruction, a black counterpublic emerged and was partially successful in gaining access to official discourse and oppositional publics before it dissolved. See Fraser "Rethinking the Public Sphere"; Joan Landes, *Women and the Public Sphere in the Age of the French Revolution* (Ithaca, N.Y.: Cornell University Press, 1988); Geoff Eely, "Nations, Publics and Political Cultures: Placing Habermas in the Nineteenth Century," in *Habermas and the Public Sphere,* ed. Craig Calhoun, pp. 289–339 (Cambridge, Mass.: MIT Press, 1992); Mary P. Ryan, *Women in Public: Between Banners and Ballots, 1825–1880* (Baltimore: Johns Hopkins University Press, 1990); Anna Yeatman, "Beyond Natural Right: The Conditions for Universal Citizenship," *Social Concept* 4, 2 (June 1988): 3–32; and Michael Dawson, "A Black Counterpublic? Economic Earthquakes, Racial Agenda(s), and Black Politics," *Public Culture* 7 (1994): 195–223. On the concept of "governing representations," see Anne Norton, *Republic of Signs: Liberal Theory and American Popular Culture* (Chicago: University of Chicago Press, 1993).

ordinates and engages their positions, if not by way of agreement, then certainly by way of critique.[9] Yet these chartings of postmodern geography issue in two radically divergent cartographic projections of the present, two contending and ultimately irreconcilable maps, which leave little room for further exploration. The result has been a debate whose terms have congealed into rigid polarities. Are we to understand the recent shifts as instances of a reactive and pathological politics generated by the unresolved contradictions within modernity itself, or as the material out of which new political subjects, selves, identities, and practices are fashioned? Do the answers to such contradictions lie in the reconstruction of reason and the reaffirmation of such universal values as liberty, autonomy, and democratic equality, or must we deconstruct reason, radically redefine those values as projections of power, and overcome all forms of universality? Can we retrieve and reinstitutionalize a democratic public sphere from the materials left us by the eighteenth century, or shall we disrupt its normatively regulated democratic code with a performative and endlessly subversive politics of parody?

These questions do not admit of easy answers, and given a contest structured by such unyielding oppositions, it is unlikely that anything new can be said in its present terms. Yet such questions need answers, and finding them is the challenge confronting us. This study forges neither a modern nor a postmodern path through the disputed terrain, siding with neither Habermas nor Foucault. Nor does it seek to reconcile the contending sides through a mediation that would, in good Hegelian fashion, effect a grand synthesis of the two positions and so cauterize the dialectic of the debate. I want, rather, to resist the terms of the debate and disturb its projections, to plot an alternative route through this shifting landscape by mapping the alien thought of ancient Athens onto the terrain of postmodernity. This mapping intends to open up fresh possibilities for dialogue by prompting new and different combinations of tired patterns and tested paths, by unsettling present accommoda-

9. The most recent are Richard Peterson, *Democratic Philosophy and the Politics of Knowledge* (University Park: Pennsylvania State University Press, 1996) and David C. Hoy and Thomas McCarthy, *Critical Theory* (Cambridge, Mass.: Blackwell, 1994); but see also Mark Poster, *Critical Theory and Poststructuralism* (Ithaca, N.Y.: Cornell University Press, 1989); Connolly, *Politics and Ambiguity;* David C. Hoy, "Foucault: Modern or Postmodern?" in *After Foucault: Humanistic Knowledge, Postmodern Challenges,* ed. Jonathan Arac (New Brunswick, N.J.: Rutgers University Press, 1988); Martin Jay, "Habermas and Modernism," *Praxis International* 4, 1 (Apr. 1984): 1–14, and the essays collected in Richard Bernstein, ed., *Habermas and Modernity* (Oxford: Blackwell, 1985).

tions with ways of being and modes of knowing that are no longer familiar. But before I begin to trace the route taken by this book, it is best to survey the terrain already mapped out in the dispute between Habermas and Foucault.

The lines of that dispute were solidified, if not drawn, some ten years ago when Habermas took up the challenge issued by the neostructuralist critique of reason. Piqued by this Nietzschean-inspired attack on the emancipatory project of modernity, Habermas initiated the first serious dialogue between the German and French intellectual traditions in recent memory.[10] Foucault died before he could actively join the dispute, so it was left to others (of whom there has been no shortage) to advance his position. As a result, the controversy over the transition from modernity to postmodernity—the "debate" between Habermas and Foucault sketched here—represents less a chronicle of actual exchanges than a charting of the significant points that structure their differences. Those differences constitute nothing less than a struggle over terms such as *enlightenment, truth, theory,* and *democracy,* which are fundamental to securing—defining—the character of postmodernity and its fate. The meaning of *enlightenment* itself, the possibility of knowledge liberated from power or interest, the status of theoretical discourse, and the future of democratic culture and practice are currently up for grabs. Although the contest sketched here must remain something of a historical fiction, it accurately and usefully represents the oppositions and predicaments in which the dispute over postmodernity has entangled itself.

To the extent that Habermas looks to the unrealized potential of modernity, he allies himself with the progressive and emancipatory claims of enlightenment. The completion of cultural modernity means for him the realization of such liberal and universal bourgeois goals as autonomy, equality, liberty, and emancipation—in short, all the goals of enlightened reason. The problem with modernity is not, as his Nietzscheans claim, too much reason—an excess—but rather too little—a deficit. Enlightenment has not reversed itself; rather, rationalization has

10. The first of these "defenses" of modernity was given as "Modernity: An Incomplete Project" upon Habermas's receipt of the Adorno Prize in 1980 and subsequently published as "Modernity vs. Postmodernity," *New German Critique* 22 (Winter 1981): 3–14. But see also Jürgen Habermas, "The Entwinement of Myth and Enlightenment: Rereading *Dialectic of Enlightenment,*" *New German Critique* 26 (Spring/Summer 1982): 13–20, republished in *The Philosophical Discourse of Modernity: Twelve Lectures,* trans. Frederick G. Lawrence (Cambridge, Mass.: MIT Press, 1987), itself a sustained defense of enlightened modernity. On the debate between French and German intellectuals, see Poster, *Critical Theory and Poststructuralism.*

either not yet been achieved, has not been institutionalized, or has proceeded one-sidedly in favor of an instrumental reason embodied in technical-scientific enterprises, the capitalist economy, and the bureaucratic state. None of this means, of course, that the enlightenment project of emancipation is unsound or that its liberatory potential is in any way seriously diminished or threatened. It does mean that the modern enlightenment has not yet achieved its potential and must therefore complete its "project."[11]

Foucault rejects the very assumptions on which enlightenment is predicated, ironically observing that the enlightenment rhetoric of liberation—whether it is bound up with the discourses of psychological, physical, or social therapies—insidiously contains and conceals its own subtle forms of coercion. Rational speech surely establishes communication, but it also establishes barriers to communication. The streamlined, functional, and efficient language of modern science—both natural and social—achieves a transparency of description that serves to exclude or silence the elements of experience that do not fit neatly into a preconceived schema. Run through the endless mills of speech, we are constantly in danger of falling prey to the various techniques of truth that promise to make us free, enlightened, autonomous beings, techniques that promise liberation even as they deprive us of our liberty. "The irony of this deployment," writes Foucault, "is in having us believe that our 'liberation' is in the balance."[12] Enlightenment thus paradoxically brings both liberation and slavery, freedom and constraint, self-conscious transparency and blind opacity about who we are and what we are doing.

To redeem the promise of the Enlightenment, Habermas elaborates a theory of communicative rationality as both diagnostic aid and normative ideal. A more differentiated concept of communicative reason allows him to preserve and pursue a selective critique of modernity, the spread of instrumental rationality, and the attendant colonization of potentially democratic political space, which further depends on the elaboration of an "ideal speech situation." Uncoerced speech guarantees a strong normative standard, freed from the constraints of structural violence, inequality, and communicative distortion. Only under

11. See Habermas, "Modernity vs. Postmodernity" and also *Philosophical Discourse of Modernity*, pp. 336–67.

12. Michel Foucault, *The History of Sexuality*, trans. Robert Hurley (New York: Pantheon Books, 1978), 1: 159.

such conditions of "rationally motivated agreement"—the telos implicit in all human speech—can we distinguish between genuine and false consensus, the legitimate and illegitimate exercise of power, just and unjust regimes.[13]

But Habermas's appeal to the "unforced force of the better argument" only works if he can specify a rationality that is truly universal, context-independent, and freed from every constraint of passion or interest. For Foucault, this quest for universal agreement is but the modern analogue of Socratic dialogue, which seeks to limit power by appealing to knowledge of the good. But since all discourse already contains its own politics of truth, there can be no truth exterior to any particular discursive regime. Power and knowledge are inextricably intertwined in a relationship of mutual constitution. The Socratic hope of a knowledge beyond the limits of power, which it would in turn limit, is a fiction. Power can neither be the manifestation of consensus nor the product of communication. Power, rather, is strategic. In the move and countermove of a game, power comes into play as "a relationship which is at the same time reciprocal incitation and struggle, less a face to face confrontation which paralyzes both sides than a permanent provocation." Neither the pristine model of Socratic dialogue nor the ideal speech situations that issue in community and consent, but the sophistic "agonism" of constant contest, struggle, and resistance, "the endlessly repeated play of dominations," best describes modern power relations, as well as Foucault's own subversion of hegemonic discourses.[14]

Although Habermas wishes to distinguish his further differentiation of reason and the selective critique of modernity that follows it from what he regards as "total" theories, he is still engaged in explaining and criticizing a societywide phenomena. Is such a global discourse so bad? After all, a conceptual system such as critical theory interprets a complex world and in that regard is a necessary component of our everyday lives. Systems call for an orderly organization and presentation of experience, without which we could not survive. Moreover, critical theory

13. On this aspect of the argument, see Habermas, "An Alternative Way Out of the Philosophy of the Subject," in *Philosophical Discourse of Modernity,* p. 315. But see also id., *Theory of Communicative Action,* vol. 1, "Intermediate Reflections," for a detailed specification of the concept of communicative reason.

14. On power as a permanent provocation, see Michel Foucault, "The Subject and Power," in *Michel Foucault: Beyond Structuralism and Hermeneutics,* ed. Dreyfus and Rabinow (Chicago: University of Chicago Press, 1982), p. 221; on agonism, see id., "Nietzsche, Genealogy, History," p. 85. See also id., *Power/Knowledge,* p. 52, and the essay "Truth and Power," pp. 109–33.

hardly constitutes an apology or justification for present social and political configurations. Unlike that master of all systems-thinkers, Hegel, Habermas in no way offers another theodicean explanation for suffering. The difficulty for theory construction—critical theory included—is to make sense out of the world of people and things while doing it, and them, the least violence possible. All conceptual thought must negotiate the distance between too much unity and coherence and too little, between the system and the individual, between global and local discourse.[15]

Where critical theory universalizes the concept of reason by implicitly relying on the enlightenment narrative of progress, Foucault suspects all master narratives as "global" theories that attempt to unify the irreducible heterogeneity of the world. For the genealogist, it is precisely critical theory's claim systematically to encompass the whole of reality that condemns it. Against a conceptual system like Habermas's, Foucault's genealogies consistently remind the reader of the tremendous and irreparable damage wrought by modernity, which the critical theorist is apt to overlook. Foucault continually invokes the lives that have been damaged, lost, or destroyed, the experiences that have been elided, subjugated, or repressed by the smooth, seamless functioning of hierarchically ordered systems of knowledge. This invocation of the suppressed contents of history—of individuals and their lives who do not fit into the system without remainder—aims to resist, disrupt, subvert, and otherwise contest the tyranny of globalizing discourses.[16]

Above all, Habermas and Foucault have underscored the dilemmas of democracy in the postmodern world. Originally construed as a radical, transformative force in modernity, democracy now appears tame, its revolutionary capacity (at least in eastern Europe) spent, channeled into the search for markets, consumer goods, and Western technology. At home, the imperatives of the accumulation of capital and power have all but eroded what democratic public space we might have had. Against this trend, critical theory aims at securing and maintaining a space for democratic speech and action that cannot be absorbed by the systemic constraints of material reproduction. This space would

15. On Habermas's own criticisms of "totalizing" critique, see *Philosophical Discourse of Modernity,* pp. 336–38, where he conflates Adorno, Foucault, Heidegger, and Derrida.

16. On genealogy as a strategy meant to disrupt globalizing discourse, see Foucault, *Power/Knowledge,* pp. 81–83, and "Nietzsche, Genealogy, History," in *Foucault Reader,* pp. 76–100.

contain institutions to guarantee an effectively functioning democratic public sphere, in which the goals of society were submitted to public discussion and decisions made based on the rational achievement of agreement. Only in this manner will deliberating citizens, speaking and acting together, secure and maintain a viable democratic public sphere.[17]

Despite this genuine concern with consensus and democratic will formation, there is a blind spot in the theory of consensus that conceals democracy's potentially normalizing effects. Although Habermas no longer posits the "ideal speech situation" as a transcendental category, his weaker claim that consensus is immanent in all speech still implies an ideal or norm that excludes other nonrational forms of expression as invalid because they fall below or outside the acceptable threshold of normality, of what counts as a reasonable or rational argument. That exclusion, of course, is all the more insidious because it is concealed by the promise of freedom. The very democratic norms that critical theory champions—in this case, those enabling the free, rational, and responsible agent to arrive at uncoerced consensus—function to delegitimate all that is "other" in self and society. Those feelings, motives, experiences, and desires that remain inarticulate within the schema prescribed by an ideal discourse subsequently become the objects of disciplinary control and normalization. What Habermas specifies as the distinctive characteristics of democratic character and culture seem to satisfy criteria of symmetry and reciprocity. Yet those necessary qualities obscure the very real power exercised by the politics of cultural hegemony. In his failure to ask which subjects and what forms of selfhood are privileged or empowered by this version of the democratic self, Habermas similarly fails to identify those selves that are silenced, subjugated, or disempowered by such a privileging. Foucault, to his credit, has taught us to recognize in the culture of democratic consensus the dangers of this drift toward those homogenizing and dividing practices that define, contain, and discipline the individual. But can postmodern democrats rest content with Foucault's concept of "resistance"—of the local struggle against regimes of power/knowledge—as a viable contribution to a theory of democratic politics?

Such are the dilemmas of postmodernity sketched within the contours of the present controversy. This contest leaves us with a series of unsatisfying choices: either an enlightened modernity blind to its coer-

17. Habermas, *Philosophical Discourse of Modernity*, pp. 362–65.

cive effects or the renunciation of all forms of emancipatory practice as subtle forms of normalizing control; either the effects of a truth that naively conceals its debt to power or an endless struggle for position and dominance; either a foundational theory unaware of its own violent exclusions or the repudiation of all theoretical foundations; and, finally, either a democratic practice and culture resting on constitutive exclusions or the rejection of democracy as one more element in the ensemble of disciplinary technologies. What these choices ultimately suggest—and why they must be resisted—is a refusal to think the difficult dilemmas of postmodernity in tension, to imagine the contradictions within these categories (and within the Enlightenment itself) as fruitful ground for further exploration, rather than as obstacles to be removed. For the very impasse of the debate indicates that the unsettling dangers of disruption, contest, contingency, and resistance that disturb our lives can no more be displaced or avoided than the comfortable seductions of order, truth, reason, and democratic progress that make such disturbances both necessary and meaningful. Whereas critical theory succumbs too readily to the easy nostalgia of settlement and permanence (while remaining fearfully impervious to the liberating aspects of disturbance), genealogy celebrates the dangerous freedom of contingency and contest, while dismissing the force and appeal of order, center, and stability. I would like to think there are choices here, but I am not willing to concede that they are the ones offered by Habermas and Foucault. In a debate that has been constructed far too narrowly, its terms overly polarized, their responses constitute subtle evasions of the difficult task of negotiating the perplexing terrain of the postmodernity these theorists have themselves so painstakingly charted.

As a preliminary indication of my own direction of travel across that terrain, I would like to pose these dilemmas differently, perceptibly altering the frame of reference. Can we remain committed to the principles of the Enlightenment, yet resist its regressive tendencies toward domination? Is it possible to pursue the truth yet relentlessly politicize the conditions of its production? Can we satisfy our profound need to make sense of the world through the construction of theoretical wholes and still disturb such orderly representations so as to resist the seductive tyranny of globalizing discourse? Finally, what are the prospects for encouraging a democratic culture and practice that simultaneously resist democracy's drift toward normalization and disciplinary control? These questions, while acknowledging the force of the dilemma, open up more room for thought, more opportunity for recombining old patterns in new ways. To think these oppositions in tension is the central object of this study, which does not rest content with *either* regulative reason codified as disciplinary norm *or* the endless subversion of all normative codes. But where shall we turn for help in negotiating the ironic reversals of the Enlightenment, the politicization of knowledge, the seductions and dangers of foundational theory, the dilemmas of democracy? My answer: the tragic poetry and philosophical dialogue of ancient Athens.

Whether we want to reconstruct an effectively functioning democratic politics or disrupt newly intensified forms of discipline, the classical past offers an alternative way of thinking about our present predicament that a thoroughgoing modern (or postmodern) perspective lacks. If, as Foucault suggests, we are indeed "normalizing" ourselves via ever more efficient mechanisms of surveillance, discipline, and subjectification, then Greek tragedy's examples of virtuosic action, as well as its preoccupation with the "other," with what falls below, behind, or beyond the threshold of the culturally and socially acceptable and intelligible, will provide an indispensable point of reference for identifying and disrupting modern forces of normalization and discipline from within a democratic tradition. If, as Habermas has argued, economic and bureaucratic forms of rationality are systematically eroding and replacing the communicative structures of public speech and action (upon which democratic politics largely depend), then the concern of Greek tragedy and philosophical dialogue with moral communication and debate—the deliberative aspects of the classical polis—can stand as a valuable resource for contemporary democratic theory and practice, even as they warn us of the potentially normalizing effects of democratic consensus. Greek tragedy and philosophical dialogue contribute most toward theorizing the present when their disturbing content is wrenched out of its original context and appropriated to disrupt the established norms and forms of democratically constituted selves and societies, even as they provide a democratic identity and practice against which to struggle.

TRAGEDY AND ENLIGHTENMENT

The theoretical and political predicament that our postmodern condition poses to contemporary thought provides the framework within which the following chapters pursue their arguments. In a series of staged encounters with four classical texts, I intervene in the current controversy over the character, legacy, and fate of the Enlightenment. Those encounters consider (1) the meaning of *enlightenment,* (2) the relationship between truth and power, (3) the nature and status of theoretical discourse, and (4) the dilemmas of democratic culture and practice. Yet these issues, and the political struggles that surround them, are neither unique nor confined solely to the present. Indeed, there is an instructive analogy here: the dilemmas bequeathed contemporary theory by the modern enlightenment are strikingly similar to those posed to classical thought by its ancient counterpart. Philosopher and Sophist, reason and rhetoric, the will to truth and the will to power, the search for ultimate foundations and the repudiation of such searches—these are a few of the recurring themes that inhabit the landscapes of enlightenment both ancient and modern. One of my aims is to press at the limits of this analogy by reading two classical tragedies and two dialogues in terms of these four "contemporary" issues. Chapter 2 considers Sophocles' *Oedipus Tyrannos* in terms of enlightenment and its consequences. Chapter 3 elaborates a politics of truth as articulated in the *Gorgias.* Chapter 4 investigates the status of theoretical foundations with the help of Plato's *Republic,* and chapter 5 turns to Aeschylus's *Oresteia* for lessons in negotiating the dilemmas of democracy.

This book also aims to challenge the privileging of the modern (or postmodern) present over the premodern past, and so to disrupt the myth of history as progress, a goal it shares with Greek tragedy. That strategy is as evident in the form or architecture of the book—in its structural articulation—as in its overt argumentative moves. By bringing the theoretical and political power of the classical past "on stage," so to speak, I hope to challenge our most deeply held assumptions about the superiority of the present associated with reason, enlightenment, progress, and democracy, and so to reveal the exclusions and acts of violence these values often conceal. The formal structure of the book reiterates this theoretical intention by reordering, and so disrupting, the usual historical (and moral) sequence in which tragedy gives way to the more theoretically "advanced" form of philosophy. I therefore order the chapters in a chiasmus (AB :: BA): tragedy and dialogue are followed by dialogue and tragedy (*Oedipus Tyrannos, Gorgias* :: *Republic, Oresteia*).

This structured destructuring of the conventional progression performs a reversal by privileging tragedy over philosophy. It also reflects the book's juxtaposition of classical past to postmodern present, an appropriation of classical tragedy's own staged confrontation between contemporary, democratic Athens and its mythical, aristocratic past. The tragedy and philosophical dialogue of classical Athens are read as expressions of the most recent political concerns, while the lineaments of the postmodern present are discerned in the contours of the most archaic past. The ancient thus appears meaningful in light of the present, while the most modern is associated with past antiquity. Such a juxtaposition disturbs both the conventional supersession of tragedy by philosophy and those comfortable teleologies that culminate in the present, thus interrupting the flow of progress by means of a device supplied by tragedy itself. The chiasmus is the structure of recognition and reversal so integral, if we are to believe Aristotle, to the power of tragedy. That structure and its sensibility inform my own attempt to read the present in terms supplied by the past, while still maintaining contemporary political and theoretical concerns.

The sophisticated literary structures of tragedy and dialogue, the way the formal elements of composition can be made to yield a critical reflection on history as progress—provide one reason for turning to these specific texts. But this book is not primarily about the literary achievements of the ancients, even if it does seek to wring out meaning precisely where dramatic structure and substantive argument intersect in complex articulation. To reiterate, my readings are intended to contribute to the contemporary struggle over the meaning of terms central to our theoretical and political discourse, terms that were as contested in fifth-century Athens as they are now.

I begin with Sophocles' *Oedipus Tyrannos* as a paradigmatic articulation of the triumphs and failures of enlightened thinking, an exemplary (and tragic) tale of enlightenment and its highly ambivalent consequences. Sophocles asks us to reflect on the nature and certainty of our knowledge, on what we know, how we know it, and what such knowledge is worth. The play presents Oedipus as supremely confident, a man of native intelligence, skill, and wit willing to abandon all inherited custom, tradition, and limits in his single-minded search for the truth. In a typically ironic reversal, however, Oedipus's upward path to enlightenment leads painfully back toward Thebes, his mother's bed, and himself. The playwright thus reveals the double nature of enlightenment—its triumphant ability to disclose and command the secrets of nature while simultaneously subjugating the subject it meant to empower. Oedipus's inquiry into his own birth reveals no happy origin, but rather the horror and violence of murder and incest. No lucky child of chance, Oedipus proves the slayer of his father and husband of his mother, the unhappy son of Laius and Jocasta, his all-too-human parents. Lurking just below the smooth contours of surface calm and light lie the rupture, turbulence, and violence upon which his identity rests. The "truth" behind Oedipus is not inviolable identity, but unutterable disparity. Oedipus learns that he is "double"—just as conscious of the powers that constitute his identity as his characteristic intellectual self-conceit allows. Enlightenment is thus both a blessing and a curse to Oedipus (and to us), revealing both the power and the limits of man's rational intelligence. Sophocles certainly celebrates the accomplishments of enlightened reason—the ordered art of his text participates in that process—but he also issues a warning to the modern reader, whose privileged historical position and tested critical methods promise to reveal the ultimate meaning of the play in all its transparency. Like Oedipus, we too are constituted by forces beyond our control, even as we try to shape the forces that constitute us. With Sophocles' hero, we seem destined endlessly to repeat incestuous beginnings despite the fact that we count ourselves emancipated, autonomous, and enlightened. This fundamental ambiguity—about the value of enlightenment—that structures Sophocles' text renders *Oedipus Tyrannos* particularly helpful in thinking through the dilemmas of postmodernity. Sophocles is particularly good to think with, I argue, because his tragedy points to an ethos that combines, in rather uneasy tension, the drive to fulfill the emancipatory project of enlightenment with a relentless criticism of enlightenment's conceits, a criticism meant to disrupt its normalizing and regressive effects. I therefore look to Sophocles for help in elaborating an epistemology of disruption, a post-Enlightenment sensibility that will reinstate a secular appreciation of the ambiguities, contradictions, and mysteries of a world that enlightenment, both ancient and modern, seems bent on suppressing.

Oedipus Tyrannos also concerns the relationship of truth to power. Does all knowledge, it asks, ultimately refer back to man himself, to his subjective purposes and plans, no matter how petty or how noble? Is Oedipus truly a self-taught, self-created man, the child of chance, able to confer meaning and produce truth at will? Is man the measure of all things, or is there an objective (in this case, sacred) order, a set of standards or an ultimate "truth" free from the manipulation of rationally ambitious humans and their quest for power? Sophocles' chorus contemplates these possibilities, when, alarmed at a growing skepticism toward the truth of Apollo's oracle, it fears for Oedipus and for itself. For if Oedipus is right, and such order as the world possesses is no more than the projection of the strong man's will to power, then it makes no sense to "join in the sacred dance to honor the gods" (894–95). The chorus would rather Oedipus prove murderer of his father and husband to his mother than the oracle false. Luckily, the oracle proves true, and Oedipus's suffering is not without transcendent meaning. There is an objective order to the world, Sophocles suggests, although knowledge of that order comes only after long and intense suffering, only in the end, and only to blind men exiled from family, wealth, and power. Truth there is, but it proves of no help in the affairs of men. That is the lesson Oedipus learns, but the play as a whole perhaps teaches the spectators something different—namely, a kind of self-knowledge that is sustained by the memory of Oedipus's own ignorance about himself. Sophocles thus anticipates Socrates by teaching through the play what Oedipus learns so painfully in it.

Socrates, too, is concerned with the relationship between truth and power, and explores it in terms of philosophy's (and the philosopher's) place in the city. In the *Apology,* Socrates gives an account of his philosophical way of life and its role in Athens. The central part of that account, and hence of philosophical activity, concerns the extent to which "truth" exists independently of the influence and effects of power. Is there such a truth, Socrates asks, or is all knowledge created, produced, and shaped in and through the workings of power and interest, as his sophistic opponents claim? Like Sophocles, Socrates also believes in an objective order of knowledge, but it is one that we as mortals can never fully grasp. We can approximate that order, but as partial beings confined to particular places, times, and physical bodies, we shall never entirely be able to apprehend it. Such a limitation does not, however, deter the philosopher from his quest for knowledge of the good. Even in the face of death, Socrates remains committed to the belief that an objective order of knowledge exists, free of the constraints of power and interest. He further believes that such knowledge ought to guide the political affairs of the city.

Socratic philosophy also suggests that such foundational knowledge is intersubjective in an important sense, achieved neither in the mantic inspiration of prophetic divination nor in the privacy of theoretical contemplation, but rather in the give-and-take of moral communication and debate. This communicative aspect of truth does not, however, obviate the problem of power. Socratic dialogues are not merely paradigms of the "ideal speech situation."[18] In fact, Plato introduces the problem of domination directly into those dialogues that aim to free themselves from just such an entanglement, and by means of a figure who professes to care more for the truth than for wealth, honor, and fame (or winning the argument). A series of questions arises regarding the aims of Socrates: is the "interest" of the philosopher in moral truth such that it transcends interest altogether? Does Socrates in fact care only for the good, or is he, as Callicles thought and Nietzsche firmly believed, concealing his will to power behind a rather thin metaphysical veil born of weakness and its accompanying *ressentiment* of the strong? The practice of Socratic philosophy, with all its claims to ignorance and the authentic search for "truth," might in the end be structured by resentment and constitute a subtle strategy of domination. The *Gorgias* shows us the stakes involved in the struggle over who will set the terms of discourse, a struggle that suggests that the norms of society are decided politically as much as they are derived theoretically.[19] In terms elaborated by Habermas, the *Gorgias* asks us to consider whether Socrates truly seeks communicatively achieved understanding through the "unforced force of the better argument" or is simply a clever player in the endless game of domination, as Foucault suspects. I argue that the dialogue resists both these alternatives, adopting an ironic stance toward the politics of truth that both projects Socratic dialogue as the ultimate arbiter of politics and contests that projection through the agonistic struggle between Socrates and Callicles—an agon that leads not to annihilation but to the perpetual activity of contests.

In chapter 3, I thus turn to the *Gorgias* for help in negotiating the unstable terrain that lies between dialogue and domination, consensus and contest, philosophical discourse and rhetorical performance, po-

18. Although Paul Friedländer's *Platon* (1928–30) predates Habermas's concept of power-free speech, Friedländer's interpretation of Socratic dialogue is remarkably similar to Habermas's formulation. See Paul Friedländer, *Plato,* trans. Hans Meyerhoff (New York: Pantheon Books, 1958), 2: 154–70.

19. E. R. Dodds explicitly links Callicles and Nietzsche in the appendix to *Gorgias: A Revised Text with Introduction and Commentary* (Oxford: Clarendon Press, 1959), trans. and ed. Dodds, pp. 387–91. On Socrates and resentment, see Friedrich Nietzsche, *The Twilight of the Idols* (1889), trans. R. J. Hollingdale (New York: Penguin Books, 1969), p. 476, and *The Will to Power* (1906), trans. Walter Kaufmann and R. J. Hollingdale (New York: Vintage Books, 1968), p. 519. But compare the *Gorgias,* 457e and 458a, where Socrates says he is interested in the truth, not in winning an argument. On the incommensurability of political and theoretical language games, a distinction drawn from Aristotle, see Jean-François Lyotard, *The Postmodern Condition: A Report on Knowledge,* trans. Geoff Bennington and Brian Massumi (Minneapolis: University of Minnesota Press, 1984), p. 66, and Lyotard and Thébaud, *Just Gaming,* pp. 19–43, 28.

larities that structure much of the opposition between critical theory and genealogy. I argue that the *Gorgias* provides us with an alternative route through that terrain, as it tirelessly searches for the truth, all the while pointing out that even the most philosophical of questions are bound to struggles for position, that philosophy indeed presupposes a politics, and that these terms—philosophy and politics, dialectic and rhetoric, prosaic truth and poetic power—remain essentially contested in the agonistic economy of the dialogue. The *Gorgias* renders problematic its own (and our) tendency to eliminate the agon, to settle once and for all the meanings of such contested terms as *virtue, justice, goodness* and (political) *health*. I thus look to the dialogue to provide a post-philosophical sensibility that reinscribes a genealogical disturbance of all philosophical foundations within the humanist goal of securing such foundations as one of the preconditions for politics.

Plato's *Republic* expresses a similar tension between the impulse to sink the foundations of politics in a ground beyond contest and a textual practice that persistently disrupts its bid for comfortable theoretical closure, between the tyranny of globalizing discourse and the genealogical mobilization of the margins against the center. In the language of tragedy, the *Republic* sustains a tension between "the search for a single form" and "the irreducible richness of human value" that attends its heroic attempt to order the world through the powers of human intellect. On the face of it though, Plato seems to reject such ambiguities and tensions. The philosopher of the ideal city controls the world, as well as the men and women in it, through reason alone. The *Republic* argues that a polis and a life can be properly ordered by knowledge of the Good so as to avoid the tragic failures of human progress adumbrated by Sophocles and suffered by his Oedipus. The *Republic* seems to banish, not only tragedy and the tragic poets, but the very conflicts born of intense human commitment to irreconcilable values. Plato so constructs a theory of the good and a hierarchy of life plans that the tragic choice of an Agamemnon would not arise as a possibility. But should we look upon this strategy as an enlightened advance over the "primitive or benighted stage of ethical life and thought" tragedy represents?[20]

There are two problems with this view. First, it fails to recognize tragedy's own impulse to create a determinate solution to the problem of conflict, an impulse present within the form and structure of tragedy

20. Nussbaum, *Fragility of Goodness,* p. 51.

itself. Alongside the tragic view of human life, tragedies contain the origin of the denial of that view. Second, although the *Republic* contains a strong impulse to deny the tragic view and impose its own totalizing vision on the world, it reveals to us the seductive dangers involved in reducing the complexity and indeterminacy of human life. The ideal city resembles a Sparta partial to philosophy, it begins to decay as soon as it is constructed, and a philosopher like Socrates would be the first person banished from its gates, all of which should make us think twice about the "wisdom" of rejecting the tragic view. Plato's *Republic* suggests (at least on this reading) that the attempt to order the world by means of a foundationalist epistemology runs the risk of a reductionism reminiscent of Agamemnon at Aulis or Oedipus at Thebes. Such grandiose schemes to assert mastery over nature, men and women, and ourselves display the fundamental ambiguity that attends even our best efforts to order and circumscribe our lives. If tragedy contains the possibility of finding "solutions" to the moral and political conflicts it explores, then the *Republic* voices its own suspicions about the very solutions to such conflicts proposed by philosophy. The *Republic,* on this reading, subtly refuses the opposition between a critical theory intent on securing its own normative foundations and a genealogical anti-theory bent on disrupting all totalizing forms of discourse. Plato's dialogue thus gives voice to a post-foundationalist theoretical imagination that proves useful in negotiating the difficult terrain of theory construction by virtue of its simultaneous construal and denial of any systematic theoretical (and political) order. The *Republic* accomplishes this task by elaborating a "textual agonistics," an orderly discourse that interrupts, subverts, and disturbs its own projections of order.

In chapter 5, I turn to the *Oresteia* of Aeschylus to confront the difficulties of democracy and to point toward the possibility of what William Connolly has called a "democratic politics of disturbance," a politics that combines the democratic aspirations of critical theory with an attendant politics of resistance that disrupts and otherwise unsettles the normalizing tendencies of democracy's stable order. Such a democratic politics would seek, like the *Oresteia* itself, to problematize the sedimentations and accretions of cultural practices and norms that constitute the self and order, even as it provides democratic norms and identities against which to struggle. In my reading of the *Oresteia,* civic discourse (centered around establishing a meaning for justice) and gender hierarchy (returning women to their "natural" places) are "normal" categories, which are disrupted and transgressed from the very beginning of the trilogy right through to the moment of their inscription on the body politic in the final and foundational act of the drama. The norms of language and the norms of sexuality, democratic politics and the politics of difference—these are the themes that govern my appropriation of Aeschylus for a contemporary politics capable of radically democratizing difference.

The *Oresteia* also broaches the themes of communication and contest, consensus and coercion, debate and domination, already raised in the *Gorgias.* Aeschylus's drama directly confronts the multiple ways in which language can be (mis)used, how it establishes barriers to, just as easily as it enhances, communication. Language most obviously serves domination in and through Clytemnestra's masterful deception of Agamemnon. A powerful king and fierce warrior, he is slain naked in the bath by a treacherous woman—a shameful death in the eyes of the Argive elders. Yet Clytemnestra's duplicitous manipulation of words and their meanings only tells half the story of the linguistic disintegration that besets Argos. It is not only this queen with a man-counseling heart who transgresses the boundaries of speech. Everyone in the trilogy manipulates language in a way favorable to his, her, or their interests: Agamemnon claims justice for his sacrifice of Iphigeneia, Apollo (defending Orestes) likewise justifies the murder of Clytemnestra, while the Furies assert the justice of their prosecution of Orestes for his act of matricide. At stake in the *Oresteia,* then, is the meaning of *justice* itself, and the trilogy dramatizes the difficulties involved in reaching an agreement on the meaning of a word to which so many forces and interests lay claim. When Athena finally establishes the law court, she also founds a discursive order and space for the city and fixes the meaning of justice within it. That order defines which principles and which interests have the greatest voice, and which are relegated to relative silence.

Aeschylus's trilogy would seem the ancient validation of Habermas's enlightenment narrative, an archaic example of reasoned deliberation or discourse: the drama moves from chaos to order, darkness to light, perversion to normalcy, miscommunication to mutual understanding and reconciliation. This movement of progress occurs within the medium of a dramatic structure that reconciles conflicting forces and competing claims: chthonic with Olympian divinities, the older with the younger generation, Greek with barbarian, men with women. The trilogy thus traces the emergence of the democratic polis back to the foundation of a civic discourse rooted in rationally achieved consensus and dramatized in the trial scene of the *Eumenides*. Successful communication replaces the deceitful manipulation of language as the new world of the democratic polis triumphs over the troubled order of the dynastic past. The rational and creative principle of free consensus replaces what is local, natural, traditional, affective, and inherited. In the language of critical theory, the *Oresteia* attains its just and legitimate order, not through normatively ascribed agreement, but through communicatively *achieved* understanding.

Yet the conclusion of the *Oresteia* is far more ambiguous than this rationalist interpretation of the play allows. The trilogy certainly legitimates a democratic civic discourse and establishes a center that values what is new, democratic, rational, and masculine over what is traditional, filial, affective, and feminine. But it also disrupts its own comfortable teleology of progress, reason, and democratic justice in a "genealogical" movement of critique. The ambiguous establishment of the Areopagus by Athena complicates any easy attempt to read the *Oresteia* as a celebration of progress, successful communication, and democratic inclusion. The figure of Athena undermines the equation between masculine reason, democratic discourse, and the ultimate (celebratory) meaning of the drama through her own ambivalent status. This trilogy, already so full of transgressions and manipulations, ends not only with the achievement of clear and transparent communication, nor merely with the restoration of conflicting forces to their proper places. Consensus of a kind is achieved, but by a manipulative rhetoric, which the trilogy seeks to overcome, and through a sexually ambivalent figure who transgresses the very norms of gender she seeks to establish. The *Oresteia* institutes and legitimates a hierarchy of values based on subsequently valorized democratic "norms" that tend to normalize its subjects by establishing what "counts" as acceptable democratic practice and discourse. But the trilogy also shows us how difference can become domination and that the hierarchy it establishes is ultimately unjustifiable in the terms of the discourse that establishes it. The *Oresteia* is instructive because it reveals how the democratic subject relies on the constitution of sexual difference, and how that difference is "naturalized" or made essential through the production of a "feminine other" as that privileged subject's founding repudiation. Aeschylus thus elaborates the contours of a democratic politics of disturbance that resists the sedimented norms of a consensually achieved self and order even as it provides democratic norms against which to struggle.

REAPPROPRIATING THE PAST

The seductions of nostalgia, of romanticizing a past that perhaps never was, threaten to disable even the most imaginative use of the Greek past. This study in no way entails a "return to the Greeks," which is neither possible (inter alia, because we have not yet taken our full leave of antiquity) nor desirable. Needed here is a strategy of appropriation, one that neither ignores the importance of historical context nor succumbs to a thoroughly unimaginative use of the past forged from a rigid obedience to the present. The strategy I propose appropriates the Greeks by means of a "conceptual displacement," a forced mapping of the Greek concepts onto our modern (or postmodern) context. Wrenching these concepts out of their ancient context does not reconcile them with contemporary social and political reality; rather, it underscores the differences between them. For to be dis-placed means to be badly or ill placed, to be placed where one does not belong, to be an ancient Athenian playwright or philosopher in a postcapitalist, postcommunist, postmodern society. It signals irrelevance. To be badly or ill placed also implies being out of place (*atopos*): to be strange, alien, or unfamiliar. To be displaced (as in physics), however, means to be placed or moved to one side, to make room or make way for someone or something.

These latter meanings are significant for my own strategy of displacement, where to be out of place or placed aside have their appropriate and useful virtues: Greek concepts and claims "inappropriately" mapped onto the alien terrain of contemporary politics and theory create visible differences, throwing into relief those practices and beliefs that routinely go unnoticed and unchallenged. By dis-placing the Greeks, we also place them alongside us, as an alien projection of what we believe we no longer are. Such a mapping enables us to see ourselves anew and stimulates fresh thought about familiar circumstances, while the juxtaposition of the Greeks as the "other" allows us to investigate questions crucial to the present, provoking us to reflect on the suppressed, ignored, or otherwise concealed aspects of our practices and identities. With Foucault, we can regard such conceptual displacement as an opportunity for "getting free of ourselves."[21]

None of this is unfamiliar to Greek tragedy. Tragedy regularly appro-

21. Michel Foucault, *The History of Sexuality,* vol. 2: *The Use of Pleasure,* trans. Robert Hurley (New York: Vintage Books, 1986), p. 8.

priated the archaisms of the city's ancient myths to illuminate and interrogate the contours of the present and its values. In its confrontation of opposites, the presentation of the strange, the alien, the unfamiliar, and the liminal, Greek tragedy called the greatest achievements and most important precepts of its civilization into question: it routinely juxtaposed heroic kingship to democratic citizenship, archaic lyric to contemporary prose, the violence of the past to the comforts of the present, all within the scope of a performance that challenged the efficacy of human progress, justice, and polis life.[22] Similarly, tragic performances created an "other" place, a city such as mythical Thebes constructed as a site of displacement, where Athens portrayed a city on stage that was radically other than itself. In that "other" scene, Athens would act out "questions crucial to the polis, to the self, the family and society" by displacing them upon a city "imagined as the mirror opposite of Athens."[23] By projecting itself onto the stage and into the mythical past of a (dis)place such as mythical Thebes, Athens confronted the subjugations, exclusions, and denials that made up the normal life of the city.

A central argument of this book is that the tragedy and philosophical dialogue of the Greek polis provide a distinctive model for appropriating the past and its critical potential. Greek tragedy and philosophy themselves offer examples of how we might "use" the past to illuminate the contours of the present. Read this way, Greek tragedy and political philosophy help us exploit the improbable relationship between the ancient concepts and our modern context, making classical Greece an "other" place for us, a topos where we can confront the implicit patterns, structures, and practices of our own lives. My fundamental premise is that the classical past can stand to our present as the plays and dialogues of the poets and philosophers stood to the ancient city. Just as Greek tragedy and political theory provided the polis with a critical view of its public and private life, the classical past can provide us with a critical view of ours. A study of how Greek tragedy and classical political theory "use" the past can teach us how to "use" Greek tragedy and classical political theory in the present.[24]

22. J.-P. Vernant, "Tensions and Ambiguities in Greek Tragedy," in *Myth and Tragedy in Ancient Greece,* trans. Janet Lloyd (New York: Zone Books, 1988), pp. 32–33.

23. Froma I. Zeitlin, "Thebes: Theater of Self and Society in Athenian Drama," in *Nothing To Do with Dionysus? Athenian Drama in Its Social Context,* ed. John A. Winkler and Zeitlin (Princeton, N.J.: Princeton University Press, 1990), pp. 130–67.

24. This is an appropriate time to acknowledge my tremendous debt to those classicists who have most shaped my understanding of Greek tragedy and political thought. The works of Jean-Pierre Vernant and Pierre Vidal-Naquet, of Charles Segal, Froma

My appropriation of the drama and dialogue of classical Athens entails a strategy of interpretation as well. Readers who insist on the canons of scholarly correctness will no doubt find themselves dismayed at my apparent disregard of interpretive probity. Although I am conscious of the political, cultural, and historical contexts in which literary and theoretical reflection occur, I am not overly concerned with identifying the discursive fields and vocabularies in which a particular utterance may be situated. While it would be foolish to ignore the debt Plato's philosophy owes to the civic institution and cultural tradition of Attic tragedy, or to discount the influence of the sophistic enlightenment, the Athenian empire, or the plague on Sophocles' tragedy, the context provided is instructive, but not determinative, for interpretation. I am even less concerned with discovering what an author "meant"—with ascribing, then uncovering, the "original" meaning of a text. Sophocles undoubtedly had some particular meaning in mind when he composed his tragedies, but such meaning eventually escapes even the most controlling and omniscient of minds, if only because our assumptions, prejudices, and commitments can never become fully transparent to us. The playwright's *Oedipus Tyrannos* provides a case study in the seductions and dangers of recovering sovereign intention, for nowhere does an actor's life (or a would-be author's) more tragically betray the noblest of intentions than on Sophocles' Theban stage. Discounting authorial intention in no way implies, as it perhaps might for Humpty Dumpty, that a text can mean anything one wants it to mean. There are limits to the interpretive imagination, and those are imposed by the text itself.

My purpose is to "use" these texts to illuminate the meaning of contemporary political and theoretical terms, to intervene in, and contribute to, the ongoing contest that constitutes our identity as modern or postmodern subjects. In the service of this cause, I sometimes read my authors and their works against themselves, often against their surface conclusions, and consistently against canonical conventions. There is complex and contradictory meaning to be wrung from these texts, and the adventurous reader does not shrink from exploiting the fissures in

Zeitlin, Martha Nussbaum, Simon Goldhill, and Josiah Ober have all been formative for me. I am not a classicist myself, and I could not have trespassed on such foreign terrain without their help. Such trespasses run the obvious risks of any amateur who steps outside the comfortable confines of his own discipline (in my case, academic political theory), and no doubt errors of a philological kind are scattered throughout this book. I can only hope that I minimally disappoint Gary Miles and John Lynch, who patiently taught me Attic Greek during my stay at Santa Cruz.

their seemingly smooth surfaces. To turn these texts to contemporary uses, it is necessary to turn them against themselves, to read them out of context, if not against their context, to search out the moments and places in and at which these texts (knowingly or not) subvert themselves, and so can be made to say more that they originally might have meant. I believe the texts of Greek tragedy and philosophical dialogue under consideration both invite and teach such a reading, that one respects a text or a tradition, not by enshrining it, and so killing it, but by using it so that it continues to live. The irony here is that the Western philosophical "tradition" contains within itself the means to think beyond the constraints it imposes, if only we are willing to refashion past stories for present purposes, as did the tragic playwrights. The chapters on Sophocles, Socrates, Plato, and Aeschylus that follow are exercises meant to push at the edges of those constraints.

I know of no contemporary theoretical work on the perplexities of postmodernity that deploys the resources of its own tradition to such good effect as Max Horkheimer and Theodor Adorno's *Dialectic of Enlightenment.* These critics of the modern enlightenment adopt and adapt elements of that tradition in order to think the contradictions of the present, and they do so in ways that directly recall the tragic playwrights. Indeed, a book that takes the tale of Oedipus's own tragic enlightenment as emblematic of man's blind attempt to assert the power of his reason appropriately ends with a reflection on the work of Horkheimer and Adorno. But there are other reasons—besides the shared trope of enlightenment—both internal to the *Dialectic* and to my own project, that invite, if not compel, such a reflection. Pairing a Greek tragedy with *Dialectic of Enlightenment* makes perfect sense when we recall Nietzsche's importance to Horkheimer and Adorno, and tragedy's importance to Nietzsche.[25]

25. Max Horkheimer and Theodor W. Adorno, *Dialectic of Enlightenment,* trans. John Cumming (New York: Continuum Books, 1969). For specific discussions of Nietzsche's influence on Horkheimer and Adorno, see George Friedman, *The Political Philosophy of the Frankfurt School* (Ithaca, N.Y.: Cornell University Press, 1981); David Held, *Introduction to Critical Theory* (Berkeley: University of California Press, 1984); Martin Jay, *Marxism and Totality: The Adventures of a Concept from Lukács to Habermas* (Berkeley: University of California Press, 1984); Nancy S. Love, "Epistemology and Exchange: Marx, Nietzsche and Critical Theory," *New German Critique* 41 (Spring/Summer 1987): 71–94, and *Marx, Nietzsche and Modernity* (New York: Columbia University Press, 1986); James Miller, "Some Implications of Nietzsche's Thought for Marxism," *Telos* 37 (Fall 1978): 22–41; Peter Pütz, "Nietzsche and Critical Theory," *Telos* 50 (Winter 1981–82): 103–14; Gillian Rose, *The Melancholy Science: An Introduction to the Thought of Theodor Adorno* (New York: Columbia University Press, 1978). For a negative assessment of Nietzsche's influence, see Habermas, "Entwinement of Myth

It is therefore not at all coincidental that Horkheimer and Adorno brought sensibilities that shared much with Greek tragedy and theory to their analysis of contemporary crisis. *Dialectic* is a thoroughly modern book, which nonetheless transgresses our modern academic categories and distinctions: as poetic as it is theoretical, as philosophical as it is political, and as archaic in its tone and language as it is modern or postmodern, *Dialectic of Enlightenment* distinctly appropriates and displays the style and sensibility of Greek tragedy and theory, while still maintaining its own contemporary concerns and purposes.[26]

I am referring here to how Horkheimer and Adorno reinsert the ancient sense of the tragic into contemporary theorizing in a way that alerts us to the tremendous losses suffered in the name, and for the sake, of modernity—losses that liberal and radical theorists alike have largely ignored. Such theorizing, I argue, is incomplete, rather than wrong, in its assessment of modernity. Perhaps Greek tragedy can indeed help "modern man . . . to confront the darker side of his own existence and explore beneath the surface of his own highly rationalized, desacralized, excessively technologized culture,"[27] and so provide a useful corrective to the pervasive view of history as unmitigated progress.

This sense of the tragic is evoked in the title of the concluding chapter, a title that is not without its own ambiguities. It is ambiguous, because "The Tragedy of Critical Theory" suggests at least two meanings. First, it alludes to a heroic struggle fought and lost by the critical theorists against the regressive advances of enlightenment: what Hork-

---

and Enlightenment." All this attention to the Nietzsche connection should not obscure the affinities between Adorno and Walter Benjamin, whose *Ursprung des deutschen Trauerspiels* (trans. John Osborne as *The Origin of German Tragic Drama* [London: NLB, 1977]) had a profound and lasting effect on Adorno's work. In fact, much of Adorno's "tragic" sensibility comes from Benjamin. See Susan Buck-Morss's *The Origins of Negative Dialectics: Theodor Adorno, Walter Benjamin and the Frankfurt Institute* (New York: Free Press, 1977), still one of the best books on Adorno's version of critical theory. For the most recent scholarship on Nietzsche's specific influence on *Dialectic of Enlightenment,* see Douglas Kellner's "Critical Theory Today: Revisiting the Classics," *Theory, Culture and Society* 10, 2: 43–60.

26. Despite its suggestive title, Paul Connerton's *The Tragedy of Enlightenment: An Essay on the Frankfurt School* (London: Cambridge University Press, 1980), makes no systematic effort to connect Greek tragedy with critical theory. In "The Theatre of the 'Other': Adorno, Poststructuralism and the Critique of Identity," *Philosophy and Social Criticism* 17, 3 (1991): 243–63, Samir Gandesha characterizes Adorno's thought (including his collaborative work with Horkheimer) as a "retrieval of the structure of tragedy" and focuses on the category of remembered suffering.

27. Charles P. Segal, "Greek Tragedy and Society: A Structuralist Perspective," in *Interpreting Greek Tragedy: Myth, Poetry, Text* (Ithaca, N.Y.: Cornell University Press, 1986), p. 23.

heimer and Adorno saw to be the irresistible development toward total social integration. The story of critical theory, then, constitutes both a theoretical and political tragedy. Horkheimer and Adorno came to see social freedom and enlightened thought, not as moments of a reconciled totality, but as opposite poles of an irreconcilable dialectic. Nevertheless, the authors faced this pessimistic conclusion with heroic intransigence, themselves confirming that "critical thought (which does not abandon its commitment even in the face of progress) demands support for the residues of freedom and for tendencies toward true humanism, even if these seem powerless in regard to the main course of history."[28] Against all theoretical and political opposition, Horkheimer and Adorno never stopped resisting forces of integration that appeared to them to be as implacable as archaic fate.

Critical theory, however, has more than just a tragic history to recommend it. It also has a tragic consciousness. Horkheimer and Adorno are thus more than tragic figures caught in a web of fate not wholly of their own making. They are also playwrights of a sort, composing a drama about the vicissitudes of enlightenment. The "tragedy" of critical theory thus refers to the tragic elements and the tragic sensibility that Horkheimer and Adorno bring to their theorizing. *Dialectic of Enlightenment* is a modern tragedy, even though its authors were convinced that the culture industry made tragedy impossible. That it *is* a work of tragedy in such an anti-tragic climate makes *Dialectic* untimely, and, if we are to believe Nietzsche, it is precisely this untimeliness that recommends it.[29]

A second reason for reading *Dialectic* has to do with how we might come to understand the classical and contemporary texts, each in the light of the other. Horkheimer and Adorno can help us read the works of tragedy and theory in a context and with an urgency and insight we would otherwise lack. Conversely, Greek tragedy and theory can teach us to recognize and appreciate the tragic components of fate, suffering, and human mutability, as well as detect the fault lines that traverse the seemingly stable foundations of our own modernized and technicized society—instabilities *Dialectic* exposes. Pairing a tragedy with a work

28. Horkheimer and Adorno, *Dialectic of Enlightenment,* ix

29. For Nietzsche, the point in studying the thought of the classical past was its ability to act "counter to our time and thereby..on our time and, let us hope, for the benefit of a time to come" ("On the Uses and Disadvantages of History for Life" (1874), in *Untimely Meditations,* trans. R. J. Hollingdale [Cambridge: Routledge & Kegan Paul, 1983], p. 60).

of contemporary theory thus enriches our reading of the latter, while simultaneously disclosing neglected or ignored aspects of the former. Here is one way in which *Dialectic* establishes a dialogue between Greek tragedy (and political theory read in its context) and the thought of the modern enlightenment.

There is one last way in which Horkheimer and Adorno's work promotes a dialogue between classical and contemporary theory, and thus one more reason for writing about it. In spite of the insistence (by Habermas and Foucault) on modernity's distinctiveness and the obsolescence of premodern concepts and categories, which seals the past off from the present, *Dialectic* manages to maintain these two extremes in uneasy and fruitful tension, much as the polis and its institutions (including tragedy) maintained an uneasy tension between myth and enlightenment, heroic individualism and democratic community, romantic legend of the past and the harsh reality of the present. Horkheimer and Adorno are able to provide a link between an irretrievable past and an almost unlivable present that threatens to accelerate out of control. Yet their project is no more an attempt to recover the past than was tragedy's. *Dialectic of Enlightenment* brings past and present together in an uneasy unity of opposites, not to accomplish the conservation of the past, but in order to use it all the more effectively for the sake of a better future.

2

Sophocles' *Oedipus Tyrannos*

The Tragedy of Enlightenment

The accompanying critique of enlightenment is intended to prepare the way for a positive notion of enlightenment which will release it from entanglement in blind domination.

—Max Horkheimer and Theodor Adorno, *Dialectic of Enlightenment*

What is found at the historical beginning of things is not the inviolable identity of their origins; it is the dissension of other things. It is disparity.

—Michel Foucault, "Nietzsche, Genealogy, History," in *The Foucault Reader*

That the tragedy of Oedipus is a tragedy of enlightenment, dramatizing the triumphs and failures attending the heroic attempts of enlightened reason to fix the identity of the rational, autonomous, emancipated, and fully self-constituted subject, is indicated by the subtitle of this chapter. As current challenges to the hegemony of Western rationality intimate, however, fifth-century Athens and the tragic theater of Sophocles are not the sole contexts of this fundamental ambiguity about reason, enlightened thought, progress, human mastery, and control. Communitarian, feminist, and especially radical postmodern critics of the "project of modernity" attest to the fact that enlightened reason has lost its universal appeal at a time when it can no longer appeal to universals.[1] The once unshakable support grounding our understanding of

1. Communitarian thinkers who have questioned the universal epistemological assumptions of the Enlightenment include Alasdair MacIntyre, Michael Walzer, Charles Taylor, and Michael Sandel. Feminist thinkers such as Carol Gilligan, Carole Pateman, Susan Moller Okin, Virginia Held, Iris Marion Young, Nancy Fraser, Drucilla Cornell, and Joan Tronto have all challenged abstract conceptions of the self that result in a subjectivity blind to the constraints of gender. The most radical criticism of the Enlighten-

nature, other men and women, and ourselves has irreparably fractured and fallen away. The meaning of *enlightenment* is now up for grabs; the territory of reason, emancipation, and progress is contested terrain.

In that contest, we are given a choice between reason defined as universal and a reason that is radically contingent, between practices that transcend the time and place of their emergence and others that bear the ineradicable marks of their earthly creation, between enlightenment celebrated as a process of self-knowledge and enlightenment exposed as a strategy of subjugation, between completing the project of modernity and disturbing all enlightenment-based narratives of emancipation. We are asked to choose between a critical theory that aims to resolve all of the contradictions that mark modernity and a genealogical critique that patiently deepens those contradictions in its effort to expose the deceptions all such smoothly functioning narratives conceal. Either enlightenment increases our autonomy, responsibility, and liberty or the very technologies of truth meant to secure such achievements conceal the workings of power from us precisely when we believe ourselves to be wholly emancipated beings. In these contending accounts, enlightenment betokens either the potential for liberation or else the effects of a subtle, disciplinary power.

Within the terms of the present contest, critical theory and genealogical criticism share precious few, if any, common assumptions about the meaning and fate of enlightened modernity. Polarized by the radical opposition between Jürgen Habermas's aim to complete the emancipatory project of the modern enlightenment and Michel Foucault's determination to disrupt its normalizing, disciplinary drift, critical theory and genealogy articulate virtually antithetical accounts of the origin(s), aims, and effects of enlightenment. The coordinates mapped out by critical theory and genealogy have so far resisted any alternative routes through the enlightenment terrain they chart. But is it possible to envision a post-enlightenment ethos that reinscribes a (genealogical) appreciation of the ambiguities, contradictions, and mysteries of the world that enlightenment, both ancient and modern, seems ruthlessly bent on suppressing, without at the same time relinquishing the positive gains provided by enlightened thought? Might we not be able to articulate a

---

ment's universal epistemological assumptions comes, of course, from "poststructuralist" thinkers such as Michel Foucault, Jacques Derrida, Jean-François Lyotard, and Jean Baudrillard.

self and order constituted from the norm of enlightened reason while allowing the "other" of reason (in its interior, internal, and external guises) to expose those arbitrary elements that comprise our own contingently constructed histories? That is, can we adopt a wholly ironic stance toward the standards of enlightened reason, a stance that combines the quest to fulfill the emancipatory aspirations of enlightenment with an unrelenting critique meant to disturb its normalizing and disciplinary effects? Is it possible to pursue a critique of enlightenment that refuses both to give up enlightened thought and to succumb to entanglement in blind domination?

Sophocles' *Oedipus Tyrannos* suggests that it is.[2] A tragedy particularly well suited for exploring the contours of a post-enlightenment ethos, the play both portrays and embodies all the tensions, ambiguities, and ironies found in enlightenment itself. Although critical of the pretensions of the (then) new sophistic learning, Sophocles' tragedy nonetheless participates in the very process of enlightenment it suspects. *Oedipus Tyrannos* structures its material with the rational will of its doomed hero in a systematic and coherent ordering of a decidedly disordered reality. Yet if it is true that "as a negation of the possibility of a systematic order of knowledge, tragedy itself is one of the finest examples of this supposedly impossible order,"[3] then *Oedipus Tyrannos* is indeed one of the finest examples of that kind of tragedy. This chapter explores Sophocles' contribution to just such an epistemology of disruption, a form of enlightened thinking that (like the play itself) sustains and celebrates the aims of enlightenment even as it exposes and opposes enlightenment's tendency to discipline and normalize the subjects it seeks to empower.

I

Enlightenment, as the word itself suggests, illuminates, reveals, or makes clear. To shed light on a subject or a problem implies replacing the darkness of ignorance and confusion with understanding and knowledge,

2. I have used R. C. Jebb's edition, *The Oedipus Tyrannus of Sophocles* (Cambridge: Cambridge University Press, 1897), with its invaluable commentary. Unless otherwise noted, all translations are by David Grene, from *Oedipus the King,* in *Sophocles,* vol. 1 of *The Complete Greek Tragedies,* ed. David Grene and Richmond Lattimore, 2d ed. (Chicago: University of Chicago Press, 1991).

3. This is part direct citation and part paraphrase of Timothy Reiss, *Tragedy and Truth: Studies in the Development of a Renaissance and Neoclassical Discourse* (New Haven, Conn.: Yale University Press, 1980), p. 21.

substituting certainty for mystery, clarity for obscurity. To be enlightened also means to make a discovery. Someone who is suddenly enlightened "sees" the truth either about her or himself, or about the surrounding world of people and things, for the first time. Such experiences of light and darkness, sight and blindness pervade Sophocles' play and plague Oedipus. For ancient Greeks, moreover, to say one "knew" something amounted to saying one had seen it: the classical Greek word *oida,* "I know," literally means "I have seen."[4] That is why Oedipus allies himself with Phoebus Apollo, the bringer and revealer of light, and proclaims continually throughout the play that he will "reveal all," "bring it all to light," and not rest until he has discovered the murderer of Laius and revealed the mystery of his birth.

Enlightenment also implies movement and progress: from blindness to sight, darkness to light, ignorance to knowledge. This further indicates a movement from illusion to reality, from appearance and seeming to essence and being. The course of Sophocles' play thus charts a journey that begins with Oedipus's ignorance concerning his parents, his home, and himself and ends in an all-too-brutal clarity that reveals his "true" identity. Such forward movement also suggests a break, not only with the past, with old ways and patterns of thought, but with nature as well, with its limits and constraints. Enlightenment thus promises freedom or emancipation from nature, from one's origin, tradition, history, and fate. For Oedipus, this means initially that he must flee his "home" in Corinth to outwit the oracle, defeat the Sphinx, that symbol of untamed savagery,[5] and assume the throne of Thebes, not as hereditary *basileus,* but as autonomous *tyrannos.*[6] Nature, custom, tradition,

4. See Bruno Snell, *The Discovery of the Mind: The Greek Origins of European Thought,* trans. T. G. Rosenmeyer (Cambridge, Mass.: Harvard University Press, 1953), esp. "Homer's View of Man," pp. 1–22. The association of truth and clarity is "characteristic of all ages of enlightenment," writes Bernard Knox (*Oedipus at Thebes* [New Haven, Conn.: Yale University Press, 1957], p. 133).

5. On the savage nature of the Sphinx, see Charles Segal, "The Music of the Sphinx," in *Contemporary Literary Hermeneutics,* ed. Stephanus Kresic (Ottawa: Ottawa University Press, 1981), p. 154. The Sphinx is a *chresmodos,* a singer of oracles (1200). But her song is harsh (36), tricky (130), and that of a rhapsode dog (391), a "hook-taloned maiden singer of riddling oracles" (1199–1200). Euripides describes her song as "unmusic (*Phoenissae* 807), and in a lost play he describes the riddle as a horrible shrieking whistle. Segal cites this as evidence that the Sphinx symbolizes the reverse of civilization: "Her song enables her to prey upon and destroy human community."

6. On the theme of emancipation from tradition, the past, and one's origins and birth, see Arlene Saxonhouse, "The Tyranny of Reason in the World of the Polis," *APSR* 82, 4 (Dec. 1988): 1261–75.

and destiny all appear to give way before the progress of Oedipus's enlightened intellect.

But Oedipus's intellectual progress also betrays the progress of a powerful (and tyrannical) intellect. The great "Ode to Man" of Sophocles' *Antigone,* an ironic meditation on the progress of enlightenment, aptly prefaces any discussion of *Oedipus Tyrannos.* The chorus extols the many powers of enlightened man: many are the wonders (and terrors) of the world, yet none more wonderful (and terrible) than man (*Polla ta deina, kouden anthropou deinoteron pelei*). Ingenious, intelligent, skillful self-taught, self-made, all-devising, all-resourceful, and all-powerful, the inventor of speech and thought, man finds his sovereignty in his knowledge. His skill overcomes all the greatest powers of the world: with the help of navigation, he traverses the stormy seas and breaks a path in the trackless wilderness; with the art of agriculture, he wearies and subdues the earth, forcing her to yield up produce and profit; the wild beasts he snares, tames, yokes, or overpowers, bending them to his will; by the art of politics, he founds cities and establishes customs, laws, and traditions peacefully to regulate a life in common. From death alone he has procured no escape, although against irresistible diseases he has devised remedies. In his knowledge and in his power, man is the measure of all things (332–52 paraphrased).

Hardly does the chorus finish its praise of man than it reflects on the radically ambiguous character of the human condition. Despite man's apparent mastery over the strange, awful, and powerful forces of the world, however, he has been unable to master the strangest, most awful, and most powerful of them all: himself. Man is *deinos* in the double sense of that word: wonderful, awesome, mighty, wondrous, clever, skillful *and* awful, terrible, dangerous, fearful, and savage. And he is most awful and dangerous to himself. The tracks we break in the wild circle back, so many endless paths to nowhere; the city that shelters us from savagery provides little security against the savagery within us; estranged and strangers, we are homeless wherever we may seek to make ourselves a home; even in our most complete knowledge, we remain imperfect; the world remains impenetrably obscure even to the most discerning gaze. Human knowledge is thus profound ignorance; our power is impotence; our greatest achievements are also our greatest failures. We are caught, Sophocles suggests, between the elusive promises of enlightenment and the surprising reversals of tragedy.

The Ode to Man, then, is not so confident in its claims about human power as might initially appear.[7] The double meaning of *deinos* and the play upon other ambiguous words, as well as the position of the ode in relation to the dramatic action, force a fundamental reorientation toward the achievements of enlightenment.[8] If, as the ode suggests, enlightened man proudly proclaims his sovereignty and control, yet has difficulty controlling himself, other men and women, and nature, then Oedipus's own enlightenment will follow no easy road that leads from darkness to light, blindness to sight, slavery to mastery. A man who trusts solely to the faulty vision of eyes that deceive him, his enlightenment lies along a slow, crooked, and cruel path, one that leads from a confident, although mistaken, knowledge to the terrible truth of his own unparalleled ignorance. Enlightened Oedipus radiates disaster triumphant.[9]

Weakest and most vulnerable precisely where he feels strongest and most capable, Oedipus embodies all the ambiguities and ironies of enlightenment itself. Sophocles' greatest play thus reflects "the ambiguity of man's power to control his world and manage his life by intelligence,"[10] and so points to the irreconcilable dialectic between the seemingly unlimited potential of our enlightened reason and our inability fully to circumscribe ourselves and our world.[11] Other tragedies, most notably Aeschylus's *Oresteia,* celebrate the civilizing power of human intelligence, extol the rational mastery of nature and glorify the hard-won law of the polis, while remembering the fearful chthonic powers that undergird the precarious achievements of civilization.[12] Aeschylus's

7. Charles Segal, "Sophocles' Praise of Man and the Conflicts of the *Antigone,*" *Arion* 3, 2 (Summer 1964): 46–66; Seth Benardete, "A Reading of Sophocles' *Antigone* I," *Interpretation* 4, 3 (Spring 1975): 148–96; J. T. Sheppard, *The Wisdom of Sophocles* (London: G. Allen & Unwin, 1947), 46–48; R. F. Goheen, *The Imagery of Sophocles' Antigone: A Study of Poetic Language and Structure* (Princeton, N.J.: Princeton University Press, 1951), pp. 97, 141; Laszlo Versenyi, *Man's Measure: A Study of the Greek Image of Man from Homer to Sophocles* (Albany: State University of New York Press, 1974), pp. 208–13.

8. The juxtapositions of resourceful (*pantoporos,* 360) and resourceless (*aporos*), and highest in the city (*hypsipolis*) and cityless (*apolis*), also point up the ambiguous meaning of *deinos.*

9. I paraphrase this line from Max Horkheimer and Theodor W. Adorno, *Dialectic of Enlightenment,* trans. John Cumming (New York: Continuum Books, 1969), p. 3, in anticipation of chapter 6.

10. For this quotation and on the theme of civilization and savagery, see Charles Segal *Tragedy and Civilization: An Interpretation of Sophocles* (Cambridge, Mass.: Harvard University Press, 1981), p. 232, and esp. ch. 8.

11. On paradox in *Oedipus,* see W. C. Helmbold, "The Paradox of Oedipus," *American Journal of Philology* 72, 3 (1951): 293–300.

12. Brian Vickers, *Towards Greek Tragedy: Drama, Myth, Society* (1973; New York: Longman, 1979), p. 425

own treatment of the Oedipus story recalls the great themes of the *Oresteia:* his trilogy casts the lame hero against a vast backdrop of dynastic ambition, salvation of the city, and an inherited curse that spans several generations. Yet the reversals from enlightenment to ignorance, mastery to impotence, remain secondary themes in both trilogies:[13] it is not his own but a family curse that dooms Aeschylus's Oedipus. Sophocles, on the other hand, forcefully concentrates the temporal and dramatic action and purposely shifts his attention to these latter themes. His *Oedipus* condenses a trilogy into one play, contracts the action to a single day, and focuses all drama on the character and fate of one individual: Oedipus commands the center of the stage.[14] Aeschylus's Oedipus kills his father at a crossroads near a shrine of the Furies in Boeotia. Sophocles' Oedipus commits the murder at a place where the three roads meet on his fate-defying flight away from Corinth, Delphi, and the sanctuary of Apollo, one of whose injunctions was "Know thyself" (*gnōthi seauton*) and whose oracle had prophesied Oedipus's horrible destiny.[15] The central theme of *Oedipus Tyrannos* is thus the ambiguous nature of (self-)enlightenment, an ambiguity the play explores in terms of fate and freedom, civilization and savagery, and through the metaphor of incest.

Sophocles considers Oedipus's "enlightened" relationship to his history, birth, and origins as a problem of fate and freedom, and introduces that problem through the figure of the *tyrannos*. The fifth-century *tyrannos* was the paradigm of the free individual—unbound by tradition, birth, history, or inherited limits. The tyrant was the man who could do and be almost anything, and who, in his escape from the past, "could become a model for human rationality and theorizing, [with] the capacity to move beyond accepted boundaries and opinions in order to imagine what was previously unimaginable, to transform the world through the power of one's mind and speech, severed from the bonds of birth and history."[16] Oedipus embodies just that combina-

13. Charles Segal, "Sophocles," in *Ancient Writers: Greece and Rome* (New York: Charles Scribner's Sons, 1982), p. 196, notes that of the three plays in Aeschylus's trilogy, *Laius, Oedipus,* and *Seven against Thebes,* only the last survives, and it is from the *Seven* and a few fragments that we are able to reconstruct the general outlines of the trilogy.

14. On this point, see Versenyi, *Man's Measure,* p. 214 and passim.

15. Segal, "Sophocles," p. 196. See also R. P. Winnington-Ingram, *Sophocles: An Interpretation* (Cambridge: Cambridge University Press, 1980), p. 178, for a discussion of Apollo's role in the enlightenment of Oedipus.

16. Saxonhouse, "Tyranny of Reason," p. 1261. This formulation is perhaps idiosyncratic to Sophocles' play, although Thucydides does make a similar distinction between hereditary kingship (*basileia*) and tyranny, the latter characterized by rule whose

tion of historical boundlessness and prideful human rationality that describes the tyrant. I have already mentioned how Oedipus solved the riddle of the Sphinx and assumed the throne of Thebes, not as hereditary *basileus* (which he in fact was), but as *tyrannos.* Yet Oedipus's attempt to escape his past, parents, and origins, and so fate, preceded his arrival at Thebes. A drunkard's insinuation about his birth first led Oedipus to Apollo's oracle (779–93), and it was the oracle's response that he, Oedipus, would murder his father and wed his mother that set him on the road to Thebes. Together with his intellectual skill, the uncertainty about his birth confers on Oedipus a sense of power, optimism, and hope, as though he could, alone and unaided, master his fate, the way he had mastered the Sphinx. When Oedipus discovers himself to be, not a child of Chance, but the accursed son of his all-too-mortal parents, Laius and Jocasta, we see before us a man with a particular history, origin, and destiny, which, no matter how hard he tries, he cannot escape, because it constitutes his very being. Watching Oedipus enlighten himself, we cannot help but recall Foucault's observation about modern disciplinary power: no matter how much in control we believe ourselves to be, forces beyond our power circumscribe our lives and direct our destinies, even as we desperately, sometimes madly, attempt to shape the forces that shape us.[17]

We should also recall, with Bernard Knox, that Oedipus's title *tyrannos* may refer, not only to the lame hero, but to Athens as well. Sophocles' Oedipus is thus "a symbolic representation of Periclean Athens," an *anthrōpos tyrannos* who resembles the *polis tyrannos* and possesses that imperial city's self-taught, self-made, and unaided ability to seize control of the environment, bending and forcing it to comply with its human designs.[18] In his role as *tyrannos,* Oedipus embodies the splendor and power of Athens: his attempt to assert dominion over nature and his unquenchable drive for human mastery; his forcefulness of purpose, his impatience, decisiveness, and daring, bordering on reckless-

---

privilege suffers no limits, hereditary, constitutional, or otherwise (Thucydides, *History of the Peloponnesian War* 1.13.1–17). The word *tyrannos* did not originally appear in the title of the play, but was assigned to it by tradition, perhaps as early as Aristotle; see Segal, "Sophocles." In any case, *tyrannos* underwent a series of transformations from its (probably) non-Greek origins in the seventh century, and it was not until the fourth century that it acquired a distinctly negative connotation; see A. Andrewes, *The Greek Tyrants,* 4th ed. (1956; New York: Harper & Row, 1962), pp. 28–30.

17. Michel Foucault, *Discipline and Punish: The Birth of the Prison,* trans. Alan Sheridan (1977; New York: Vintage Books, 1979), "The Carceral Archipelago."

18. Knox, *Oedipus at Thebes,* p. 107.

ness; his intoxication with his own accomplishments, his liberation from the constraints of all traditional pieties; his restlessness, innovation, and ingenuity; his designs that are swift alike in conception and execution, all recall the "fierce creative energy, the uncompromising logic, the initiative and daring which brought Athens to the pinnacle of worldly power."[19] To put matters this way suggests that the audience watching Oedipus also watched its own tragic power on stage.

If Knox is right about Oedipus, Athens, and the play's concern with the political context of its performance, then *Oedipus Tyrannos* is also about the Athenians' own collective self-knowledge, the limits of that knowledge, and the limits of the city's drive for empire. Through the mantic vision of the poet, the audience witnessed in "symbolic, riddling, and prophetic terms" the utter disaster immanent in Athenian intellectual and political greatness.[20] Encoded in Oedipus's name and role as *tyrannos,* then, is also the riddle of the character and fate of the Athenian citizen audience watching the play; for both "come to disaster through the valiant exercise of the very qualities that have made them great."[21]

The humane and humanizing power of Oedipus's (and Athens's) intellect proves, in this tragic reversal, to be the obverse of a savage bestiality. All the achievements of the human intellect centered on Oedipus "point to the ironies that attend [his] intellectual mastery as a civilizing hero." His powerful intellect can neither know nor master his own nature—that of a plowman who furrows forbidden fields, a hunter who tracks and snares himself, a pilot who scuttles his craft in safe harbor, a doctor who cannot diagnose his own dreadful disease, a seer blind to the circumstances of his name, place, and birth. He who finds unity beneath diversity, identity in plurality, and the universal in the particular does not see the excess of his own unity: that he is both husband and son to the same woman, both father and brother to the same children—that he himself is the exception to the riddle of the Sphinx, the murderer of Laius, and cause of the plague.[22]

19. Ibid., p. 105.
20. Ibid, p. 99.
21. Ibid, p. 106. Allusion to the plague that struck Athens (and claimed the life of Pericles) shortly before Sophocles' play was produced must also be counted along with references to Pericles, Athens, and empire as evidence that Sophocles was commenting on contemporary Athens. On the relation of history to Sophoclean tragedy, see, too, Victor Ehrenberg, *Sophocles and Pericles* (Oxford: Oxford University Press, 1954).
22. The quotation and the characterization of Oedipus come from Segal, *Tragedy and Civilization,* p. 232.

Oedipus divides and arranges the contents of the world, yet at the same time unwittingly obliterates the most sacred of boundaries. The forcefulness of intellect with which he crosses the boundaries that separate the particular from the general, the many from the one, parallels the transgressions that characterize the private and public aspects of his life. In breaking the taboos against patricide and incest, Oedipus destroys the boundaries that separate the civilized city from savage nature, humanity from bestiality. By killing his father and wedding his mother, Oedipus disrupts the "natural" succession of generations. Both inside and outside, a foreigner in his own land, an anomalous man who touches both gods and beasts at once, powerless where he ought to rule most securely, Oedipus embodies a tragic perspective in which men and women (and their actions) are seen, "not as things that can be defined or described, but as problems." Tragedy presents them "as riddles whose double meanings can never be pinned down or exhausted."[23] Enlightenment and Oedipus both ultimately founder on the rock of impenetrable mystery, their intellectual power no match for the ironies of human life.

Sophocles directly broaches the paradoxical course of Oedipus's enlightenment in the staged confrontation between Oedipus and Tiresias. Tiresias's insightful blindness provides, in both spectacle and substance, the dramatic counterpoint to Oedipus's own blind sight. The seer's prophetic, riddling, and symbolic knowledge stands in direct opposition to the king's analytical rigor, coherent logic, strict method, and highly structured and structuring intellect. Like the Sphinx and Apollo, Tiresias neither speaks out nor conceals, but gives a sign. And Oedipus is as impatient with the perplexing and ambiguous signs of the prophet as he is with all the other riddles of life. Where Oedipus demands unequivocal answers, clear solutions, and decisive action, Tiresias offers impenetrable riddles, ambiguous enigma, and is at first reluctant to speak at all, wishing he had never come before the king. Oedipus, of course, has neither ears to hear nor eyes to see what is plainly before him. Even when the prophet speaks and reveals the unambiguous truth, Oedipus is constitutionally incapable of receiving it. Blind, dependent on guide and staff, the prophet summoned by Oedipus is a helpless picture of the king's own broken future. The prophetic wisdom of Tiresias stands as

23. Jean-Pierre Vernant, "Tensions and Ambiguities in Greek Tragedy," in id. and Pierre Vidal-Naquet, *Myth and Tragedy in Ancient Greece,* trans. Janet Lloyd (New York: Zone Books, 1988), p. 38.

a rebuke to the mastering intellect of Oedipus, even as it foreshadows Oedipus's own insightful blindness.[24]

The scene juxtaposes two kinds of knowledge, a juxtaposition that recurs in the unreconciled dialectic between the play's "message" and its dramatic "structure." Oedipus's fall, as the chorus in the central stasimon acknowledges, certainly vindicates the pious rebuke of the prophet. At the same time, though, the play organizes, structures, and clarifies the world with the will of an Oedipus. The heroic impulse embodied in the form of the drama itself works to subvert the experiences of hierophany, enigma, and perplexity and to engender in the spectator a profound sense of tension and ambiguity. The play asks us both to be analytical, logical, and rigorous *and* to attend to the enigmatic, prophetic, and poetic. Where Oedipus's tyranny of mind constantly drives the world apart into polarities, which eventually collapse around him, the play itself holds both sensibilities in uneasy and unreconciled tension. Sophocles' play both participates in, and is critical of, the fifth-century enlightenment, with its faith in emancipation through the progress of knowledge. From an ironic stance that resists the settled terms of the current controversy over modernity and the Enlightenment, *Oedipus Tyrannos* both embodies the powerful drive toward the clarity, understanding, and rational discourse that marks Habermas's critical theory and constitutes a cautionary tale about the deployment of enlightened discourses that parallels Foucault's warnings about the insufficiencies of reason. Sophocles' play thus both encourages us to cherish the mysterious, the enchanted, and the enigmatic as indispensable allies against the increasing disenchantment of a fully enlightened world and counsels us not to abjure what is implicit in even the most critical and painstakingly genealogical of discourses: the profound need of enlightened men and women to structure and order the world by means of reason and in their own image.

II

Through the metaphors of sight and blindness, Sophocles weaves the themes of enlightenment and its reversal into the very fabric of the

24. On the paradox of sight and blindness in the *Oedipus,* see R. G. A. Buxton, "Blindness and Limits: Sophokles and the Logic of Myth," *Journal of Hellenic Studies* 100 (1980): 22–37

hero's name, one possible meaning of which derives from the Greek root *oidi-* (*oidanō, oideō,* "to swell"). Coupled with *pous* (foot) this etymology, all too well known to Oedipus, refers to his pierced ankles and pronounced limp; hence the name means "swell-foot." We are thus simultaneously reminded of the outcast child he was and of the exiled man he will soon become. In a series of ironic phrases, Sophocles focuses attention on Oedipus's feet as a clue to the knowledge of his origins: "The Sphinx induced us to look at what was at our feet" (*to pros posi skopein,* 130); "the dread footed curse" (*deinopous,* 418); forlorn and with miserable foot (*meleos meleōi podi chēreuōn,* 479); "The highfooted laws of Zeus" (*hypsipodes,* 866), and, finally, "pride . . . plunges into sheer necessity where it uses a useless foot" (*ou podi chrēsimōi chrētai,* 876). Moreover, since *dipous* means "two-footed," and *Oi* is an untranslatable expression of grief and pain, *Oidipous* (Oedipus) can also mean "alas, two-footed" (*oi-dipous*). As Knox observes, all of these phrases point with horrible irony to the maimed foot of Oedipus, which forms part of his name and is a clue to his birth. Two of them, *hypsipodes* and *deinopous,* pun on the king's name itself.[25]

Another meaning, playing on the similarity between *oidi-* and *oida,* "to have seen," hence, "to know," suggests the name "know-foot," an appropriate appellation for the man who solved the riddle about feet.[26] *Oida* in one form or another occurs constantly throughout the play, and the words "I know" are never far from Oedipus's lips. This meaning connects Oedipus directly to the play's central themes of sight and blindness, light and darkness, knowledge and ignorance.[27] Early in the play, the priest says to Oedipus, "perhaps you know [*oistha pou*] something from a man" (43). This "perhaps you know" points to a different, more damaging sense of the meaning of *oida-pou,* because *pou* with a circumflex means "where," but without it, as here, it means "somewhere," "perhaps," "I suppose." But nowhere does Sophocles trade on the ambiguous sense of his hero's name with such ironic force as when the Corinthian messenger etymologizes Oedipus's name in a

25. I have consulted Knox, *Oedipus at Thebes,* pp. 182–84, on the significance of Oedipus's foot. All translations are his, except for line 130, where I have adopted Grene's "induced" for Knox's "forced" as a rendering of *prosēgeto.*

26. Sophocles, *Oedipus Tyrannus,* ed. M. L. Earle (New York: American Book Co., 1901), p. 40.

27. Both Snell and Heidegger discuss the relation between verbs of sight and verbs of knowledge: Snell, *Discovery of the Mind,* pp. 1–22; Martin Heidegger, *Being and Time,* trans. John Macquarrie and Edward Robinson (New York: Harper, 1962), pp. 214–17.

series of puns on "know where" (*mathoim' hopou / Oidipou / katisth' hopou,* 924–26), ironically pointing to the fact that Oedipus does not know who or where he is.[28] The ambiguous status of Oedipus's knowledge and place thus sounds in his very name, while the confident knowledge expressed by the king is rebuked by an uncertainty and indeterminability at the heart of his shifting identity. Just as the narrative structure of the plot and the waywardness of the action overturn Oedipus's too-confident assertions about his ability to "see" the truth, the fearful indeterminacy of his name similarly reverses its own claim as an expression of triumphant knowledge with the recognition of ambiguity, uncertainty, and ignorance that lies at its core.

Finally, in response to a query about the origin of Oedipus's name, the messenger at line 1038 says "*ouk oid'; ho dous*" (I don't know; the giver . . . [knows]).[29] *Oid' ho dous* surely echoes the king's name in an exchange about that naming and its very sense, while the words "I don't know; the giver knows" underline a central ambiguity in the story. But *ouk oid' ho dous* also means "I don't know the roads" and points, not only to Oedipus's decision to flee Corinth to avoid fulfilling the prophecy and to his encounter with Laius at the place where three roads meet, but also to his inability correctly to decipher the signs on the roads and thus control the direction of his travel and of his life.[30]

Oedipus perhaps best reveals the paradoxical nature of enlightenment encoded in his name through his self-proclaimed riddle-solving ability, a boast that is not wholly without merit. We learn in the prologue that Oedipus's position in Thebes derives directly from his intellectual skill: he won his rule in a contest of wits.[31] Where others, most conspicuously the blind prophet Tiresias, had repeatedly failed, Oedipus's own unaided intellect overcame the death-dealing Sphinx by identifying the two-, three-, and four-footed creature of the riddle as man. Oedipus founds his political rule in Thebes on the solid ground of his superior knowledge, and as his solution to the riddle illustrates, the power of his intellect lies in his uncanny ability to divide, order, and

28. On the puns on Oedipus's name at lines 924–26, see Knox, *Oedipus at Thebes,* pp. 183–84.

29. Here I follow Simon Goldhill, *Reading Greek Tragedy* (Cambridge: Cambridge University Press, 1986), p. 218.

30. On etymologies of and puns on Oedipus's name, see Segal, *Tragedy and Civilization,* p. 207; Jean-Pierre Vernant, "Ambiguity and Reversal: On the Enigmatic Structure of *Oedipus Rex,*" in *Myth and Tragedy,* pp. 123–24; Goldhill, *Reading Greek Tragedy,* pp. 216–18.

31. Although we also learn that no one has more of a right to rule than Laius's son.

clarify the world.[32] He sees unity in diversity, identity in plurality, and equality in difference. Oedipus's intellectual power is in an important sense the power of abstraction: by simplifying, clarifying, and reducing the enigmatic elements of experience to their lowest common denominator, he sees patterns and discerns order where others see only chaos; by penetrating surface particularities, he reveals essential unity and perceives coherent structure, solid form, and clear shape where others see constant change, shifting forms, and shapelessness. His powerful gaze pierces the veil of illusion to uncover the solid bedrock of truth.

Oedipus's characteristic knack for abstract intellection, for seeing unity in multiplicity and equality in difference, proves to be both his greatest asset and greatest liability. In this way, he introduces a dangerous equality into language, which affects his relations with the city, his family, and the gods: he will not recognize claims to equality in judicial procedure, exhibits an "unstable arithmetic of the self"[33] in effacing generational difference, and finally threatens to destroy the difference between mortal men and the gods. In Greek, *isos* refers to the equality of political status (as in *isonomia,* equality before the law; and *isēgoria,* equality of speech), as well as to the sameness of logical identity. In the case of Oedipus, "equality" spans both these meanings. Oedipus must be expelled from Thebes, not only as a man who exceeds the upper limits of equality (a god among men), but also as a man who falls below the lower limit—the *pharmakos,* or ritual scapegoat, who bears the pollutions of the city.[34] "Equal to the gods" (31) and "equal to nothing" (1187–88) converge in the figure of Oedipus and mark one aspect of his double identity as both savior and destroyer: in saving Thebes once more, Oedipus will destroy himself. This doubling or equating of the saving with the destroying capacity occurs at lines 425 and 443 in an exchange between Oedipus and Tiresias. "The evils that will make you equal with your children" (*exisōsei*) are here equated with "saving the

32. A. J. A. Waldock, *Sophocles the Dramatist* (Cambridge: Cambridge University Press, 1951) suggests, on the contrary, that Oedipus "does not possess, as far as we can make out, an intelligence of piercing quickness or very remarkable reach" (p. 144) and thus finds it odd that Oedipus solved the riddle.

33. Froma I. Zeitlin, "Thebes: Theater of Self and Society in Athenian Drama," in *Greek Tragedy and Political Theory,* ed. J. Peter Euben (Berkeley: University of California Press, 1986), p. 111.

34. Cf. Aristotle *Politics* 1253a9: a man without a city is either a god or a beast. Oedipus seems to oscillate between these two poles, denying the possibility of a third, mediating term.

city" (*exesōsa*). The close juxtaposition and coincidence of sound in the two near homophones *exisōsei* and *exesōsa* point to Oedipus's "equality" as incestuous polluter and savior of the city.[35]

In his violent exchange with Creon, Oedipus demonstrates a fundamental denial of juridical and political equality. Oedipus would deny Creon the right of equal speech and equal hearing (408–9; 544). Creon appeals to the equality of power, property, and honor he shares with Oedipus (579, 581–87), and indeed Oedipus has shown himself to be a fair and equitable ruler, one who is not only generous, but who respects the rights of other citizens. At least, he does so until he suspects a plot, and when he does, he would not merely exile Creon, but put him to death. Oedipus relents, however, and Creon's last word is "equal" (676–77), meaning that Creon himself is equal to his former honor. Oedipus is found both "unknowing" and "unknown" (*agnōs* is ambiguous here), and so stands in an uncertain relationship to the civic equality or fairness of the good ruler.[36]

As we saw in the scene with Creon, Oedipus was the respected, much loved and admired ruler of Thebes. Having saved the city once from the Sphinx, Oedipus would prove himself as good, compassionate, and generous in the face of the new crisis as he was before. Granting all that the suppliants ask, he takes upon himself the pain, burden, and sickness that each individual Theban suffers separately. "Your several sorrows each have single scope and touch but one of you. My spirit groans for city and myself and you at once" (62–64). "There is not one of you whose disease is equal to mine," Oedipus tells the suppliants in the prologue (60–61). And the grief Oedipus bears for the city he loves, he bears in public. "Speak it to all," he tells Creon, when his wife's brother returns with Apollo's command. His is an extremely open and public rule, which he shares with Jocasta and Creon. Yet this great, good, and compassionate ruler who cares for his city more than for himself utterly conflates and confounds his relationship to what he loves the most. He does not uphold the demarcations that set the city apart as a distinct space, but dissolves those boundaries that differentiate the city from his family, the public from the private domain, and civic from personal rule, in a threatening equation of sameness. In his role as patriarch, Oedipus treats the city more like a household than a *polis,* and himself more as its master (*despotēs*) than as its political leader (*anax, hēgemōn,*

35. See Segal, *Tragedy and Civilization,* pp. 209, 213–14, for this discussion of equality.
36. Ibid., p. 214.

basileus). As with the intellectual riddles he solves, Oedipus would reduce the plurality and diversity of the city to a unity, embodied first in his household and finally in himself. He would destroy the city so dear to him by obliterating the very differences that define and sustain it. It is as though Oedipus's patricidal and incestuous relationship with his literal parents, Laius and Jocasta, extended to Thebes, his other, figurative, parent. Private and public incest are thus of a piece in this play.[37]

Oedipus violates not only the juridical and political equality upon which the city is founded but the differences that distinguish mortal men and women from the immortal gods as well. As it does the rest of the play, this conflation marks the prologue, in which Oedipus appears before the plague-stricken citizens of Thebes as caring father, powerful ruler, and, above all, godlike savior. Although the priest carefully avoids identifying the king as a god (30), this opening scene systematically undercuts his public display of piety. Amid the mingled sound of hymns and smell of incense, the wreathed suppliant Thebans prostrate themselves before Oedipus as before the altar of a god. And the king assumes his godlike role with the easy nonchalance of a man who knows his worth and knows that others share thoughts similar to his own: the characters on stage and the chorus acknowledge Oedipus's quasi-divinity and revere him accordingly. The irony, of course, is that although the suppliant citizens approach Oedipus as if he were a god (16, 31), and, at the opposite extreme, as a *pharmakos,* he has no right to any altars at all.[38]

Oedipus emerges unsummoned from the palace as a godlike figure, consciously allying himself with Apollo, the bringer and revealer of light. This alliance should also draw us up short, for although Oedipus professes piety in associating himself with Apollo and swears that he will "do everything the god commands" (76), it is Apollo who connives in the king's destruction. Yet even as Oedipus is at first quick to associate himself with the god, the nearer he draws to his own truth, the farther he removes himself from the truth of Apollo, the oracles, and the gods in general. As Jocasta and Oedipus lose faith in the oracle, the balance between Oedipus and Apollo, precarious as it was in the prologue, is altogether lost. When Oedipus thinks his fortunes are on the

37. Seth Benardete, "Sophocles' *Oedipus Tyrannos,*" in *Sophocles: A Collection of Critical Essays,* ed. Thomas Woodward (Englewood Cliffs, N.J.: Prentice-Hall, 1966), pp. 107ff., has some suggestive remarks concerning the political and family crime.
38. Segal, *Tragedy and Civilization,* p. 243.

rise, Apollo begins to fade; what was once a holy alliance is now a confused and desperate enmity, man against god.[39] With Apollo in eclipse, the oracle abjured, and nothing certain, Oedipus exults in the possibility that he is the child of beneficent Chance, son of immortal parents, unconstrained by time, place, or birth. This wild imagining is but pregnant prelude to certain disaster, the supreme delusion before the most hideous revelation. Following that revelation, Oedipus's destruction and impending exile reverse the priest's praise of his ruling power in Thebes, while the final judgment of the chorus, that Oedipus is equal to nothing (*isa kai to mēden* [1187]), demolishes the suppliants' previous hope that he was equal to the gods (*isoumenos theous*).

Another instance of equality within difference that illustrates enlightened thought's confusion between the one and the many confronts Oedipus at the beginning of the play when he hears of the discrepancy concerning the number of "robbers" who put an end to Laius (118–25). Oedipus's error, "robber" (*ho lēistēs*), after Creon insists on "robbers" in the plural (*lēistai*), together with the occurrence of the word *one* four times in eight lines and the juxtaposition of "one" and "many" twice in four lines, underscores what seems to be an almost deliberate blindness to the difference between unity and diversity, and so to a deliberate blindness about himself.[40]

The final instability inherent in Oedipus's relation to equality is no where more evident than in his transgression of the incest taboo. As an incestuous son, Oedipus collapses the distinct and successive generations of the city, which differentiate past, present, and future. This confusion of generations, sounded in the first line of the play, "O children, young brood of old Cadmus" (*palai nea*), is hideously revealed when herdsman and messenger confirm Oedipus's identity. As husband to his mother and father to his brothers and sisters, Oedipus unites the opposites of "sameness and difference, unity and multiplicity" in himself.[41] Just as he fails to solve the riddle of the robbers ("If he still says the same number, I am not the robber; for one would not be equal to many" [843–45]), fails to see himself as the exception to the Sphinx's riddle (since Oedipus has always walked with three feet, he short-circuits the usual progression from four to two to three), he fails to see that he is

39. See David Seale, *Vision and Stagecraft in Sophocles* (Chicago: University of Chicago Press, 1982), esp. ch. 8.

40. On the significance of this exchange, see Segal, *Tragedy and Civilization*, p. 215.

41. Ibid., 214.

two where he ought to be one, and one where he ought to be two. Oedipus is both king and scapegoat, husband and son, brother and father, *tyrannnos* and *basileus*. His ultimate failure is that he fails to discover, or rather discovers too late, the answer to the riddle of his own life.[42]

Sophocles also plots the reversal of enlightenment through the ambiguous status of language in its relation to truth. "No play," writes Charles Segal, "is more about language than *Oedipus Tyrannus* . . . Human communication here parallels the communication by ritual and oracle between man and god. Continually breaking down, this communication either ceases prematurely because of fears, or knowledge that cannot be spoken or runs to excess because of passion and anger. Apollo's oracles from above and the Sphinx's riddle from below provide models for human discourse, but both also short circuit the significative function of language." Oedipus, the expert at decoding difficult messages, cannot solve the riddle of his own name.[43] An enigma to others, he is above all an enigma to himself. Such ambiguity, central to Oedipus's character, fate, and language (and the language of the play), differs significantly from the ambiguity that marks other Greek tragedies.[44] The ambiguous use of language in *Oedipus Tyrannos* marks neither a conflict of values nor a duplicitous character; rather the ambiguity of Oedipus's speech translates the duality of his being. Oedipus's language is double because he himself is double, and he is doubly deceived by it because he is self-deceived. Through the words he exchanges on stage, Oedipus conceals, from himself and others, who he is and what he is doing to himself and to those around him. Instead of establishing communication and community, instead of promoting self-knowledge and wisdom, Oedipus's speech underlines the impermeability of his mind and the opacity of his words, imposing barriers to human communication and comity. This is not to neglect the connivance

42. On the problems of identity in Oedipus, see also Zeitlin, "Thebes: Theater of Self and Society," pp. 103–6, 111–13.

43. Segal, "Music of the Sphinx," pp. 151–52.

44. All tragedy rests on a double reading of Heraclitus's famous dictum "*Ēthos anthrōpou daimōn*" ("Human character is destiny") (Hermann Diels, *Fragmente der Vorsokratiker, Griechisch und Deutsch* [1934; Dublin and Zurich: Weidmann, 1972– 73], fr. 119), R. P. Winnington-Ingram aptly remarks (*Sophocles: An Interpretation* [Cambridge: Cambridge University Press, 1980], p. 177). Both character and destiny constitute the space in which tragic action occurs. In *Antigone,* for example, the same word takes on multiple and contradictory meanings in the mouths of different characters. Thus, for Antigone, *nomos* designates the opposite of what Creon means by the word. In *Agamemnon,* Clytemnestra uses ambiguous language to deceive her husband, fooling him even as she reveals her sinister purpose to the spectators.

of Apollo in Oedipus's fate. The play unfolds simultaneously on human and divine planes, which in the end meet. Until they do, all Oedipus's utterances double themselves.[45] Oedipus's speech proves to be just as elusive, enigmatic, and mysterious as the world it, and he, purports to clarify. His words systematically conceal as much as they reveal; they encode as well as decode, obscure as they illuminate, and miscommunicate as they seek to communicate. Oedipus discovers that in leading the play from beginning to end, it is he himself who has been led; seeking to be master of his speech, and so of his fate, he finds that it has mastered him.[46]

As these examples indicate, the play is also about the necessity of sharing clear understandings, unambiguous interpretations, and transparent meanings, about the way in which speaking structures and constitutes a community and the irreducible need we have for collective interpretations, understandings, and meanings. Yet our need for clarity, transparency, and certainty, for a common set of stable linguistic structures, can, when pursued with Oedipus's character and fate, undermine the very stability we seek to preserve. Impatient with multiple meanings, diverse voices and contradictory or incompatible points of view, Oedipus seeks to impose his unitary voice upon all others, silencing varied and variegated possibilities. The unity achieved he attains at the expense of a diversity that makes agreement and political community possible in the first place. By insisting that words, and the world, have only one meaning; by reducing the complexity and flexibility of language; by diluting the richness and unifying the plurality within the community itself, Oedipus seeks to fool others as he has fooled himself and paradoxically threatens to destroy the city he set out to save. For these reasons, the play is also about the difficulty of achieving clarity, transparency, and certainty. For speaking always entails misspeaking and engenders the tragic possibility of destroying the tenuous political and intellectual relationships that bind us together, even as we desperately seek to establish them. *Oedipus Tyrannos* dramatizes the temptation to transparency in speech as very real, indeed, as almost given by the inadequacies and partialities of our understandings of ourselves, of others, and of the world. For the characters in the play, however, there is

45. On the human and divine aspects of Sophocles' drama, see H. D. F. Kitto, *Sophocles, Dramatist and Philosopher* (Westport, Conn.: Greenwood Press, 1981).

46. Jean-Pierre Vernant, "Ambiguity and Reversal: On the Enigmatic Structure of *Oedipus Rex*," in *Myth and Tragedy*, p. 116.

no stable, unshifting, ultimately unshakeable ground on which to stand and from which to speak (clarity is only given to blind, exiled members of the community).

My earlier characterization of Oedipus as a man who can discern pattern or order where others see only chaos describes only half the matter and half the man. For one thing, it suggests that Oedipus's knack for discerning pattern, order, and structure in a seemingly incoherent world is the achievement of an all-too-passive will and intellect. Although Oedipus does not ask for, but is given, power by the people of Thebes, his character inextricably binds together the will to truth and the will to power. Oedipus does not merely discern shape, pattern, and order in the world; nor is his intellect merely a passive receptacle for information; it is also a "structure of intentions"[47] that actively and aggressively shapes, patterns and imposes order on nature, circumstance, and human action. Oedipus relies on his intellect to clarify, divide, and arrange the world. He has mastered savage nature by mastering the Sphinx and will master the city and men by tracking the murderer and driving the polluter from Thebes. Under the pressure of a new crisis, Oedipus is confident that he can save Thebes once again. He has only to depend on his intellect to track the murderer, gather evidence, make inferences, impose logical order on chaotic events, clarify present mystery by uncovering past deeds, and reconcile conflicting reports from reluctant witnesses. He is sure of what he already knows, confident of his ability to discover what he does not, and positive that it will be what he most wants to find out.

No one wants to know more than Oedipus, and no one asks so many questions or takes the quest so seriously.[48] Spurred on by Apollo's riddle, Oedipus's unquenchable desire for truth drives him ineluctably toward his prophesied fate and self-destruction. On his way to disaster, he "investigates, examines, questions, infers; he uses intelligence, mind, thought; he knows, finds, reveals, makes clear, demonstrates; he learns and teaches."[49] It is this overwhelming love for the truth and his magnificent will to reveal it, no matter what the consequences, that sustain

47. Sheldon Wolin, "Political Theory as a Vocation," *APSR* 63, 4 (Dec. 1969): 1078.

48. "It is not the question that is difficult; it is the rigidity of the questioner," says Cedric Whitman (*The Heroic Paradox: Essays on Homer, Sophocles and Aristophanes* [Ithaca, N.Y.: Cornell University Press, 1980], p. 26). Few questioners in Greek tragedy are as rigid as Oedipus.

49. Knox, *Oedipus at Thebes,* p. 117. On the medical, legal, forensic, and scientific terminology current at the time, see ibid., pp. 107–46.

him through to the final, horrible revelation that he is an incestuous patricide. Neither the obstinacy of Tiresias, the traditional counsel of Creon, nor the wild and desperate entreaties of Jocasta deter Oedipus from this unwavering commitment to "bring it all to light" (133). He stands steadfast against all opposition, imagined or real, even against warnings that he will destroy himself and the city. Such warnings and cautions only goad him on and strengthen his resolve. Poised alone on the pinnacle of impending disaster, Oedipus will know the truth, whatever the cost to his city, his house, and himself: "With such clues I could not fail to bring my birth to light"; "Break out what will, I shall at least be willing to see my ancestry"; "Such is my breeding, and I shall never prove so false to it, as not to find the secret of my birth" (1059, 1076, 1085).

On the point of revelation, as Oedipus imagines himself the son of no mortal parents, but the self-made, self-taught offspring of the gods, the child of Chance, the king's intellectual journey (and his life) comes full circle. Having begun his quest as an ally of the gods in a common search for a murderer and polluter, on the brink of the horrible revelation, he questions the validity of the oracles and the existence of the gods themselves. Oedipus's "enlightened" intelligence threatens to destroy the very order and coherence that give it meaning. Fortunately, the old herdsman enters and confirms the oracle by setting in place the last piece of the puzzle that is Oedipus's life. That life is left shattered, but the world's meaning is restored. He is indeed murderer of his father, husband to his mother, and vile polluter of Thebes, yet the oracles prove good, chance does not completely rule human life, and the gods are not indifferent to the plight of mortals. The quest that began in enlightenment and light reveals the most profound personal ignorance and ends in darkness, destruction, and exile for the quester.

Oedipus, the man of knowledge and of action, seeks to "conquer complete prosperity and happiness" (1197–98).[50] As investigator, prosecutor, judge, and executioner, he seeks to solve the riddle of Laius's murder, as he thinks he has solved the riddle of his own fate by fleeing Corinth. But events prove otherwise. The riddles he solves and the solutions he offers create new riddles to solve and new solutions to be sought. The world proves elusive, slippery, hard to define, and even harder to grasp; the tighter he holds on, the quicker he loses his hold. Oedipus's quest for knowledge and mastery defeats itself. The fate he would master masters him, his

50. On these lines, see ibid., p. 107.

magnificent energy accomplishes his own ruin, his decisive action loses the character of action altogether. Oedipus investigates the investigator, prosecutes the prosecutor, condemns the judge, and punishes the executioner; he is both subject and object, actor and sufferer, victor and victim, seeker and thing sought, the sole author of his actions and a player performing a divinely authored role.[51] In a script authored jointly by the mortal hero and the immortal gods, the power of Oedipus's intellectual progress proves to be the progress of his own tyrannical power.

Oedipus's attempt to unravel this ambiguous and tangled web of meaning so as to discover the murderer and the identity of his parents, and finally of himself, drives the action of the play. It also threatens to destroy the actor, the city, and the intelligible order of the world itself. The play thus unfolds a tragic vision of the tyrant's splendor, vigor, and inevitable defeat, a vision that contemplates no possibility of escape, because Oedipus's defeat is immanent in his very greatness.[52]

III

In the end, Oedipus recognizes his fate, embraces it as his own, and thereby confirms the truth of the oracle for himself, the chorus, and the audience. However painful the search and discovery, his suffering ultimately validates the principles of linguistic, intellectual, political, and ritual order on which the human community rests. His self-blinding and exile mend the fractures in a ruptured order where the ruler is the murderer, the savior the destroyer, the self-taught, self-made man the utterly ignorant and impotent puppet of the gods. In this reaffirmation

51. Vernant summarizes tragic ambiguity this way: "But perhaps the essential feature that defines it is that the drama brought to the stage unfolds both at the level of everyday existence, in a human, opaque time made up of successive and limited present moments, and also beyond this earthly life, in a divine, omnipresent time that at every instant encompasses the totality of events, sometimes to conceal them and sometimes to make them plain but always so that nothing escapes it or is lost in oblivion" ("Tensions and Ambiguities," pp. 43–44).

52. Knox, *Oedipus at Thebes,* p. 105. E. R. Dodds, "On Misunderstanding the *Oedipus Rex,*" in *Greek Tragedy: Modern Essays in Criticsm,* ed. Erich Segal (New York: Harper & Row, 1983), p. 186, argues against what he believes to be the overly allegorical interpretations of Knox and of Ehrenberg in *Sophocles and Pericles,* pp. 141 ff., who contends that the character of Oedipus reflects that of Pericles. Although I agree with Dodds that Ehrenberg goes too far in conflating Oedipus with the historical Pericles, if only for the reason that their characters differ too substantially to sustain such a comparison, I am sympathetic to Knox's view that Oedipus and Athens share a similar character, especially if we accept the Corinthians' description of the Athenians in Thucydides' *History,* bk. 1.

of ritual and religious meaning, Sophocles seems critical of the fifth-century enlightenment and sophistic intellectual and political tyranny; and in the dramatization of Oedipus's self-defeat, the playwright seems to castigate as impious the Protagorean dictum that "man is the measure of all things." Before an implacable, mysterious, and impenetrable fate that shapes us even as we desperately try to shape ourselves, human intelligence and power, for all their great achievements, ultimately achieve very little.[53]

But surely this reading does justice to neither the complexity of Oedipus's character nor that of the play itself. Such a chastening of the emancipatory impulse of enlightenment embodied in Oedipus is too easy, too neat, and makes him all too familiar. Oedipus is himself a riddle, a paradigmatic hero who cannot be assimilated to comfortable categories. The unity of opposites he embodies, "quasi-divine power and bestial rage, strength and weakness, self-affirmation and utter helplessness, confident knowledge and abysmal ignorance, proud rationality and uncontrolled passion,"[54] makes him a human enigma that defies solution. He is both "the measure of all things"—equal to the gods—and equal to nothing. Horrified as the chorus may be at Oedipus's self-apotheosis, it does refers to him as a paradigm (*paradeigma* [1193]), an example or model for all time, and thereby celebrates the fallen hero.[55] The play remains disturbingly ambivalent about Oedipus's character and fate, an ambivalence that echoes the ambiguity of his paradigmatic status: he commits unspeakable crimes and suffers untold agonies, yet in the same position and with such a character, no mortal could or would do otherwise. Oedipus is thus both object lesson and noble exemplar: in his tragic suffering, he has indeed reconciled himself to his fate, and in this sense, he has gained a kind of heroic stature with his

53. This is C. M. Bowra's interpretation in *Sophoclean Tragedy* (Oxford: Clarendon Press, 1944), p. 175: "The gods have contrived an awful fate for Oedipus in order to display their power to man and to teach him a salutary lesson." As will become clear below, I do not think such a reading does justice to the ambivalence of the play. In *Sophocles the Dramatist,* p. 168, Waldock, on the other hand, finds no meaning in the play, merely terrible coincidence.

54. Charles Segal, "Greek Tragedy and Society: A Structuralist Perspective," in *Interpreting Greek Tragedy: Myth, Poetry, Text* (Ithaca, N.Y.: Cornell University Press, 1986), p. 37.

55. In *The Heroic Temper: Studies in Sophoclean Tragedy* (Berkeley: University of California Press, 1964), pp. 146–47, Bernard Knox argues that Oedipus is the paradigmatic hero who cannot be assimilated to familiar categories, but fails to recognize the presence of that same heroic impulse in the structure of the play itself.

wisdom. Yet the price of that wisdom—impotent, wandering, blind exile—is a price no ordinary mortal could bear, and it threatens to nullify the prize. For these reasons, a merely "pious" Sophocles will not do, any more than will a simple assessment of the play as a "tragedy of fate," for to read the playwright as a nostalgic conservative evades the tragedy's all-too-evident "heroic temper."

This ironic assessment of the paradigmatic status of Oedipus, and so of enlightenment, finds expression at several other levels and layers of the text. At the intersection of dramatic text and ritual context, by the form of the drama itself, through its structure, and in its refusal of final narrative closure, *Oedipus Tyrannos* subverts both a rationalist, progressivist *and* an anti-enlightenment, nostalgic appropriation. These subversive textual strategies all conspire to articulate the enduring ironies of enlightenment embodied in a play that forcefully strives to fulfill the emancipatory claims of enlightened reason even as it resists and otherwise disrupts the disciplinary effects of enlightenment. It is to these levels and layers that I now turn.

In ancient Greece, tragedy was not only an art form, but also a social institution, which the city, by establishing competitions in tragedies, set up alongside its political and legal institutions. As part of a festival in honor of the god Dionysus, tragedy renewed and reaffirmed the ritual, institutional, and cultural order in which it participated. The city established "in the same urban space and in accordance with the same institutional norms as the popular assemblies or courts, a spectacle open to all citizens, directed, acted and judged by qualified representatives of the various tribes. In this way it turned itself into a theater. Its subject, in a sense, was itself and it acted itself out before its public."[56] Thoroughly rooted in the social and political order of the city, a tragic performance such as *Oedipus Tyrannos* helped confirm and sustain the civic and ritual context that shaped it. As such, tragedy was conservative and opposed the fifth-century enlightenment.

A tension emerges, however, between the conservative context of tragedy as ritual public performance and the disturbing content of the enacted drama. We have seen that as a transgressor, Oedipus is a paradoxical figure who stands at the point where contraries converge, at the intersection of simultaneously present polarities. As he pushes relentlessly forward toward the discovery of the murderer and so the identity

56. Vernant, "Tensions and Ambiguities," p. 33.

of the hero himself, the normally coherent and balanced order of the play's world breaks down. The narration and enactment of the tragedy stretch that order to its limits and suspend its intelligibility: knowledge becomes ignorance, power becomes powerlessness, and civilization reverts to savagery. In its portrayal of a relentless search, the drama moves forward with a desperation marked by the confused intermingling of opposites: in its political, social, and ritual reversals, in its inversion of identifications that replace reassuring and familiar demarcations and differentiations, in its violent action, and in the sudden irruption of the unexpected and unforeseen into human life the play deranges the normally related aspects of the human, divine, and natural order. It deliberately distorts, manipulates, and transforms the patterns, structures, and divisions by which we live.[57]

The tragedy of Oedipus thus calls into question the most solid structures of meaning, the most carefully guarded boundaries, and the most piously observed limits. In depicting a social order on the verge of dissolution, Sophocles' tragedy turned that order into a problem; as a violent performance, tragedy negated and radically questioned the moral, political, and intellectual arrangements of the culture that made that order, and tragedy as a part of it, possible. A play such as *Oedipus Tyrannos* subjected the established order to searching criticism. A "structured deconstruction" of the social order,[58] the play stands in critical opposition to its social and ritual context, even as it reaffirms that context, and Sophocles stands in an uneasy tension, both with and against, enlightenment.[59]

The playwright is thus neither merely a sophistic critic of tradition nor a naive believer in traditional pieties. He is critical of the extant cultural order from a position within tradition and in a way that self-

57. Segal, "Greek Tragedy and Society," pp. 36–39.

58. Ibid., p. 47. My interpretation does not only differ from a poststructuralist reading by virtue of its extratextuality. Where Maurice Blanchot, *L'Entretien infini* (Paris: Gallimard, 1969), and Franco Tonelli, *Sophocles' Oedipus and the Tale of the Theatre* (Ravenna: Longo Editore, 1983), for example, interpret the play as a continuous process of loss—the dissolution of meaning into nonmeaning, of identity into nonidentity, of transparency into nontransparency—I take the view that the "text" not only "deconstructs" itself but pushes back and against that deconstruction.

59. On festivals and the ritual aspects of tragic performance, see A. Pickard-Cambridge, *The Dramatic Festivals of Athens,* 2d ed. (Oxford: Oxford University Press, 1968). For an opposing interpretation that discounts the importance of the ritual, religious and institutional context of tragedy, see Oliver Taplin, "Emotion and Meaning in Greek Tragedy," in *Greek Tragedy: Modern Essays in Criticism,* ed. Erich Segal (New York: Harper & Row, 1983).

consciously uses the past. Sophocles' play expresses the opposition between the myths of the archaic past and the forms of enlightened thought peculiar to the city, not only in the tensions and ambiguities that mark the characters and their action, but in "the very form of drama, by the tension between the two elements that occupy the tragic stage."[60] On one side, there is the chorus, a body of trained citizens that expresses the collective achievements of Athenian democracy. Opposite it, there is the protagonist, a legendary hero estranged from, and a stranger to, the collectivity of citizens. This juxtaposition of present democratic citizenship and past heroic kingship establishes enough distance between the spectators and their immediate context to allow them to reflect, not only on the meaning of the action on stage, but on the meaning of their own past and present actions.[61] The dichotomy between the citizen chorus and the tragic hero is further complicated by another opposition, which cuts across the first, further jarring expectations, discomfiting sensibilities, and demanding reflection. Where the democratic chorus chants its songs in the traditional lyric of a poetry that celebrates the heroic virtues of the archaic world, the tragic heroes speak their lines in the language of the present, in a meter close to that of prose.[62] A hero like Oedipus, projected into the mythic past, would embody the character and perform the actions of a legendary king, while at the same time seeming to live and act in the present, speaking the same language and confronting the same problems as the city. This unsettling juxtaposition of past and present in the form of the drama reiterates the thematic oppositions in the tragedy between knowledge and ignorance, power and powerlessness, enlightenment and myth. Here is one more way in which Sophocles' *Oedipus Tyrannos* turned the "enlightened" present into a problem that the mythical past could illuminate from within the tradition of a public festival.

Sophocles sustains this "dialectic of enlightenment" in another way too. Oedipus is a paradigm, not only for the chorus (and perhaps the audience), but for the playwright as well. This is to say that the play

60. Vernant, "Tensions and Ambiguities," p. 10.

61. Cf. Albert Cook, *Enactment: Greek Tragedy* (Chicago: Swallow Press, 1971), pp. 34–35.

62. Vernant, "Tensions and Ambiguities," p. 34. On the role of the chorus in Greek tragedy, see G. M. Kirkwood, *Sophoclean Drama* (Ithaca, N.Y.: Cornell University Press, 1957); R. W. B. Burton, *The Chorus in Sophocles' Tragedies* (Oxford: Clarendon Press; New York: Oxford University Press, 1980); C. P. Gardiner, *The Sophoclean Chorus* (Iowa City: University of Iowa Press, 1987).

also celebrates, if not emulates, the paradigmatic status of its hero.[63] Yet if Oedipus is so strange and so awful and suffers the monstrous fate he does, the attempted celebration and emulation are impious, if not an invitation to certain failure. But that is precisely what the play itself does.[64] It both represents and emulates Oedipus as *deinos:* as wondrous, awesome, marvelous, powerful *and* terrible, fearful, destructive, and violent. Insofar as the drama itself pursues the task of clarifying, ordering, and interpreting the perplexities, ambiguities, and mysteries of an opaque world, it participates in the movement of enlightenment that defines Oedipus's own intellectual and political feats, even as it warns against defeat. In this attempt to create an ordered and meaningful whole, *Oedipus Tyrannos* reveals its affinities with the hero's quest for enlightenment and the emancipation it brings. For even as Oedipus's defeat and suffering educate the citizens who witness it, in the tragedy wrought by Sophocles, the audience also witness one of the finest examples of the shaping and ordering power of the rational intellect. This is one way in which the dramatic structure of the play reflects its substantive teaching about the ultimate irony of enlightenment.

Lastly, I want to say something about how the play resists final narrative closure and so keeps alive the tension between tragedy and enlightenment. In the final moment of the drama that follows the self-blinding, when we see Oedipus again, bloodied and sightless, he is groping for his two daughters and uttering for one last time his first word of the prologue: "Children." This reunion seemingly brings Oedipus's story to a close and the play full circle. The image of the closing tableau reflects, with almost mirrorlike exactitude, the image of the play's opening movement.[65] But I am not convinced that Sophocles' theatrical symmetry supplies his spectators with the narrative closure they might want or expect. Oedipus does, indeed, reemerge from the privacy of the palace into the publicity of day, but shrouded in his own darkness, not in his previous godlike radiance. His impending exile will re-

63. John Jones, *Aristotle and Greek Tragedy* (London: Chatto & Windus, 1962), p. 265, disagrees: "The word exemplar is inadmissible because it declares a distinct moralising intent and a way of looking at the stage figure which Sophocles' play is without." This seems to stem more from a failure to extend an ambiguous reading of Oedipus to the play as a whole than from any confusion about Oedipus himself.

64. Winnington-Ingram recognizes this when he says that Sophocles was no prophet of *sōphrosunē:* "All we have to do is contemplate a world of Creons and wonder whether it would be any place for a tragic poet" (*Sophocles,* p. 204).

65. Seale, *Vision and Stagecraft,* ch. 8.

store order to the blighted Theban landscape. We have only to wait for his departure.

This departure never comes. If it did, it would in any case suggest a kind of comfortable closure that unjustifiably reconciles the tensions and oppositions Oedipus embodies and the play dramatizes. In fact, the play ends on a fragmentary note. First of all, Oedipus's reunion with his daughters, the loved ones he had all but forgotten in his single-minded purpose, is not only fleeting, but tainted. Blind Oedipus "sees" them now for the first time, yet they are as polluted as he. These girls will not be able to regenerate a city that has endlessly polluted beginnings. Secondly, all the previous action, including Tiresias's prophecy and Oedipus's own decree, leads us to expect that Oedipus will go into exile, exiting stage, theater, and Thebes for the last time. But this does not happen. Instead, Creon insists that Oedipus go indoors to await the word of the god. Creon acts in cautious character, but nevertheless, we want Oedipus to go. Until he does, the drama cannot be over. This ending, with Oedipus brought back inside the palace, disconcerts. Oedipus, the play, and the spectators all oppose it. The drama thus does not give us the final and satisfying conclusion that we want, but only a certain respite from the uncertainties and vicissitudes of life lived as mortal men and women. This refusal of closure is the final reversal of our expectations in a play so full of reversals: "We are left with Oedipus's reentry into a house that has already seen too much."[66]

IV

The strategies of internal subversion outlined above constitute Sophocles' *Oedipus Tyrannos* as an instructive political and theoretical alternative to the terms of the current debate over the meaning and consequences of enlightenment. Sophocles' attitude toward the fifth-century enlightenment certainly shares Habermas's concern for the ideas of reason, liberty, and self-determination that characterize the modern enlightenment. Reason distinguishes humans from nature, dispels the archaic forces of myth and superstition that impede freedom and threaten autonomy, and, as *Antigone*'s Ode reminds us, provides the material needs of civilization on a hitherto unprecedented scale. Moreover, to

66. Ruth Scodel, *Sophocles* (Boston: Twayne, 1984), p. 72. Tonelli, *Sophocles' Oedipus,* p. 165, calls the final exodus a non-ending.

the extent that Greek tragedy participated in this process of rationalization in the ways elaborated above,[67] Sophocles is at one with the modern defenders of reason and enlightenment.

Yet Sophocles is at pains to warn such defenders of enlightenment to educate themselves about the blindnesses, obscurities, and instabilities within enlightened thought itself. Enlightenment promises freedom from fate and from the overpowering forces of nature, yet all too often, it enslaves us to a "second" nature (in the form of economic, technical, or disciplinary necessity). It provides us with the knowledge and power to fashion our world and ourselves, yet reveals our ignorance and our powerlessness. Enlightenment brings us, as it brought Oedipus, both freedom and constraint, self-conscious transparency and ignorant opacity about what it is we are doing in and to our world. This Sophoclean warning parallels Foucault's ironic observation that the modern enlightenment rhetoric of liberation—whether it is bound up with the pseudo-scientific discourses of psychological, physical, or social therapies—simultaneously contains and conceals its opposite.

But Sophocles offers us no mere cautionary tale. Insofar as the play embodies the rationalist and progressive moments of enlightenment, it sustains Habermas's attempt to achieve that clarity of communication and mutual understanding that signals progress toward a rational society. To this end, *Oedipus Tyrannos* makes a coherent point about incoherent speech, establishes communication with its audience as it eventually reestablishes communication onstage, and so participates in the invention of a reason that is also the subject of sustained criticism. The language of reason surely blinds us, as it blinded Oedipus, to the patterns of our repeated mistakes, enslaves as it liberates, and dominates as it promises to empower. But reason also discloses aspects of ourselves and of the world in which we live. Rational speech certainly establishes communication, but it also establishes barriers to it. The confrontation between Oedipus and Tiresias stands as mute testimony to such a communicative failure. The streamlined, technical, and overly abstract language of communications theory achieves a transparency of description that parallels Oedipus's own (failed) attempt at clarity. The irony here is that such language works to ignore, exclude, or silence the multi-

67. In the ways we have seen: tragedy reshaped the archaic myths, juxtaposed myth to enlightened thought, and embodied reason in the very structure of the dramatic performance.

faceted, varied, and heterogeneous elements of experience that do not fit neatly into its schema. What enlightened Oedipus suppresses in the world, he suppresses in himself.

Sophocles' play, like one of Foucault's genealogies, also alerts us to the unexpected, the ambiguous, and the enigmatic, and points to ways of being and modes of knowing that disrupt our comfortable reliance on the enlightenment alliance of reason, science, and progress. Sophocles would thus chasten Habermas's commitment to enlightenment, and in a manner that recalls Foucault's own caution about privileging the "progress" of human reason and intellect. The playwright warns us against our own intellectual and political conceits, lest we fall prey to the various techniques of truth that promise liberation even as they strip us of our liberty, and so questions the enlightenment assumption that we are fully conscious actors, always in control of the consequences of our speech and action.

Of course, Oedipus is a hero; he does avert the plague and save Thebes. The "natural" order is restored, Oedipus is reunited with himself, and the paradoxes and ironies presented onstage are "solved" by the spectators. Moreover, the play's aesthetic structure is itself a paradigmatic example of the clarifying and ordering reason it seems to reject. Lest it seem that the Sophoclean narrative of enlightenment is a continuous and constant process of loss, in conclusion I want to reemphasize its positive—rational—achievements. By holding the two contending narratives of progress and reversal in mind, as the play in fact asks us to do, Sophocles offers an alternative to current thought on enlightened reason by reminding us (as well as Habermas and Foucault) that we, too, are incurably full of irresolvable tensions, ambiguities, and oppositions. Like Sophocles' king, we children of the modern enlightenment embody a unity of opposites, "from palace to wild, city to mountain, man to beast..highest to lowest, king to scapegoat. At the point of intersection stands Oedipus, whose identity consists of this intersection of contradictions."[68] Those ambiguities and oppositions find consummate expression in a play that requires us to appreciate both the analytical, logical, and rational *and* the enigmatic, surprising, and mysterious as irreducible elements of the human condition. *Oedipus Tyrannos* does not in any conventional sense resolve the contradictions, ironies, and dilemmas of enlightenment. Rather, the play's great

68. Segal, "Greek Tragedy and Society," p. 29.

achievement lies in its ability to hold these conflicting impulses in a productive tension that thinks both the seductions and dangers of enlightenment *together* rather than driving those impulses apart through acts of evasion or (dis)solution. While too much rationally achieved (imposed?) order certainly exacts high psychic and political costs from those selves who fit poorly into its confines, the clarity and certainty that enlightened thought brings remain just as necessary as the genealogical subversions that disturb such order, and not only because the former make the latter intelligible. If there is a post-enlightenment ethos that reinscribes an appreciation of the ambiguities, perplexities, and contradictions of the world while simultaneously conserving the positive elements of enlightened thought, then Sophocles' *Oedipus Tyrannos* embodies just such a sensibility.

V

I want to end this chapter and prepare for the next by introducing the figure of Socrates. For, like Oedipus, Socrates seeks enlightenment. The philosopher's desire for the truth, his commitment to his native city, and his association with Apollo all connect him to Sophocles' Oedipus. Like Sophocles' hero, Socrates begins his quest in an attempt to solve a riddle set by Apollo: "How can a man who knows he is ignorant be called wise?" In his search for an answer, Socrates questions, cross-examines, and interprets men and evidence in order to bring to light the truth hidden in the oracle's enigmatic pronouncement. In the process, Socrates becomes a spokesman for Apollo, the bringer and revealer of light.

Yet Socrates' character hardly resembles Oedipus's: where Oedipus is a king, Socrates is a private citizen, and where Oedipus is a man of aggressive will, tremendous energy, and tireless action, Socrates possesses a character of unparalleled equanimity, is deliberate and deliberative, contemplative and reflective, deeming it better to think carefully rather than to act rashly. More important, though, Socrates searches for wisdom fully aware of his mortality and is not surprised at the limits this human knowledge imposes. Oedipus, absolutely convinced of the unlimited capacity of his intelligence, the truth of his knowledge, and his supreme ability freely to shape his fate, cannot imagine that he has constructed a whole life upon an utterly false assumption. Socrates' search for knowledge and his attempt to enlighten his fellow citizens is ironically nourished by the consciousness of his own ignorance, while

Oedipus learns (tragically) that ignorance is the foundation of knowledge.[69]

If this characterization is right, then Socrates' purposeful interrogation of the unexamined components of "normal" life in Athens indicates that a comparison between Socrates and Sophocles is more appropriate. Whereas Oedipus himself is not initially conscious of his own transgressions against the ritual, political, and linguistic norms of the city, a good case can be made that *Oedipus Tyrannos* is. The confrontation between Oedipus and Tiresias, and its place in the structure of the play, illustrates this point. It also recapitulates, with painful intensity, all of Oedipus's conflicts with an enigmatic, unforgiving world.

Sophoclean wisdom, then, prefigures itself as something of a Socratic enigma. In its "structured deconstruction"[70] of the social order, and of itself as a part of that order, *Oedipus Tyrannos* anticipates the manner in which Socratic philosophy questions, transforms, and affirms the cultural, political, and intellectual structures that make it possible. In the same way that Sophocles' drama provokes and admonishes its citizen audience to reflect on the conventions the play dramatizes on the stage and embodies in a public festival, Socrates challenges his interlocutors to reflect on their own contemporary practices, beliefs, and values: like Sophoclean drama, Socratic philosophy was an Athenian critique and therefore refused to abandon Athens. This is to say, Socratic philosophy, like Sophoclean tragedy, is a form of immanent critique. With Sophocles' theater, which participated in the very traditions it subjected to criticism, Socratic philosophy reorganized the material of the Athenian political tradition in order to rethink the present and guide action in the future.

More specifically, in Plato's *Gorgias,* Socrates mounts a sustained attack on the tradition of Athenian politics and on that tradition's most celebrated statesmen. That tradition was founded on rhetoric and includes such eminent names as Themistocles, Cimon, Miltiades, and Pericles. Socrates challenges rhetoric—which he defines as the knack (*empeiria*) of clever speaking—with dialectic or philosophy—which he defines as the true art of politics (*technē politikē*)—and transfers the authority of the Athenian political tradition from its greatest statesmen

69. J. Peter Euben, *The Tragedy of Political Theory: The Road Not Taken* (Princeton, N.J.: Princeton University Press, 1990), p. 126.

70. Segal, "Greek Tragedy and Society," p. 47.

to himself. Socrates seeks, then, to reconstruct Athenian politics on the unshakeable ground of philosophical truth, caring more for the argument than for honor, more for truth than for victory, more for mutuality and agreement than power and domination. Yet the perils of less-than-ideal communication—of mishearing, misspeaking, and misunderstanding—so powerfully dramatized by Sophocles, as well as the attendant difficulties of establishing a secure ground for community (both inside and outside the dialogue), haunt Socrates in *Gorgias.* For all its radical "destructuring" of the familiar codes, Sophocles' tragic performance was ultimately hedged in and bounded by the space and confines of the tragic theater as ritual performance and public festival. Unlike tragedy, Socratic philosophical dialogue cannot rely on a secure context of shared understandings external to the dialogue's "performance." It is precisely that context, at least in *Gorgias,* that is in question. If Socrates cannot establish grounds for clear communication within the dialogue, he has no recourse to stable structures outside it. Socrates performs, as it were, without a net.

Gorgias is, at least in part, about the difficulties that attend the establishment of shared understandings, projects, and lives. Socrates' attempts to establish a level of mutuality or agreement with his interlocutors are largely unsuccessful: the necessary conditions for philosophical dialogue go unmet. Yet as the dialogue proceeds, we begin to see how the goal of philosophical "truth" through the achievement of shared understanding is in part the product of a subtle strategy of power. Quite early in the dialogue, Socrates deploys a set of extraphilosophical tactics designed to control the terms of political discourse. As the dialogue progresses, it reveals the origins of philosophical "truth" to be as closely connected to power and politics as to the unprejudiced pursuit of pure knowledge. Power, jealousy, envy, strife—these are the weapons that philosophers have used to forge the truth. Similar to Oedipus's rule in Thebes, which rested not on his intellectual achievements alone, but on an identity that was dispersed, fractured, and fissured by murder and incest, the "truth" of *Gorgias* might be fabricated, not discovered, philosophy thoroughly politicized, and morality produced by power. *Gorgias* at least suggests as much: it reveals the machinations of power behind even the most (non)disingenuous search for truth, the implication of power in all discourse, and the dependence of the rule of right—of law, morality, and ethics—on the right of rule.

This final comparison between Sophocles' *Oedipus Tyrannos* and Socrates in *Gorgias* invites an additional comparison between Sophocles and Plato. I want to look ahead and suggest further that Sophocles' *Oedipus Tyrannos* and Plato's *Republic* share important continuities of substance, aim, and structure. This is not merely because Oedipus, the paradigmatic tragic hero, stands to the greatest work of Greek tragedy as Socrates, the paradigmatic philosophical hero, stands to the greatest work of classical political theory. Plato's *Republic* is more complex than such a simple and direct analogy between the hero of the play and the chief interlocutor of the dialogue suggests. And, as I have already indicated, Socrates' temperament, circumstances, and character differ too much from that of Oedipus. Not only the activity of Socrates, but political theory itself, is the subject of the *Republic* and supplies the missing term in the analogy.

That Socrates leads the discussion in a dialogue that, as I shall argue, does not wholly identify political theory with his style of philosophy, suggests an implicit criticism of that activity. That the figure of the philosopher-king unites quasi-divine knowledge with political rule should also remind us of Oedipus, while my characterization of Oedipus's controlling intellectual purpose as a "structure of intentions" should recall the "epic" theorist Plato and the "global" theory of the *Republic*. This ambiguity, between the "Socratic" practice of dialogue and the product of that practice in the *Republic* (the philosopher-king), an ambiguity concerning what political theory is, or can or ought to be, suggests that its very definition is at stake in the dialogue. Two forms of knowledge vie for preeminence in the *Republic* in ways that suggest a structural affinity with the tension between intellectual (and political) mastery and the wisdom that suffering brings in Sophocles' play.

3

Liberating Discourse

The Politics of Truth in Plato's Gorgias

And not only Aristotle but the whole of Greek antiquity thinks differently from us about hatred and envy, and judges with Hesiod, who in one place calls one Eris evil—namely, the one that leads men into hostile fights of annihilation—while praising another Eris as good—the one that, as jealousy, hatred, envy, spurs men to activity; not to the activity of fights of annihilation but to the activity of fights that are *contests.*

—Friedrich Nietzsche, "Homer's Contest," in *The Portable Nietzsche*

We are subjected to the production of truths through power and we cannot exercise power except through the production of truth.

—Michel Foucault, "Two Lectures," in *Power/Knowledge*

According to Diogenes Laertius and the medieval manuscript tradition, Plato's *Gorgias* bears the subtitle "or on rhetoric" (*ē peri rhetorikē*), a perhaps all-too-obvious designation, arising out of the initial question posed by Socrates to Gorgias: "What is rhetoric?"[1] Modern critics allow the formal correctness of this designation but deny its adequacy as a description of the dialogue's scope or purpose. This is a preliminary question about the function of rhetoric, they argue, not the subject of the dialogue. The main themes emerge gradually in the course of the conversation: the problem of justice, the question of whether it is better to do injustice or suffer it, and the value of the philosophical over the

1. I have relied primarily on *Gorgias: A Revised Text with Introduction and Commentary,* ed. E. R. Dodds (Oxford: Clarendon Press, 1959), and *Gorgias,* trans., with notes, by Terence Irwin (Oxford: Clarendon Press, 1979). Translations are Irwin's, unless otherwise noted.

political life. The topic of rhetoric would seem incidental, then, to these more weighty issues. The subject matter here is the moral basis of politics—the dialogue is centrally concerned with how one ought to live—not the rhetor's craft.[2]

But rhetoric has experienced a revival of late, and perhaps this renewed interest helps reveal a dimension of the dialogue previously elided. For contemporary philosophers and literary theorists, the rhetorical turn is not incidental to the pressing questions of power and morality, but involves them directly. Consider Michel Foucault's redeployment of the Sophists, Jacques Derrida's engagement with Plato's *Phaedrus,* Jean-François Lyotard's appropriation of the "pagan" philosophy of Aristotle's *Rhetoric,* or Jürgen Habermas's defense of an antirhetorical discourse ethic. For Foucault, the Sophists and rhetors reveal the will to power behind the pretensions of the philosophers. For Derrida, rhetoric provides the necessary tools to unmask the origins and practices of Western logocentrism. Lyotard relies on the *Rhetoric* to debunk claims that "the political can be derived from the theoretical."[3] Habermas appropriates a tradition of civic virtue that reaches back to Aristotelian deliberation and Socratic dialogue in his formulation of a communicative ethics. While I do not want to deny that *Gorgias* is about "how one ought to live," especially since I take up the issue of power and morality as a central theme in the dialogue, my own purposes are best, and most interestingly, served by paying attention to

2. In evidence that the dialogue is not about rhetoric, *Gorgias,* ed. Dodds, p. 1, cites Max Pohlenz, *Aus Platos Werdezeit: Philologische Untersuchungen* (Berlin: Weidmann, 1913), 142, 151; Ulrich von Wilamowitz-Moellendorf, *Platon: Sein Leben und seine Werke,* 2 vols. (1919; Berlin: Weidmann, 1959–62), 1: 234; A. E. Taylor, *Plato: The Man and His Work* (1926; 3d ed., New York: Dial Press, 1929), 106 ("Life and the way it should be lived, not the value of rhetoric, is the real theme"), and André Festugiere, *Contemplation et vie contemplative selon Platon* (Paris: J. Vrin, 1936), 382 ("The true subject is the knowledge of what is the life that a man worthy of the name ought to lead"). Exceptions to these interpretations are Eric Voegelin's "The *Gorgias,*" in *Plato and Aristotle,* vol. 2: *Order and History* (Baton Rouge: Louisiana State University Press, 1957); Paul Friedländer, *Plato,* trans. Hans Meyerhoff, vol. 2 (New York: Pantheon Books, 1958), and Werner Jaeger, *Paideia,* vol. 2 (New York: Oxford University Press, 1943). Charles Kahn, "Dialogue and Dialectic in Plato's Gorgias," in *Oxford Studies in Ancient Philosophy,* vol. 1, ed. Julia Annas (Oxford: Clarendon Press, 1983), and Richard McKim, "Shame and Truth in Plato's *Gorgias,*" in *Platonic Writings / Platonic Readings,* ed. Charles Griswold, pp. 34–48 (New York: Routledge, 1988), are attentive to the inseparable connection between the craft of rhetoric and the morals of the craftsman.

3. See, e.g., Michel Foucault, "Nietzsche, Genealogy, History," in *The Foucault Reader,* ed. Paul Rabinow (New York: Pantheon Books, 1984); Jacques Derrida, "Plato's Pharmacy," in *Dissemination,* trans. Barbara Johnson (Chicago: University of Chicago Press, 1981); and Jean-François Lyotard and Jean-Loup Thébaud, *Just Gaming,* trans. Wlad Godzich (Minneapolis: University of Minnesota Press, 1985), pp. 26–28, 74–75, 78.

what has passed as the obvious: that *Gorgias* is about rhetoric, and that rhetoric matters. I think that the dialogue acknowledges the force and importance of rhetoric, as do these contemporary theorists. What better text, then, to illuminate the present controversy over truth's relationship to power than *Gorgias?*

In that dispute, Habermas and Foucault offer us a choice between deriving norms communicatively or imposing them politically, between achieving consensus cooperatively or vanquishing an opponent strategically, between assenting to the "unforced force of the better argument" or winning that argument in order to dominate the conversation and others. Where Habermas reckons that "reaching understanding is the inherent telos of human speech,"[4] Foucault argues that truth is produced through multiple forms of constraint and dismisses the project of dissolving relations of power in a "utopia of perfectly transparent communication."[5] Put as a question, the opposition between Habermas and Foucault reads something like this: "Can we limit the rights of power, or does power implement the rules of right by which we live?"

But perhaps this opposition is somewhat overdrawn. The prospect of communication free from domination is an attractive goal (who now wants to remain dominated?), but we ought not to foreclose the possibility of a world in which not all communication is transparent, in which agreement might be achieved by more mundane linguistic mechanisms, such as courtesy and politeness (or even lying), or by such rhetorical tropes of speech as irony, satire, or hyperbole. Why discount the positive effects of ambivalence or ambiguity in words (even if that were possible), why privilege the prosaic over the poetic, the logical over the rhetorical, the illocutionary over the perlocutionary?[6] Ultimately, it is the latter terms in these pairs that make politics and political theory possible (even if at times confusing, perplexing, and frustrating), and certainly they enrich them. We surely ought to heed Foucault's warning against hypostasizing a state of communication "without obstacles,

4. Jürgen Habermas, *The Theory of Communicative Action: Reason and the Rationalization of Society,* trans. Thomas McCarthy (Boston: Beacon Press, 1984, 1987), 1: 287.

5. Michel Foucault, "The Ethic of Care for the Self," in *The Final Foucault,* ed. James Bernauer and David Rasmussen (Cambridge, Mass.: MIT Press, 1988), p. 18.

6. Such a discounting characterizes Habermas's criticism of the rhetorical in Derrida. See Jürgen Habermas, "On Leveling the Genre Distinction between Philosophy and Rhetoric," in *The Philosophical Discourse of Modernity: Twelve Lectures* (Cambridge, Mass.: MIT Press, 1987), pp. 185–210.

without constraints, without coercive effects,"[7] lest we be seduced by the cult of the dialogue and blithely fail to recognize when, where, and how power is at work. From this perspective, the seductions of a romanticized "ideal speech situation" are just as dangerous as the cynical strategies of a thoroughly hardheaded realism. Yet if all speech is not ultimately about reaching rationally grounded agreement, neither is it always the case that "to speak is to fight."[8]

The opposition sketched here, between dialogue and domination, consensus and contest, reasoned discourse and rhetorical performance, seems as intractable as that between sight and blindness, freedom and fate, autonomy and subjection explored in chapter 2. In a contest that replays the struggle between Socrates and Callicles in *Gorgias,* Habermas and Foucault advance apparently irreconcilable arguments concerning the possibility of liberating truth from power. But is it possible, in the face of these oppositions, to cultivate a philosophical ethos that is both prosaic and poetic, theoretical and political, dialectical and rhetorical, a sensibility attuned to the desire for a philosophical foundation beyond political contest and the drive to disturb such foundations? Can we formulate a post-Platonic practice that combines a healthy dose of genealogical suspicion of all teleological forms of truth with the humanist goal of securing philosophical standards of the good available to everyone? Might we envision a "politics of truth" that sustains such standards, yet that also exposes the political character of truth and resists its pretensions to uncontestability? Can we adopt an agonistic ethos and adapt it to our search for philosophical or theoretical certainties, an ethos that would amount to a wholly ironic stance toward "truth," its conditions and its possibilities? *Gorgias* explores just such an agonistic ethos by advancing as a theoretical and political paradigm something very much like the unconstrained communication of an ideal speech situation, even as it interrogates the very possibility of that ideal by dramatizing the rhetorical moves in the struggle, which occur below or outside the dialogue's argument, between Socrates and his interlocutors over who will control the terms of political discourse,[9] both within and outside of the parameters of the dialogue.

7. Ibid., p. 18.

8. Jean-François Lyotard, *The Postmodern Condition: A Report on Knowledge,* trans. Geoff Bennington and Brian Massumi (Minneapolis: University of Minnesota Press, 1984), p. 10.

9. William Connolly, *The Terms of Political Discourse,* 2d ed. (Princeton, N.J.: Princeton University Press, 1983).

That struggle is played out on a number of levels, both dialectical and dramatic, logical and psychological, philosophical and political, discursive and rhetorical, between several characters and through a number of themes. To get at this layered complexity, I want to analyze the dialogue by paying attention, not only to *what* the interlocutors say, but to *how* they say it. This means analyzing the dialectical progression of the argument as well as the parallel dramatic action, attending to a method that is logical as well as psychological, rhetorical as well as discursive, exposing the political in the philosophical. Indeed, as I argue, *Gorgias* subtly articulates how it is that Socratic philosophy presupposes a politics, or, more precisely, how the search for truth is at the same time a struggle for power, the inscription of philosophical discourse on the Athenian body politic itself a political act. The political continually encroaches upon the philosophical in *Gorgias,* and in a way that heightens, rather than resolves, the contradiction between them. Philosophy and politics, dialectic and rhetoric, truth and power—these remain the essentially contested terms in the agonistic economy of *Gorgias.*

I

The occasion for the dialogue is the visit of the rhetor Gorgias to Athens. Gorgias is receiving visitors at the home of his host, Callicles, and Socrates wishes to find out from the expert exactly what his craft is and what value it has. As the dialogue progresses, however, this initial theme broadens and multiplies: the conversation begins with Gorgias and rhetoric, then moves to Gorgias's pupil Polus and the question of committing or suffering injustice, and finally takes up with Callicles the question of how one ought to live, as a philosopher or a politician. The dialogue concludes with Socrates' claiming for himself and philosophy the true arts of politics and rhetoric. Thematically, the dialogue returns to its starting point, the symmetry of *Gorgias*'s conclusion brings us back to its beginning through a Socratic redefinition of rhetoric: true rhetoric is practiced only by Socrates, he is the one citizen practicing the art of politics (*politikē technē*), that art is identical with philosophy, and it aims to make Athenian citizens better. This expansion of the initial theme of rhetoric is also accompanied by an intensification of the discussion: as the dialogue enlarges its scope, the stakes involved in the discussion escalate accordingly. The question concerning rhetoric soon involves questions of responsibility, justice, civic education, and political leadership. *Gorgias* ends with an attempt (and, as we shall see, an ambiguous one) to transfer moral and political authority to philosophy and Socrates.

For all his incoherence, Gorgias is a gentleman and knows how to conduct himself decorously in public. He remains friendly to Socrates and encourages him to define rhetoric, even when that means defining it as flattery (463ab). Indeed, later in the dialogue, when Callicles threatens to withdraw, Gorgias reenters the conversation as Socrates' ally and urges the recalcitrant politician to continue the discussion. Polus is a different story altogether, and only with him do we see the problems with the teaching of his master. The product of Gorgianic education is boorish and ill-bred. What had been a rather friendly and intellectually abstract discussion among polite company quickly turns hostile and personal, potentially a game of domination. Polus is right, of course, to understand Socrates' attack on rhetoric as an attack on his chosen profession. For Socratic elenchus not only refutes an argument, it also refutes the way of life on which that argument rests. The stakes in the dialogue increase again when Callicles enters the discussion. Here is an opponent truly worthy of Socrates. Although Callicles pretends goodwill, at issue in this intellectual drama is nothing less than the life of the philosopher, a situation Callicles does not hesitate to point out, and about which he is correct. The focus of the struggle is multiple: a sophistic amoralism versus justice, politics versus philosophy, and Athens versus Socrates.[10] How Plato has Socrates navigate this dangerous terrain in his pursuit of knowledge is instructive for the way in which we view a politics of truth.

Gorgias is constructed as a series of dialectical engagements, in which Socrates converses with three very different characters about ostensibly different topics. Gorgias, the professional orator, is concerned with rhetoric; Polus, his rather clumsy pupil, praises, then defends, injustice over justice; Callicles, the Athenian politician, champions the free and powerful life of the statesman over the slavishly weak philosopher. Despite this diversity of topics and interlocutors, however, one issue runs like a thread throughout the dialogue and provides it with thematic unity: power and its relation to morality. When Socrates opens the dialogue by having Chaerephon ask Gorgias, "Who he is," he wants to know about the power (*dunamis*) of rhetoric and how Gorgias uses it. When Polus indignantly leaps into the fray in defense of his master, he

10. Friedländer, *Plato,* 2: 261.

identifies the rhetor with the tyrant, but with one difference: where the tyrant achieves power through violence and force, the rhetor achieves it by artful persuasion. Callicles goes to the heart of the matter when, in his first speech, he unmasks law, equality, and justice as inventions of the naturally weak and inferior, designed to shackle the naturally strong and superior. There is only one law, insists Callicles, and that is the law of the powerful. All other talk is merely specious pretense. Against this array of arguments, Socrates must demonstrate that the power of true rhetoric serves justice, that the tyrant is powerless, and that the philosophical commitment to truth sets the moral standard for human action.

In his first response to Socrates' question about the power of the rhetorical craft, Gorgias links rhetoric to power and freedom, to the field of politics in the broad sense. Gorgias defines rhetoric as the craft that possesses the power to persuade by speech. Under Socratic cross-examination, he narrows this broad definition down to the persuasion of the mob (*ochlos*) about the just and the unjust. The politician who wishes to succeed in those political debates taken up by the law courts, the council, or the assembly will find rhetoric indispensable. A neutral tool that allows its user to pursue whatever ends he chooses, rhetoric provides a power that enslaves others, be they physicians, athletic trainers, or moneymakers. This first definition of rhetoric is significant for two reasons. First, there is its amoralism. Rhetoric will serve any ends its master wishes. It is a practice radically ungrounded and unguided by the values of the community it seeks to persuade, both self-interested and self-serving. Second, its power depends upon a distinction between the one who knows and the many who do not know, between the educated initiate (presumably the rhetor himself) and the ignorant, ill- or misinformed demos. Where the former distinction leads to tyranny, the latter reveals a contempt for the demos. That contempt, however, must remain unspoken and be carefully concealed, given the rhetor's dependence upon those he must persuade.

Before Socrates begins his refutation of Gorgias, he has been at work making his own distinctions. In friendly preliminaries with the great orator, Socrates has already pointed out the difference between rhetorical display (*epideixis*) and dialectical conversation (*dialegō*), a point Gorgias says he understands (447c1–4). He follows Socrates' request with the boast that he is just as adept at giving short answers as at making long speeches, a boast that reveals his fundamental misunderstanding of Socrates' dialectical art. For Gorgias, short answers and long speeches are both part of rhetorical display. But Gorgias does not suspect that his eagerness to give the short answers Socrates' requests involves him in a subtle contest. He does not realize that, in submitting to questions by Socrates, he has had Socrates' "own law imposed upon him."[11] Rhetoric, which Gorgias proclaims is the most comprehensive of the arts and the most powerful, is unattuned to the immediate struggle over its scope and status. Gorgianic rhetoric will prove no match for Socratic dialectic.

In the discussion that follows, Socrates makes a further distinction between conviction and knowledge, where rhetoric merely produces conviction without knowledge, and does not teach about the just and the unjust. Gorgias admits that the rhetor does not teach (*didaskein*) but merely persuades (*peithesthai*) the mob. As an example, Gorgias refers to the building policies of Themistocles and Pericles to demonstrate the power of rhetoric over the craftsmen responsible for the actual construction. Gorgias continues to extol the powers of rhetoric with another example: the rhetorician, who knows nothing of the doctor's craft, can more easily persuade the patient to submit to an unpleasant treatment than the doctor himself. Moreover, in a competition with a doctor or any other craftsman, the rhetor can persuade his audience to choose him rather than the expert, so powerful is his craft.

The power of this craft does not, however, entitle the pupil to abuse it. The student should use it justly. But if it turns out that he does not, we should not blame the teacher, for he is not responsible, nor is the craft itself, but rather the man who does not use it rightly. And Gorgias himself would justly "hate and expel from the city and put to death" (457c) a student who used rhetoric unjustly. Gorgias defends himself this way on three occasions, driving home the point that, as a foreigner who potentially exerts great influence on the Athenian young, he must watch his step. He is in a vulnerable position and so must exercise caution by claiming moral neutrality for his teaching.[12] Socrates, of course, will make it a point to contrast his true rhetoric with Gorgianic flattery. But there are two larger points that follow here: one concerns the teacher's responsibility for his pupils, the other concerns the possibility of moral neutrality. Socrates will later point out that the great Athenian statesmen did not make the citizens better, and that he, practicing the true art of rhetoric, is the only one now also undertaking the true art

11. Ibid., 247.
12. Kahn, "Dialogue and Dialectic," p. 81.

of politics. But this claim is complicated by the fact that Socrates will be convicted of corrupting the young and, to the extent that he counts Alcibiades his protégé (481d), is implicated in the corrupt behavior of his pupil.[13] This "failure" of Socrates in the education of Alcibiades undermines his own claim about the benefits of philosophy and ironically links him to Gorgias.

The dialogue here raises a question about the professed moral neutrality of Gorgias's craft. Does not some "interest" inhere in all knowledge? If the interest of medicine, for example, is the health of the patient, the interest of rhetoric is the flattery of the demos, and so the power of the rhetor. Whether the rhetor persuades his audience in the cause of justice or injustice is incidental to the fact of persuasion. What guides the oration is the "victory" of the orator, whether for good or evil. Rhetoric that regards itself merely as a tool or technique is thus more seductive and dangerous than a rhetoric that honestly proclaims its will to power, for it conceals its interest behind a neutral façade, lulling us into a false sense of its benignity. Socrates will argue that dialectic or philosophy has an "interest" too, but its interest lies in pursuing the truth, an interest shared by everyone, and hence not an "interest" in the conventional sense at all.

Under the pressure of Socratic cross-examination, Gorgias changes his position a third time, finally assenting to Socrates' view that if the teacher of rhetoric teaches just things, then he himself must be just. Once Gorgias has made this admission, he must agree with Socrates that the rhetor cannot use rhetoric unjustly. Thus Gorgias himself must teach justice and take responsibility for his pupils if he is not to be seen as a corrupter of youth and regarded with hostility and suspicion. Socrates shames the teacher of rhetoric into this admission because he is not willing to admit in public what would condemn him before his Athenian hosts. Socrates thus catches Gorgias in a contradiction between the amoralism of rhetoric and his own conventional morality, a morality dictated by the paying fathers of his would-be pupils. The refutation thus shows us the dependence of rhetoric on public opinion: Gorgias cannot say what he really thinks without undermining the power of his craft, and Socrates demonstrates that rhetoric is powerless

13. Alcibiades' relationship to Socrates is evidenced in *Symposium* 212d—223d, and his less-than-exemplary behavior is depicted in Thucydides *History of the Peloponnesian War* 6.28.2 and 6.61.1–7, on the affair of the Hermai; 6.89.1–6 and 6.92.1–7, where he goes over to the Spartans; 8.44.1–8.56.5, where he intrigues with the Spartans; and 8.86.4–7, where he reverts to the Athenian side.

to negotiate this dilemma. The freedom and power of which Gorgias initially boasted (452d5) cannot be delivered by rhetoric after all: the rhetor is not free to speak his mind and is powerless before the public he must obey.

II

This rather reluctant admission by Gorgias is more than Polus can bear. If rhetoric does not produce the power necessary for dominating debate in the assembly, defending oneself in court, or taking whatever one wants, then what does it produce? At this juncture, "the situation of the dialogue enters into the argument."[14] Gorgias is shamed into silence, not only because Socrates has exposed the contradictions in his position, but because of the embarrassing presence of the vulgar and immoral Polus, a specimen of Gorgianic education. Polus is quite ready to admit what Gorgias is not—that he studies rhetoric because he wants power in the city. For is not the rhetor, like the tyrant, able to kill, expropriate, or imprison anyone he wishes at any time? To prove that the tyrant is both powerful and happy, Polus praises a contemporary tyrant, Archelaus, who had recently risen to the rulership of Macedonia through a series of particularly vile crimes.

The would-be tyrant Polus cannot believe that Socrates does not think Archelaus the happiest of men by virtue of his tyrannical power and envy him it accordingly. What is revealed here is the measure of Polus's own tyrannical impulses as he gropes his rather inarticulate way toward the distinction that Callicles will make between nature and convention. Socrates, he thinks, is trapped by a conventional morality that does not give free reign to a man's true impulses, calling "just" what the mass of men believe. He is not strong enough to break out of the conventional mold, as does Polus, who appeals, however inchoately, to a law of nature under which the stronger and superior rule. What Socrates conventionally calls "injustice" is naturally just. But as Callicles points out, Socrates manipulates Polus into confusing nature and convention in his answers and so traps Gorgias's pupil into an admission he does not believe, that doing injustice is worse than suffering it, and further, that not paying the penalty for an injustice one had committed is worst of all.

The exchange with Polus is instructive because of Polus's reliance on

14. Voegelin, *Order and History*, p. 25.

the many, the democratic practice of the vote, and his appeal to the example of the tyrant Archelaus. Polus associates rhetoric, democracy, and tyranny, implying that the democratic rhetor is really a tyrant at heart, willing to use the intimidation of numbers to get what he wants. Against this identification of power with tyranny and numbers, Socrates opposes his elenchus. Socratic elenchus appeals, not to the many, but to only one, and in that appeal seeks to produce real conviction in the listener. Its power depends on the "unforced force of the better argument," not the thoughtless votes of the many. Nothing could be farther from the conventional conception of democratic power (as Gorgias and Polus represent it) than this model supplied by the practice of Socratic dialectic. And in this model, rhetoric has no place, unless it is to persuade the tyrant or would-be tyrant to pay restitution for the evils he has done. True rhetoric, then, is not in the service of a tyrant like Archelaus, who would use it to gain power over others, but in the service of justice, in order to gain control over oneself and learn moderation.

Socrates' conversations with Gorgias and Polus reveal a fundamental antagonism between Athenian political practice and Socratic dialectic, an antagonism that culminates in Callicles' prediction of Socrates' death and Socrates' assumption of the mantle of Athenian statesmanship. The rhetors and politicians merely flatter the demos, gratifying the citizens with pleasing words, as a cook gratifies the palate with pleasing food, in order to gain their favor and then their votes. Unlike the true politician or the doctor, the rhetor does not need to know anything, he only needs to seem to know, and just enough to be persuasive. Socratic dialectic, on the other hand, forces its participants to reflect on the nature and patterns of what they believe and do in order, not to persuade a mob, but to choose the good. Whereas rhetoric is given over to displays of verbal pyrotechnics as a means of concealing its ignorance, dialectic argues for the most important matters of justice in a singularly mundane fashion, which begins with familiar examples from everyday life—shoemakers, pastry cooks, and doctors. After the unhealthy display of the rhetors, Socrates will welcome the candid speech (*parrhēsia*) of his next interlocutor, Callicles.

III

Callicles is a formidable and worthy opponent. The very antithesis of Socrates, he opposes rhetoric to dialectic, politics to philosophy, the naturally powerful to the conventionally just, and Athens to Socrates as his ultimate standards of judgment.[15] Yet Callicles possesses all the qualities Socrates admires most: knowledge, goodwill, and free speaking. That is why Socrates refers to Callicles as his "touchstone" (487a). If Socrates succeeds in convincing the politician, then the substance of his argument must be true, since no one's agreement could be counted worthier than that of Callicles (487e5). In a perverse sort of way, Callicles turns out to be the "ideal" interlocutor. If Callicles can truly be persuaded, then philosophy does have a point and place in the city and there are good reasons to believe that a philosophically grounded politics is possible. The outcome of that contest is far from certain, however, and how one "reads" that outcome will determine any assessment of where *Gorgias* stands on the relationship between philosophy and politics, dialectic and rhetoric, truth and power.

Socrates begins that persuasion by laying the groundwork for the mutuality and friendship that meaningful dialogue requires. Callicles and Socrates both share the same experience (*pathos*) in the form of two loves: Socrates loves Alcibiades, son of Cleinias, and philosophy; Callicles loves Demos, son of Pyrilampes, and the demos of Athens (481d). This parallelism tends, however, to drive Socrates and Callicles apart rather than bind them together.[16] Socrates juxtaposes the inconstancy of Alcibiades to the constancy of philosophy, which he, Socrates, follows, and then juxtaposes himself to Callicles, who flatters both the demos of Athens and Demos, son of Pyrilampes. Implicit in these pairings is the opposition between politics and philosophy, rhetoric and dialectic, which will emerge again at the end of the dialogue, when Socrates characterizes the great Athenian statesmen as flatterers of Calliclean stripe. The comparisons, in addition to prefiguring the contours of the dialogue in so compact a space, underline the vast difference between the "partners" in conversation and point to the irreconcilability of the opponents. If Socrates cannot replace the love of the demos with

15. Ibid., p. 31; Jaeger, *Paideia,* 2: 138; *Gorgias,* ed. Dodds, p. 267.

16. This point is complicated by the fact that Plato shows Callicles able to play a similar game as well. At 485e the orator introduces the characters Zethus and Amphion from Euripides' lost play *Antiope,* suggesting that he, Callicles, will play Zethus to Socrates' Amphion in their argument over which life, the active and political or the contemplative and private, is best. The point, of course, is that Zethus and Amphion are *twins,* and the strategy has obvious implications, not only for Callicles' friendly relation to Socrates, but also for philosophy's relation to politics. On the significance of *Antiope* for *Gorgias,* see Andrea Nightingale, "Plato's *Gorgias* and Euripides' *Antiope:* A Study in Generic Transformation," *Classical Antiquity* 11, 1 (Apr. 1992): 121–41.

the love of philosophy in Callicles, then it is unlikely that the experience they share will provide sufficiently fertile ground for communication. It is against this background, the pathos of communication, that the rest of the dialogue unfolds.

Callicles is a worthy opponent, because he is unafraid to assert aloud what Gorgias conceals, and what Polus has only inadequately articulated: the justice of domination. Unlike his guests, Callicles will not be shamed into admitting what he does not believe merely to satisfy conventional morality. Indeed, he has seen how Socrates trapped the two rhetors by appealing now to nature, now to convention, whenever it suited his purpose in the argument. Callicles will successfully avoid such Socratic sleight of hand if only he holds fast to the one objective standard there is: nature (482d—483a). In that way, he can unmask Socrates' claims to truth for what they really are, the philosopher's will to power, which hides behind the pretense of intellectual respectability.

In the great speech that follows, Callicles elaborates a genealogy of morals worthy of (perhaps inspiration for) Nietzsche himself.[17] Socrates is advancing nothing but a slave morality, a set of conventions made by the weak and for the weak, when he argues for justice. Such conventional lawmakers cannot defend themselves and so must define justice to their own advantage and for their own protection. They then call themselves virtuous and just for refraining from taking more than their share, and call shameful and unjust those who would take more than others (*pleonektein*) (483c). Thus do the weak and inferior manufacture virtue out of their weakness and tame the naturally stronger and superior into submitting to convention. But if we hold to nature (*physis*), we shall see how things really stand. It is the same among men as it is among animals and cities: the strong rule where they can, and the weak suffer what they must.[18] The law of nature (*nomos physēs*) prescribes as much, and it is only by rules contrary to nature that the weak and slavish hold the strong and noble in check. If only he would leave off philosophizing and turn to more important things, Socrates would come to his senses and understand that this is to "turn the whole of human

17. On Nietzsche's relation to the dialogue, see *Gorgias*, ed. Dodds, appendix, "Socrates, Callicles, and Nietzsche," pp. 387–91, where Dodds gathers a wealth of references in Nietzsche's corpus relating to Callicles, Socrates, Plato, and the Sophists.

18. Dodds (ibid., p. 268) has not failed to notice the parallel with the argument made by Athenian generals at Melos according to which cities obey the rule of the stronger (*upo phuseōs anangkaias*), which is later referred to as a law (*nomos*) in Thucydides' *History* 5.105.2. Cf. Callicles' *kata nomon ge tēn tēs phuseōs* (483e3).

life upside down" (481c). That is not to say that philosophy has no place in the education of a gentleman (*kalos k'agathos*), but when pushed to extremes, as in the case of Socrates, the result does not befit a free man. He will be unacquainted with politics, he will not be able to hold his own in debate, and, what is more, if he is dragged into court by an inferior man, he will be unable to defend himself. What good is a man who cannot protect himself from his enemies, a man whom one may hit with impunity? Better to leave off philosophy, Callicles admonishes, and tend to more important matters. Philosophy pursued in excess makes a man effeminate: he will be forever hanging about in corners with lisping boys, shy at public gatherings where great matters are at stake and reputations are won. The philosophical life is the life of a slave, hardly worthy of a free man and an Athenian.

Callicles champions the master morality of the "just by nature," although his preliminary definition is none too exact. Socrates forces him to revise that definition and eventually prove the position untenable. Callicles argues that the tyrant, the man who gives his desires free reign and possesses the capacity to satisfy them, is the model of nobility. Socrates opposes the tyrant with the model of the philosophical man, who strives, not to gain more than his share, but to make his fellow citizens more just by teaching them successfully to rule themselves. Callicles first identifies the strong with the good: rule by the strongest is justice (488c). As with men, so too with cities. If it is just for a strong man to rule the weak, then a powerful city like Athens rules weaker cities with justice as well. Socrates directs his attack against this position by undermining the identification of the strong and the good. Do the numerous weak not prove better than the few stronger ones when the former impose their hated conventions on the latter? And then wouldn't equality and justice be according to nature (*physis*) and not convention (*nomos*)? Callicles is outraged by the prospect that a rabble of slaves, superior in strength alone, should rule their superiors. He immediately withdraws the argument and redefines the good as the "better" (*beltion*).

After a short Socratic cross-examination, the "better" as defined by Callicles turn out to be those men who are wise and brave with respect to the affairs of the city. They ought to rule, and it is fair for them to have more than their subjects (491b—d). Callicles is then brought up short by the Socratic query, "Ought the rulers to have more than themselves?" He quickly denies that such a man should be ruled at all. On the contrary, he should let his desires grow to their fullest and then possess the power to satisfy them: "luxury, intemperance and freedom" (*tryphē, akolasia, eleutheria*) are truly virtue and happiness, and their pursuit right according to nature (492c). Socrates then offers a series of examples meant to shame Callicles into admitting a distinction between good and bad pleasures: hunger satisfied by food, thirst by drink, an itch by a scratch. But what about the sexual tickle of the catamite? Callicles bridles at this last suggestion, and even goes so far as to upbraid Socrates for such a shameful example, but for the sake of argumentative consistency, maintains his position (494e—495a).

Socrates pushes the inquiry and Callicles further by attacking the equality of good and bad pleasures through the same appeal to "convention" that defeated Gorgias and Polus: Callicles implicitly admits the distinction of good and bad pleasures because he accepts a ranking of the virtues in which wisdom and courage are better than folly and cowardice. If, as Socrates concludes, the weak and base can experience more pleasure than the strong and brave, then by Callicles' account, the former are better than the latter. This is a conclusion Callicles cannot bear, and it forces him into the grudging admission that all along he has thought "some pleasures are better and others worse" (499c). Once Callicles has made this concession to conventional morality, Socrates will, step by step, prove his case for the superiority of the life of justice and temperance over the life of tyranny and license, for the superiority of the Socratic will to knowledge over the Calliclean will to power. As he does so, Callicles withdraws from the discussion. He first pretends ignorance (497b), then answers only to gratify his guest Gorgias (501c, 505c), and finally breaks it off altogether when he suggests that Socrates either let the discussion go, have a dialogue with someone else, or ask and answer for himself (505e).

The discussion so far has juxtaposed two models of power, the Calliclean and the Socratic. For Callicles, political power is the power of domination, the ability of one man or one city to fulfill his or its unlimited desires. Political greatness means dominating debate in the assembly, gaining fame, honor, wealth, and reputation, or, in the case of a city, being powerful enough to dominate other cities, "leaving behind monuments, whether for good or evil."[19] For Socrates, being powerful does not mean dominating other men or cities, but dominating and controlling ones' own desires and appetites, ordering the self and city

19. This is, of course, Pericles, in the Funeral Oration. Thucydides *History* 2.41.4–5.

(508a) in a just and lawful manner (504d). The best life is the life of the philosopher, because he has power over himself, is not dependent on the many as are the politicians, and will never commit injustice. Being great means being good, which entails forsaking honor, wealth, and reputation as those things are commonly conceived. Given this conception of "power," Callicles "rightly sensed the revolution in the words of Socrates,"[20] for the Socratic criticism of Athenian politics has turned Callicles and his world completely upside down.

There is one more model of power in the dialogue, however, one given by the practice of dialectic itself. In that practice, power is dispersed among the participants in the conversation. The point of dialectic is not the domination of one interlocutor over another, but the mutual search for truth. Dialogue and dialectic serve no one person's particular interest in getting or having more, but rather harmonize a plurality of interests in the common search for the good (*to agathon*) (500a). If there is competition, it is for mutual enlightenment, not personal gain or aggrandizement. Socrates reminds his partners in dialectic that he has no more knowledge than they, and that he searches in common with them for the truth (506a). The dialectical model of power resists tyranny and closure by insisting on the equality of the participants and honoring the diversity and multiplicity of viewpoints that characterize dialogue as the collective search for wisdom.

Yet *Gorgias* culminates in Socrates' famous claim that he alone of the Athenians practices the true art of politics (*politikē technē* 521d). The great statesmen of Athens's past—Themistocles, Cimon, Miltiades, and, most important, Pericles—did not practice real rhetoric, but Socrates does, because through philosophy he makes the Athenians better citizens. Socrates advances a similar claim in the *Apology,* where he exhorts the jury, as he has exhorted his fellow citizens all his life, to care more for the goodness of their souls than for wealth, honor, and fame—the stuff of the conventional Athenian political life that Callicles so readily praises. But it is only in *Gorgias* that Socrates claims philosophical dialogue as a paradigm for political deliberation (527d) and identifies philosophy as the practice of the true art of politics.

The contours of the paradigm delineated by Socrates in *Gorgias* are familiar from the early or aporetic dialogues and from his defense speech in the *Apology.* Socrates goes about the city testing and examin-

20. Voegelin, *Order and History,* p. 28.

ing all whom he meets for their wisdom, ever the ironic man, always inquiring, searching, and professing ignorance. Philosophy, in contrast to rhetoric, entails the open-ended search for knowledge, wisdom, and justice, unpretentious in its claims and conscious of its mortal limits. Unlike his opponents, Socrates is more interested in following the logos of the argument wherever it may go than in winning a contest, as willing to be refuted as to refute (458a). Implicit in Socrates' transfer of political authority to himself and dialectical examination is the claim that if the Athenians were to follow this Socratic practice in their political deliberations, the city would now be healthy rather than bloated with harbors, docks, and walls (519a), and the citizens "good" rather than the idlers, cowards, prattlers, and spongers they are now (515e5). As partners in a dialogue share a mutual commitment to the argument (*logos*), so too would deliberating citizens be united by a commitment to the good of the city. Debate in the Assembly would then resemble the dialectical search for the truth, a search that would result in the adoption of the best policy, that decision influenced neither by the most rhetorically persuasive speech (as opposed to the most logically persuasive) nor by any particular individual's or group's interest. Inside the dialogue as well as inside the Assembly, "the unforced force of the better argument" would ideally prevail. Moreover, the richness of the dialogical community defined by a plurality of voices and a multiplicity of perspectives would reflect a similar diversity in the Assembly, where plurality is the irreducible condition of successful moral communication and debate. Such is the practice and the promise of Socratic dialogue, both for us and for the citizens of Athens.

IV

But I am not sure that so easy an identification of philosophical dialogue with political deliberation is possible. For one thing, the very practice of Socratic philosophy begs the question of where, when, and how philosophy is political. Unlike the assembly, council, law court, or even tragedy, philosophy had no prescribed institutional status in Athens (although Socrates' suggestion in the *Apology* that he be maintained at public expense indicates that he thought it ought to). That Socratic philosophy had no recognized public form or forum is bad enough, but the fact that Socrates deliberately avoided the official spaces and places of politics only made matters worse. To claim a monopoly on the true art of politics and then refuse to participate in the "official" discourse of the city (or to do so incompetently)[21] indicates either a wholesale rejection of that discourse, the failure of philosophy as a political ideal, or the failure of Athenians to respond to Socratic philosophical education. In each case, Socratic dialogue remains marginalized, performing its work at the interstices between public and private, trespassing on both, at home in neither, but always standing as a rebuke to Athenian political practice.

For these reasons, *Gorgias* leaves us with an ambivalent message, both about the practice of Socratic philosophy itself and about its promise for the reform of the city's politics. This ambiguity makes it difficult for critical theory's ideal of unconstrained speech readily to absorb or assimilate the dialectic of *Gorgias.* While I do not doubt that *Gorgias* offers philosophical dialogue as something like an analogue for political deliberation (whether that deliberation will take place in the assembly or law courts is unclear), the dialogue nonetheless reveals that such a model is problematic, for the lasting impression of *Gorgias* is more complex, more nuanced, and certainly more ambivalent than such an "ideal" reading suggests. A number of disturbing ambiguities mark the course of the dialogue, ambiguities that challenge the idealized image of an egalitarian speech community in search of the truth. These ambiguities tend to disrupt and so challenge as disingenuous the explicit arguments in favor of philosophy put forth by Socrates. They are generally dramatic in character, sometimes acknowledged by Socrates, but always reveal how the text subverts its manifest content in the rhetorical surplus of meaning it generates. The atmosphere of *Gorgias* contributes to this impression in a number of subtle ways. Unlike a dialogue such as *Protagoras,* with its humorous and good-natured ambience, the fate-laden gloom of tragedy pervades *Gorgias,* casting a somber shadow on the proceedings. Whereas the former dialogue portrays the exaggerated vanity of the Sophists as harmlessly comic, and Socrates as a jester poking fun at such seriousness, here the menacing tone of Callicles[22] points to Socrates' own trial and death and the "limits" of philosophy. More than once Callicles reminds Socrates of the fate that

21. See Socrates' allusion to his inexperience in legal procedure at *Gorgias* 522b3—c2, and his opening speech in the *Apology,* where he confesses his unfamiliarity with the procedures of the law court.

22. Werner Jaeger, *Paideia,* 2: 141.

awaits a man who devotes too much of his life to philosophy: he will be accused with impunity, unable to defend himself in court (486b4–6).[23] Moreover, unlike the two other great antisophistic dialogues, *Protagoras* and *Euthydemus,* Plato presents *Gorgias* in direct dramatic form, without the benefit of mediation by a narrator.[24] The characters confront one another, directly expressing themselves and their objective differences. The absence of narrative mediation and the dramatization of direct confrontation underscore the agonistic elements of the dialogue. Here direct drama subtly and effectively heightens the tension of the contest: the form of the dialogue rearticulates its content in the agonistic clash of opposites, where once-decorous speech threatens to drop all pretense to civility and is exposed as verbal combat.

The tone and texture of its language, the examples used, and the images evoked suggest another way in which *Gorgias* deploys rhetorical strategies to achieve a certain philosophical effect. It is no coincidence that Callicles opens the dialogue with the words "of war and battle" (*polemou kai machēs*), a hint that the impending philosophical conversation between Socrates and Gorgias will be "the continuation of politics by other means."[25] Nor is it a coincidence that Plato sets the dramatic date in such a way that, although it is impossible to fix with any certainty, there is no doubt that the war with Sparta provides both dramatic background to, and substantive content of, the dialogue.[26] The war of each against all, portrayed by Thucydides' accounts of the stasis at Corcyra and the "dialogue" at Melos, has now moved to Athens. The repeated assurances of mutually friendly competition to the contrary, the form of the agon and the tone of war undermine the professed comity of intellectual exchange. As the dialogue progresses, the social veneer of urbanity wears thin. In the communicative struggle between Callicles and Socrates, we must hear, not the achievement of consensus—as Habermas would have us believe—but rather, as Foucault re-

23. Both Voegelin, *Order and History,* p. 34, and Friedländer, *Plato,* 2: 261, see this touch as distinctly authorial and suggest Plato's own doubts about the success of the Socratic enterprise.

24. Friedländer, *Plato,* 2: 245.

25. *Gorgias,* ed. Dodds, p. 384, quotes V. De Magalhaes-Vilhena, *Socrate et la legende platonicienne* (Paris: Presses universitaires de France, 1952), p. 128. The phrase is, of course, from Clausewitz.

26. References in the dialogue cover a span from 429 B.C., the year of Pericles' death, to 405 B.C., the year after the trial of the generals responsible at Arginusae. See *Gorgias,* ed. Dodds, pp. 17–18, and Arlene Saxonhouse, "An Unspoken Theme in Plato's *Gorgias:* War," *Interpretation* 11, 2 (May 1983): 142–44.

minds us, in a different, though related, context, "the distant roar of battle."[27]

Finally, *Gorgias* concludes with a Socratic myth full of religious imagery and symbols, the first intimation, Jaeger argues, that "behind the infinitely subtle dialectic distinctions in which his moral principles are concealed, there is a metaphysical transformation of the whole of life."[28] Socrates quotes Euripides' "Who knows if life here be not really death, and death in turn be life?" Earlier in the dialogue, Callicles was right to sense the revolution in Socrates' exchange with Polus, a revolution that would turn political life upside down. Now, at the conclusion of the dialogue, not only the conventions of the would-be politician, but the orientation of human life itself is reversed. Socrates leaves us wondering if he prefers death to life, and if he has abandoned Athenian politics altogether. Despite the cheery confidence of Socrates' convictions about the virtue of the philosophical life, the dialogue ends on a note of pessimistic resignation.[29]

The somber atmosphere, the reality of external and the imminent threat of internal war, and the reminder of Socrates' impending death all provide a context for the "failure" of Socratic philosophy to reform even the individual Athenian citizen, never mind the whole city. That failure seems nearly complete: Socrates points out on several occasions that the purpose of debate is to persuade one's opponent, and he himself admits that if he succeeds in convincing Callicles, whom he deems his "touchstone," he will have arrived at the truth of the matter. But by the end of the dialogue, Callicles is not persuaded that the virtuous life of the philosopher is better than a life of *pleonexia,* even though Socrates has demonstrated the incoherence of that position. As in so many other dialogues in which Socrates outargues his interlocutor, Socrates here re-

27. Michel Foucault, *Discipline and Punish: The Birth of the Prison,* trans. Alan Sheridan (1977; repr., New York: Vintage Books, 1979), p. 308.

28. Jaeger, *Paideia,* 2: 141.

29. Cf. the *Apology,* which concludes on a similar note: Socrates remains calm in the face of death and professes ignorance about life after death, as he does here, but is pessimistic about the political efficacy of philosophy in a city like Athens. Pessimistic resignation is perhaps too strong, however, because in the end, Socrates is vindicated. In the story of the afterlife, it is Callicles the politician who will "reel and gape" before his divine judges, just as Socrates did before his human ones. This is the argument of Nightingale, "Plato's *Gorgias* and Euripides' *Antiope.*" This may be true, but it indicates Plato's judgment, certainly, and is decidedly a turn away from the political life. My argument, of course, is that *Gorgias* holds these two impulses in tension, so I do not read the mythos that concludes the dialogue as a definitive vindication of the philosophical life. Callicles has some, although not all, of my sympathy.

futes Callicles, yet fails to change his way of life. In spite of Socrates' repeated efforts throughout the dialogue to establish a minimum level of comity and mutuality, the Socratic elenchus fails to encourage in Callicles that agreement or conviction (*homologia*) necessary to establish and maintain the speech community. Callicles, like Polus before him, slowly withdraws from any "honest" engagement with Socrates. As a consequence, Socrates fails to meet the standards of dialogical success he himself has set.

Closely related to this failure of philosophy is the failure of the dialogue form itself. Socrates repeatedly juxtaposes dialectic to rhetoric and insists on conducting the conversation in the form of question and answer as a way of ensuring a kind of communicative equality: no one speaker will be permitted to dominate the discussion. But under the relentless questioning of Socrates, first Polus and then Callicles retreats from the dialogue. Callicles' answers become increasingly perfunctory, and he admits that the only reason he submits to what he considers Socrates' impertinent questioning is to please his guest Gorgias and maintain some semblance of decorum in public. At the conclusion of *Gorgias,* Callicles finally refuses to answer: dialogue becomes monologue, and Socrates is left, not for the first time, talking to himself. The only voice we now hear is the voice of Socrates. The irony is that Socrates himself has brought about what he (said he) most feared: that Gorgias (or someone trained like him) would dominate the conversation, silencing other views and other voices. Despite Socrates' best efforts (or perhaps because of them) to save appearances, as the once actively engaged participants in the discussion withdraw from the community of the dialogue into private silence, dialogic give-and-take succumbs to the centripetal forces of Socratic oration.

To the extent that Socrates proclaims himself to be the only Athenian practicing the true art of politics, and so claims philosophical dialogue as a paradigm for political deliberation, the failure inside the dialogue also indicates its failure outside. Despite Socrates' claims on behalf of philosophy, it is unlikely that it can successfully guide the politics of the city, either as a model for speech in the assembly or as a force for individual moral reform outside it. If Socrates cannot convince Callicles in private conversation, how will he (or anyone else) be able to convince the Assembly in public deliberation? And does not the concluding Socratic monologue simply imitate the rhetorical display (*epideixis*) that Socrates deems inappropriate in both private philosophical conversation and public deliberation? How can philosophy guide political deliberation in any meaningful sense? Indeed, if Alcibiades represents another example of the limits of Socratic philosophical education, then perhaps it is best that philosophy stay out of the Assembly and away from politics. This purposeful mention of Alcibiades alerts us to what Socrates suppresses in his account of statesmanship. One might then ask the same question of Socrates that Socrates asks of Pericles: has philosophy made any citizens better? If the presence of Polus gives the lie to the success of Gorgias's education in rhetoric, the career of Alcibiades likewise raises a doubt concerning the dialectical education practiced by Socrates. If Alcibiades is the product of Socratic education, then Socrates is indeed corrupting the Athenian youth.[30] These ambiguities in the *Gorgias* suggest that perhaps Plato believes there is less to Socrates' boast about statesmanship than meets the eye. Such failures (with Callicles and Alcibiades) certainly indicate that Socratic dialogue is not possible "anywhere and at any time" and that it provides no unproblematic paradigm for political deliberation.

Except for the *Republic,* perhaps, *Gorgias* is the dialogue most aware of its enabling context, most conscious of its own preconditions. It is a dialogue about dialogue, contains speeches about speech, and frequently pauses to reflect on the grounds of its own possibility. It is a dialogue that takes itself as its theme, a metadialogue. The subject of *Gorgias* is the relationship between power and morality. But below or alongside the arguments about the value of rhetoric, the worth of justice or injustice, and the question of how one ought to live, *Gorgias* portrays a struggle over who will set the terms of political discourse and so control both the dialogue and what counts as "moral" in it. In Foucault's terms, it dramatizes how power implements the rules of right by which we live. If we pay attention to this subtext, we see a struggle over *what* the interlocutors will talk about and *how* they will talk about it. And, as I hope to make clear, Socrates sets the terms of discourse in such a way that he violates them in the act of establishing them. By articulating this paradox, *Gorgias* indicates that no morality is free of power, no theory not implicated in political struggle, no logic without its rhetorical effects, no speech situation so ideal that it can escape the violence of its own founding. If philosophy is to replace rhetoric as the

30. This is further complicated by the fact that Alcibiades was Pericles' ward. Socrates and Pericles both share, then, in the forming of Alcibiades. Socrates' condemnation of Pericles then begins to reflect on himself and brings Socrates closer to Gorgias in the dialogue, insofar as Gorgias admires Pericles and the tradition of Athenian statesmanship.

foundation of politics, as Socrates seems to teach, can it do so only by extraphilosophical means?

The answer to that question requires a further exploration of the dialogue's highly reflexive deployment of rhetorical effects. Recent critics have noticed the importance of dramatic structure in *Gorgias,* in particular how the complex nature of the elenchus "is reflected artistically in the interplay between the personal and the dialectical, between the dramatic and the logical structure of the refutation." Every dialectical encounter with Socrates turns into a critical examination of the interlocutor's own life.[31] In *Gorgias,* Socrates relies as much on personal as on dialectical argument, as much on shame as on logic. As Socrates moves closer to the conclusion of a refutation, the personal becomes the dialectical. Socrates' method then becomes an attempt less to argue Callicles into accepting his proposition than to maneuver him into acknowledging that he has really believed it all along. Socrates' weapon in this psychological warfare is shame.[32] This exchange is significant for two reasons. On the one hand, it demonstrates the dependence of the rhetorician upon the *dēmos.* If the conventional morality of the city requires a conventional belief, then the rhetor or politician who, like Callicles, really holds unconventional (i.e., natural) beliefs about justice, cannot divulge them safely in public. On the other, it shows Socrates doing exactly what Callicles' charged: appealing to either nature or convention when the occasion (and argument) suits him, and appealing to public opinion to intimidate an opponent. Read this way, can we understand Socrates' claim—that in the pursuit of truth he is just as willing to be refuted as to refute—without irony? Or is truth fabricated piecemeal and out of alien forms by the hatred, passion, envy, and the will to power of philosophers, who are not averse to deploying a variety of strategies, including that of shame, to maneuver their opponents into defeat?

Socrates reveals those strategies at the dialogue's outset. He insists on conducting the conversation in the form of question and answer. Socrates is not interested in witnessing a rhetorical display, but in engaging his interlocutor in a frank discussion. Gorgias agrees to this Socratic condition, boasting that he is capable of short answers as well as long speeches (449c). Polus is a different matter. He does not so readily submit to the Socratic condition when Socrates asks him to restrain his

31. Kahn, "Dialogue and Dialectic in Plato's *Gorgias,*" pp. 75–76.
32. McKim, "Shame and Truth in Plato's *Gorgias,*" p. 37.

long speeches. But Polus is either a slow study or else he willfully and subtly evades the condition: he either cannot or will not learn the elenchus. Socrates' ironic response is to provide a display himself, at the end of which he points out the violation of his own prohibition, one suspects both for Polus's edification and ours. Socrates (or Plato) is playing with Polus. At the same time, Socrates drops the reader a clue: the dialogue too transgresses Socrates' prohibition against rhetoric.

Socrates continues to set the terms of the dialogue—how the discussion will be conducted—by threatening a walkout. If Polus refuses to restrain the prolixity of his speech, then what choice does Socrates have but to leave? Here again, Socrates sets the terms in which the discussion will be conducted, but those terms are themselves beyond contestation. And he does so by appealing to the crowd, who wish the conversation to continue. Polus would like to resist, but finds himself in a bind: if he refuses to grant Socrates' conditions, he shows bad form; if he grants them, we all know he is no match for the master dialectician. We also feel that Socrates knows this and so engineers the dilemma in order to gain the upper hand. At this point in the dialogue, once Socrates has maneuvered his opponents onto dialectical territory, he can surprise and ambush them at will, carrying out a successful campaign of elenchic warfare. Successfully setting the terms of the discussion means that Socrates has already won half the battle.

Gorgias dramatizes the struggle over *what* the interlocutors will discuss as well as *how* they will discuss it. If Socrates sets the formal parameters of the dialogue, he also sets the substantive agenda of the discussion. The Socratic maneuver is subtle, but Plato supplies enough clues so that we do not mistake its significance. Polus and Callicles both defend some version of the thesis that it is better to commit injustice than suffer it. To argue the other way round, as does Socrates, is a ploy to force a slave morality on the strong and noble natures of the masters. The argument Socrates pursues here, however, does not concern the superiority of the life of justice over the life of injustice, but rather whether everyone already believes as much. Socrates defends the following position: "I believe that you and I and all men consider doing injustice to be worse than suffering it" (474b). Polus, apparently unaware of the subtle, although crucial, shift in the epistemological stakes of the debate, responds accordingly with the counter: "I believe that neither you nor I nor anyone else believes that" (474b6). What is plain from this passage is that Socrates and Polus are arguing about what they already *believe* about justice and injustice, not what is in fact the case. We always prefer justice to injustice, Socrates argues, even if we do not always choose it, since we are often wrong about what is truly in our best interest. By moving the discussion onto the terrain of "what you and I and all men already believe," Socrates does not have to prove anything about justice and injustice.[33] He merely has to maneuver his opponent into a position where he will capitulate out of shame. By (re)establishing the terms of the argument, Socrates is free to wage the conversational equivalent of guerrilla warfare: he catches his opponent in a contradiction between belief and action, between what a character says and how he lives his life, in order to change, not only his beliefs about his life, but his life itself.

I have been arguing that *Gorgias* is a complex, nuanced, and multilayered dialogue that violates the expectations of those who would defend the idea of uncoerced speech (even if Habermas sometimes rejects Socratic dialogue as a naive example of ideal speech) and of the genealogical critic who would unmask all claims to truth (especially Platonic ones) as so many instances of the will to power, and so reject even the ironic truth, grounded in ignorance, of Socratic philosophy.

That Socrates offers philosophical dialogue as a paradigm for political deliberation is a serious, although I think ironic, gesture. The "failure" of either side to convince the other implies that there are certain inescapable constraints on the ideal speech situation and Socratic dialogue understood in its terms. To the extent that knowledge is virtue, rationally grounded agreement would have to result in conviction. But it is apparent from the dialogue that intellectual agreement does not necessarily produce existential conviction. Unlike critical theory's faith in the "unforced force of the better argument," *Gorgias* acknowledges the concrete realities that condition the search for truth. *Gorgias* shows us that pure Socratic dialogue is, indeed, "not possible anywhere or at any time" by showing us the structural, material, and existential realities of power that disable the mutually beneficial search for truth.[34]

33. See ibid.

34. Jürgen Habermas, *Knowledge and Human Interests,* trans. Jeremy J. Shapiro (Boston: Beacon Press, 1971). On this point, Habermas and *Gorgias* agree: a critical theory exposes the power and asymmetry that obscure or otherwise distort speech situations so as to clear the way for the "unforced force of the better argument." On this reading, Socrates, too, has an interest, but it is in the "truth." I argue that *Gorgias* and critical theory part ways precisely at the point where the dialogue concedes the irreducible presence of rhetoric in even the most honest of philosophical dialogues, whereas Habermas aims to purge all speech of its rhetorical contaminations. For the technical discussion of illocutionary and perlocutionary speech acts, which correspond to the difference between propositional statement and rhetorical effect, and of how this dis-

At the same time it shows us, negatively perhaps, those qualities—honesty (*parrhēsia*), goodwill (*eunoia*), mutuality (*homologia*), and fearlessness—that enable a philosophical as well as a political dialogue.

In the "end,"[35] Socrates defeats Callicles but does not persuade him: the politician withdraws from the conversation. But the purpose of debate is to persuade one's opponent to change his life as well as his beliefs. Formal refutation is insufficient: knowledge must become virtue. To the extent that this manifestly does not occur with Callicles, Socrates fails to meet his own "self-set standards of success."[36] The dialogue is, then, a failure, because it does not reach Callicles on its own terms. Socratic philosophy is a failure, because if it cannot reach the "touchstone" Callicles, it has little point or place in Athens. Socrates, and Socratic philosophy, then, is more appropriately characterized as an object lesson to be avoided, rather than as a paradigm to be emulated or imitated.

Certainly, *failure* is too strong a word. After all, Callicles cannot put Socrates down. More than once he rejoins the conversation after lapsing into silence. Echoing an observation made earlier by Polus (480e), Callicles admits that he is at once attracted to, and repelled by, Socrates. "I do not know how it is," Callicles admits in what is perhaps one of his more truthful utterances, "but your words attract me Socrates. Yet as with most people you do not quite convince me" (513c5). Although Socrates has not quite made his case, still Callicles cannot stop talking to him. There is no final closure here: Socrates is not persuasive, and Callicles has not quite severed the tenuous bond that holds them together. The politician and philosopher will continue talking to each other, for politics will not submit, and philosophy has not yet had the last word. There is still work to be done, for the ground of philosophy (and of politics) remains essentially contested and contestable. Knowledge of that contestability, at least in *Gorgias,* is what makes Socratic philosophy *political* philosophy. More important, Socrates' "failure" to convince Callicles does not signal the failure of the dialogue. After all,

---

tinction is possible, see Habermas *Theory of Communicative Action,* vol. 1, "Intermediate Reflections."

35. I put it this way because, as will become clear, I'm not sure *Gorgias* really ends. Of course, the dialogue stops in a conventional sense, but its lasting impression is one of further provocation, not final closure.

36. James L. Wiser, "The Force of Reason: On Reading Plato's *Gorgias,*" in *The Ethical Dimension of Political Life,* ed. Francis Canavan (Durham, N.C.: Duke University Press, 1983), p. 56.

the dialogue is not trying to convince Callicles, but rather its potential readers, who are, beyond Plato's immediate students, an audience of unspecified and unknown readers. And if I am right, *Gorgias* contains a lesson about its (and philosophy's) own rhetoricity.

Gorgias thus does not leave matters with an unsuccessful Socrates and an incorrigible Callicles. As we have seen, the dialogue periodically alerts its readers to the way in which what counts as true is determined by extraphilosophical means, by means outside, below, or prior to the "agreed upon" parameters of Socratic dialectic.[37] This subtext in *Gorgias* largely concerns who will control the terms of philosophical discourse, and that control is the substance of the *agon* between Socrates and his interlocutors. For once Socrates' partners submit to the condition of question and answer, to dialectic instead of rhetoric, the dialogue has shifted decisively in philosophy's favor. That Socrates aims to set the terms of discourse, and so control the dialogical as well as the political community, creates a paradox. Does not the dialogue instantiate a paradigm of uncoerced communication by means of subtly coercive rhetorical strategies while it simultaneously denies the operation of these tactics through its commitment to "the argument" (*logos*)? Has not Socrates transgressed the rules of philosophical discourse at the very moment and in the very act of establishing them? *Gorgias* must then "conceal the gaps it opens by recourse to tactics it opposes."[38] Callicles is right, it seems: Socrates hides his will to power behind the philosophical façade of truth.

All this implies that *Gorgias* contains its own rhetorical dimension, that its dramatic structure (broadly understood) tellingly reveals those gaps the dialogue opens by pointing explicitly to the "tactics" used by Socrates but opposed by "Socratic" philosophy. *Gorgias* both posits an ideal speech situation as a model for politics and reveals the intricate (and perhaps ineluctable) workings of power involved in the collaborative search for incontestable political foundations. The dialogue thus forces us to reflect, not only on the difficulties (which are formidable enough) that attend communicatively achieved understanding, but also

37. This point is similar to Giovanni Ferrari's reading in his *Listening to the Cicadas: A Study of Plato's Phaedrus* (Cambridge: Cambridge University Press, 1987), p. 66, where he argues that "philosophy . . . has the peculiar quality of instantiating itself even as it examines its own conditions of possibility." Ferrari offers this assessment in the context of Socrates' mythmaking, but structurally our points are the same.

38. William Connolly, "Democracy and Territoriality" in *Millenium: Journal of International Studies* 20, 3 (Winter 1991): 468.

on what is suppressed, neglected, or ignored in the process of attaining such rationally motivated agreement. Socrates insists that truth is intersubjective and rests in an important sense on freely given conviction, and his efforts are in good part given over (unsuccessfully) to establishing the basis for such meaningful communication. Yet *Gorgias* makes an even stronger claim about the impurities of reason in its account of rhetoricity. The dialogue's irreducible rhetorical dimension—dramatized in the *agon* between Socrates and Callicles over who will control the terms of discourse—further alerts us to a lacuna in critical theory's account of uncoerced speech, a lacuna that makes the theory not especially attentive to the subtle workings of its own linguistic "power" to constitute what counts as "truth."

Although Habermas no longer posits an "ideal speech situation" anchored by transcendental moorings, his qualified claim that communicatively achieved agreement is immanent in the anthropologically deep-seated structure of everyday speech still implies an ideal or norm that excludes other forms of speech as valid because they fall below its threshold of rationality.[39] The very norm of rationality—in this case of the free, reasonable, and responsible agent to achieve a common situation definition based on valid criteria—constitutes a subtle mechanism of power that predefines what is reasonable and rational, and so systematically excludes what is other, alien, or different in both individual and society.[40] Those feelings, motives, experiences, and selves that remain inarticulate or indistinct within the schema of rationally sanctioned discourse subsequently become the objects of disciplinary control, a control that tends to vitiate difference, contribute to uniformity, and hasten the conformity and thoughtlessness that any critical theory rightly sus-

39. In *Zur Rekonstruktion des Historischen Materialismus* (Frankfurt: Suhrkamp, 1976), p. 241, Habermas finds "anthropologically deep-seated general structures" in all speech. These structures predate humanity as such: "Labor and language are older than man and society" (Habermas, *Communication and the Evolution of Society,* trans. Thomas McCarthy [Boston: Beacon Press, 1979], p. 137).

40. For an account of this norm as it functions in a discourse ethics, see the essays in Jürgen Habermas, *Moral Consciousness and Communicative Action,* trans. C. Lenhardt and S. Nicholsen (Cambridge, Mass.: MIT Press, 1990), esp. the title essay and "Discourse Ethics: Notes on a Program of Philosophical Justification." In those essays, Habermas sets out his principle of universalizability: a norm is universal if "the consequences and side effects that its general observance can be expected to have for the satisfaction of the particular interests of each person affected must be such that all affected can accept them freely" (pp. 65, 120). My account of *Gorgias* means to show that this principle of argumentation, which rests on the "free acceptance" of validity claims, presupposes—indeed conceals—a standard of and procedure for rational discourse that is itself *contestable.*

pects and fears.[41] If genealogy does not readily acknowledge that "to speak is [not always] to fight," then critical theory is not always sufficiently attuned to the effects of power that produce its own possibility nor to the effects of power it produces. *Gorgias* indicates how a critical theory that does not make itself the subject of its own genealogy of truth runs the risk, too, of concealing or denying those subtly coercive rhetorical strategies and tactics that attend even the best-intentioned attempts at unconstrained communication.

Does such a deconstructive reading of the dialogue, and of the ideal speech situation, abandon all potentially universal moral standards for the endlessly repeated play of domination? Does *Gorgias* in the end really confer victory upon Callicles and rhetoric, Nietzsche and Foucault, while Socrates and philosophy, Habermas and reason, are unavoidably implicated in the workings of power? Can the dialogue be reduced merely to a struggle over who will control the language in which citizens speak, as this interpretation suggests? Callicles himself provides one indication that reasoned agreement is possible and so partially validates Socrates' preference for the truth. That admission comes at the point in the exchange between Socrates and Callicles when the latter defends good pleasures against bad, the strong and noble against the weak and base (499c). Callicles has appealed to an *implicit* standard all along, a standard that Socrates exposes by suggesting a pleasure so ignoble that even Callicles squirms. This reliance on an implicit standard of judgment reveals a telling gap in Foucault's own account of genealogical critique that belies the possibility of the critic's own professed "happy positivism." Foucault steadfastly refuses (perhaps this is his blind spot) to inquire into the motivations that guide his own critical activity. If he did, would he not have to admit, with Callicles, that some regimes of power are not just different, but better than others?[42] And is an unreflective genealogy that fails to investigate its presuppositions not in danger of becoming the new norm, standard, or center, which would then require its own genealogical critique? *Gorgias* dramatizes—and

41. This paragraph borrows from the discussion of Habermas in my essay "Between Modernity and Postmodernity," *Political Theory* 22, 1 (Feb. 1994): 87.

42. Nancy Fraser, among others, has asked this question about implicit normative standards. See her "Foucault on Modern Power: Empirical Insights and Normative Confusions," *Praxis International* 1, 3 (Oct. 1981): 272–87. I agree in general with her point, but in polarizing the contradictions in the relationship between power and normativity, rather than thinking them in tension, as Socrates does in *Gorgias,* she, like Habermas, tells only half the story. See also Habermas, *Philosophical Discourse of Modernity,* ch. 10, "Some Questions Concerning the Theory of Power: Foucault Again."

the historical triumph of Socratic—Platonic philosophy over sophistic rhetoric confirms—the susceptibility of critical and even revolutionary movements to travel from the margins toward the center, from the outside to the inside, so that the radicalism of today becomes the party of order tomorrow. *Gorgias* thus contains a profound irony, all but lost on the canonists, rationalists, and other self-proclaimed enemies of deconstructive play: in an effort to disturb its own (and all?) drive toward closure, the dialogue portrays a Socrates more attuned to the subtle workings of rhetoric and power than his formidable adversary Callicles, a philosophy that acknowledges its own implicit reliance on politics, even as it tries to transcend that reliance, and a philosopher who resists canonization by the hagiographers of truth, even as Plato places him at the head of the Athenian political hierarchy.

Gorgias pushes at the limits of both the ideal speech situation and the obstacles that inhibit its attainment, at the search for truth and the realities of power, at the practices of dialectic and rhetoric, philosophy and politics. This perspective on *Gorgias* alerts us to the insufficiencies in the accounts of truth's relation to power given us by Habermas and Foucault. If critical theory ultimately succumbs to a blind spot in its attempt to disentangle power from knowledge (as I think *Gorgias* reveals), then genealogical criticism suffers from a similar debility in its refusal to acknowledge that its own deconstructive energy feeds upon the existence of ideals that make intelligible the real, upon norms to define what is deviant, upon a center against which to mobilize the margins. If critical theory too readily posits its own version of reason as an incontestable final marker, genealogical critique too readily dismisses those traditional signposts (truth and reason included) that help us negotiate the difficult terrain of a postmodern geography virtually without landmarks. Finally, if critical theory ultimately fails to make itself the subject of its own critical inquiry, then genealogical play, while it certainly deconstructs final markers, similarly fails to excavate its own origins and thereby tends to reinstate itself as another marker of finality. *Gorgias* neither calls for the "dissolution of final markers"[43] *tout court* nor posits a teleological truth that will secure the horizons of our identities, practices, and institutions once and for all. Rather, the dialogue maintains in productive tension two contradictory, but no less necessary, impulses: it both projects philosophical dialogue as a foun-

43. Claude Lefort, *Democracy and Political Theory,* trans. David Marcy, (Minneapolis: University of Minnesota Pess, 1988).

dation for politics and contests that projection through the agonistic struggle between Callicles and Socrates—a struggle that leads not to annihilation but to the continuous activity of contests. *Gorgias* thus cultivates an agonistic ethos that is both philosophical *and* political, dialectical *and* rhetorical, aware of the acute desire for philosophical foundations beyond political contest *and* of the need to disturb such foundations. The dialogue's great achievement is to keep these contradictions—which are our contradictions as well—alive and so prohibit us from privileging either side of the contest and slipping into a forgetfulness about the political character of truth, a politics dramatized by *Gorgias* itself.

A retrospective glance back over *Gorgias* shows it to be concerned with foundations, with the need to establish a solid philosophical ground for Athenian politics. On close inspection, however, that philosophical foundation appears less than stable, built on shifting rather than permanent soil, a fractured mass traversed by fissures and cracks, shot through with paradox and contradiction. As we have seen, the dialogue hints at various solutions to finding (or founding) a stable basis for politics beyond question, opposition, or rhetorical manipulation, yet it returns us again and again to that essentially contested terrain. The dialogue searches, now hopefully, now resignedly, for a ground beyond politics—beyond power—in the dialectical philosophy of Socrates, only to reveal philosophy's founding moment as—political. *Gorgias* cannot, or does not, wholly disentangle truth from power, but rather implicates each in the construction of the other. One way to characterize this inability, or refusal, to separate philosophy from politics, truth from power, and anchor the latter in the former, is as a "failure." But we have also seen that *failure* is perhaps too strong a word, not only because the contest ends inconclusively and so keeps the *agon* alive, but also because, as one might imagine, *Gorgias* is nothing like Plato's final word on the subject. The intractable problems of politics and the genuine yearning to place those problems and their solutions beyond contestability persist in Plato's theoretical imagination well beyond the writing of *Gorgias*. Plato continues that effort in what is perhaps the founding work of Western political philosophy: the *Republic*. It is to that formidable and foundational dialogue that *Gorgias* points, and to which I now turn my attention.

4

Plato's *Republic*

(Con)founding the Theoretical Imagination

Nothing in man—not even his body—is sufficiently stable to serve as the basis for self-recognition or for understanding other men.

—Michel Foucault, "Nietzsche, Genealogy, History," in *The Foucault Reader*

The philosophers have only *interpreted* the world, in various ways; the point, however, is to *change* it.

—Karl Marx, "Theses on Feuerbach," in *The Marx-Engels Reader*

The whole is the false.

—Theodor Adorno, *Minima Moralia*

Plato's *Republic* is a founding text.[1] When Alfred North Whitehead remarked, in a famous and often-quoted phrase, that the European philosophical tradition "consists of a series of footnotes to Plato," he might justly have added that the European tradition of *political* philosophy consists of a series of footnotes to the *Republic*.[2] Certainly no work of political thought has more vigorously captured the utopian political imagination. From Cicero to the Neoplatonists, from Thomas More to Thomas Hobbes, and from the socialist utopias of the nineteenth cen-

1. I owe the title of this chapter and much else of what is good in it to Mark Reinhardt. See his *The Art of Being Free* (Ithaca, N.Y.: Cornell University Press, 1997), esp. ch. 3. I have used the Greek text of John Burnet, vol. 4 of *Platonis Opera* (1902; Oxford: Clarendon Press, 1962). I have also relied on the commentary by R. C. Cross and A. D. Woozley, *Plato's* Republic: *A Philosophical Commentary* (New York: St. Martin's Press, 1964). Translations are from various sources and I note them where appropriate.

2. Alfred North Whitehead, *Process and Reality: An Essay in Cosmology*, ed. D. R. Griffin and D. W. Sherburne (New York: Free Press, 1978), p. 39.

tury to the science fiction utopias of the twentieth, the *Republic* has endured as a benchmark, a standard from which to begin thinking about the fundamental problems of politics. Of course, Plato's utopian dream has not gone uncriticized. Thinkers as diverse as Hannah Arendt and Karl Popper have denounced the *Republic* as a dystopian nightmare bordering on totalitarianism. For them, Plato certainly continues to instruct us, but his most salutary lessons are negative. They construe Plato's *Republic* less as an appealing paradigm than as an object lesson to be avoided.

Today such instruction by way of criticism continues, even as contemporary critics shift accents and alter inflections. Two examples should clarify this point. For those excluded from the European tradition, the *Republic* is indeed a founding text, but what it founds is a tradition of Western cultural hegemony. At a time when the currency of the classics has been devalued by a multicultural economy that daily disinvests in the "tradition," Plato's *Republic* says less and less to more and more people. In these diverse and divisive times, any expectations that the *Republic* might supply us with congenial answers to our most pressing political problems have been dispersed in a solvent of cultural, religious, and ethnic differences, differences that have increasingly come to define the contours of contemporary politics. For their part, modernists and postmodernists alike decry any return to Plato's founding vision as a desperate flight into an irrecoverable past, a retreat into coercive community that flirts with profoundly dangerous consequences. At a time when the sovereign, territorial nation-state has been rendered increasingly porous—and perhaps anachronistic—by the rapid globalization of permanently destabilizing forces, Plato's vision of a homogeneous, face-to-face, territorially organized, and hierarchically ordered moral community cannot appear as anything but dangerously nostalgic.[3] To think that the ancient concepts can be wrenched from their institutional context and put successfully to work amid the complex realities of the postmodern nation-state is an exercise as futile as it is foolish.

Despite these most recent criticisms, the *Republic* persists. Such per-

3. Among such recent critics of Platonic political philosophy, and of ancient Athens in general, see Robert A. Dahl, *Democracy and Its Critics* (New Haven, Conn.: Yale University Press, 1989), esp. introduction and ch. 1; Stephen T. Holmes, "Aristippus in and out of Athens," *APSR* 73, 1 (Mar. 1979): 113–27; Michael Ignatieff, *The Needs of Strangers* (New York: Viking Press, 1984), esp. conclusion; see also the essays collected in *The Phantom Public Sphere,* ed. Bruce Robbins (Minneapolis: University of Minnesota Press, 1993).

sistence might be explained by Plato's residual status as a "classic," by the sheer weight and inertia of a yet-to-be-overcome tradition. Or perhaps Plato continues to haunt our political and theoretical imaginations because the *Republic* addresses our profoundly felt and permanently unrelieved yearnings for community, solidarity, and authority. The resurgent wave of communitarian nostalgia that has emerged as a prominent feature of our shifting postmodern landscape articulates just such a yearning for the warmth of home, the solidity of place, and the security of a fixed cultural identity. Certainly, all these longings find seductive expression in Plato. Whether as utopian dream to emulate or dystopian nightmare to denounce, whether we think with it or against it—the *Republic* remains a founding text. To acknowledge it as such (and Plato as a founder), is not, however, to give the book the first (or last) word in the matter, nor yet to succumb to its nostalgic seductiveness. At a time when those few foundations that have not (yet) cracked are suspect, such acknowledgement need not, and must not, place Plato's work beyond criticism. Yet to ignore its importance or to dismiss its considerable power to nourish thought is to do so at one's peril. The *Republic* may not be a text to revere or privilege, but it is certainly one to respect. Nietzsche's remark that a friend ought to be a worthy enemy applies no less to Plato. *That* kind of respect, the respect for one's opponent, informs my own relationship to Plato's *Republic* and guides my appropriation of it.[4] But my aim in offering one more reading of the *Republic* is neither to rediscover "what Plato said"[5] nor to recover the context in which he was able to say it in the first place. I am not interested in rescuing a liberal Plato, reviving a communitarian Plato, or denouncing a totalitarian one. I want to turn Plato to other, more radical, purposes by using him (often against himself) to intervene in the current struggle over the nature, status, and politics of theory.

As we have seen, that struggle presents us with a choice between a critical theory and a genealogical critique of society, between a theory confident of its ability to distinguish between legitimate and illegitimate regimes, just and unjust exercises of power, and an anti-theory suspicious of all such attempts to ground politics in a theoretical discourse that reconciles contradictions in an all-encompassing totality. Where the critical theory of Habermas requires an enlightenment meta-

4. To honor one's enemies is the lordly way, as Nietzsche puts it in the first essay of *The Genealogy of Morals* (1887; New York: Modern Library, 1918), 1.10.

5. Paul Shorey, *What Plato Said* (Chicago: University of Chicago Press, 1933).

narrative of emancipation, in which all particular positions, practices, and identities might be harmonized through a set of universally valid rules of argumentation, Foucault's antitheoretical genealogies expose the foundationalist pretensions of such globalizing discourses as so many regulative ideals that conceal their normalizing and disciplinary effects for the self and order. This controversy leaves us, then, with the choice between validating action and judgment in the give-and-take of moral communication and debate or participating in a game of global consensus that regularizes the rules of rationality and thereby also normalizes the differences among acting and speaking subjects themselves.

Polarized by the opposition between a critical theory that would think and judge the whole and a genealogical wariness of the tyranny of all globalizing discourses, Habermas and Foucault construct mutually antagonistic accounts of the theoretical impulse to stabilize all politics in a ground beyond contest. Where critical theory seeks ultimately to construct a systematic discourse that harmonizes all its components into a conceptual order that goes into reality without remainder, genealogical critique mobilizes those (inevitable) remainders—the selves and subjects that do not fit neatly into the order—against the accretions and sedimentations of an orderly theoretical discourse (and social system) that creates them as its founding repudiation. If critical theory in the end projects stable arrangements, genealogy disrupts those settlements, exposing the lie in all systems founded on such stability and order. But might it be possible to cultivate a theoretical imagination that both construes and denies such ultimate grounds, a discourse that sustains the (useful) fiction of a theoretical (and political) totality and at the same time disturbs that totality by means of a subversive (textual and political) practice? In other words, can we articulate a postfoundationalist sensibility that introduces heterogeneity, difference, and contest into our theoretical visions without at the same time relinquishing the need for (temporary) resting spots such textual and political agonistics are intended to disrupt?

Plato's *Republic* suggests a way to elaborate just such an agonistics, an appropriate sensibility for the work of (con)founding the theoretical imagination now required. Put in simple, although not altogether misleading, terms, the *Republic* attempts to sink the foundations of politics—of rule, authority, and order—in an unshakeable truth beyond contest or question. Plato offers the strongest possible case for such a grounding, and although that project ultimately fails (and I think it fails on its own terms), it nonetheless offers valuable lessons about the tragic shortcomings of the Platonic theoretical imagination. To this end, the present chapter explores those foundings and foundations that the *Republic* constitutes (as foundationalist philosophy) and that constitute the *Republic* (as canonical text) for their *con*founding possibilities. By turning the text against itself, by searching out the gaps, the cracks, and the irregularities that traverse its landscape, this chapter appropriates the *Republic* as a book that not only founds, but also disturbs, the Western theoretical imagination. My hope is that Plato will provide salutary lessons in the seductions and dangers of global political theory, and I approach him as an important teacher on these matters. I also, indirectly, challenge those readings that interpret the *Republic* too comfortably—as either utopian dream or dystopian nightmare—readings that tame its disturbingly radical vision through dismissal or assimilation. My intention is to pursue Plato's ability to provoke thought about the possibilities of theory and politics by appropriating a *Republic* that is theoretically and politically provoking. Perhaps the *Republic* can disrupt our familiar categories because it is such an unsettling and disruptive book itself, a book that challenges contemporary theoretical and political principles no less than it challenged the principles of the Athenian democracy of its day. Such a *Republic* would contribute to the work of (con)founding the theoretical imagination, a perpetual task that sustains the fiction of all theoretical foundations even as it disrupts the tyranny of theory's globalizing discourse and resists its attempt to constitute reality without remainder.

The *Republic* is a foundational text in more ways than one. For not only does it found (for good or for ill) a tradition of political philosophy, but its philosophy is itself in an important sense foundationalist. If in *Gorgias,* Socrates mentions the form of the Good once and merely in passing, the *Republic* places it at the center of its ontology and makes it the ground of its politics.[6] And while the earlier dialogue abounds

6. The presence or absence of a theory of the forms is sometimes used to distinguish, along with other criteria, between early, middle, and late dialogues. The *Gorgias* is usually considered a "late" early or aporetic dialogue, while the *Republic* is generally agreed to be from Plato's middle period. For this generally accepted schema, see W. K. C. Guthrie, *Plato: The Man and His Dialogues,* vol. 4 of *A History of Greek Philosophy* (Cambridge: Cambridge University Press, 1975), p. 236. On dating *Gorgias* as a very early, or presystematic dialogue, one written before the so-called "Socratic" dialogues *Laches, Charmides, Lysis,* and *Euthyphro,* see Charles Kahn, "Did Plato Write Socratic Dialogues?" in *Essays on the Philosophy of Socrates,* ed. Hugh H. Benson (New York: Oxford University Press, 1992), pp. 35–52. I am less concerned with the dating of the dialogues, which is inexact in any case and cannot determine an interpretation, than with the contending and contradictory impulses that inhabit the dialogue.

with craft analogies—Socrates compares the art of politics to other crafts, such as medicine—no account of the goal of the political craft is elaborated in such detail as in the *Republic.* Indeed, when Socrates says in *Gorgias* that the purpose of the political art is to make the citizens better, he gives little systematic substance to what he means by that claim. Justice—or the just life—remains largely undefined. Even though *Gorgias* raises justice and injustice as central issues, it is left to the later dialogue to supply both the ground for, and the details of, the argument that a life of justice is preferable to its opposite.[7] The *Republic* specifies with excruciating precision exactly how justice is to be produced in citizens, and that precision flows directly from the philosopher's privileged access to the truth and subsequent knowledge of the Good. In the *Republic,* the philosopher and the *technikos* are one and the same. To employ Plato's own metaphor, the philosopher-king cares for the body politic as the physician cares for the individual bodies of the citizens. Of course, Plato never suggests that the medicine dispensed by either civic or somatic physician will be easy to swallow.

The *Republic* thus elaborates solutions only hinted at in the earlier dialogue. As I presented it in chapter 3, *Gorgias* reveals the problems of politics to be a source of frustration (to the philosophically minded), as well as of constant energy and change, and repeatedly circles around the proffered solutions, only to reject (or at least only partially, with qualifications, to accept) them. *Gorgias* presents the ground of politics—including the possibility of its philosophical grounding—as always already contested. Even Socratic dialectic—the proposed model for the true political art—was implicated in the virtuosity and agonism of the rhetorical contest for power. The *Republic,* however, anchors politics firmly in the Real, positing an unchallengeable epistemology, which provides the stable basis for the order of both soul and society. In *Gorgias* Socrates somewhat ironically transfers political authority to himself (and to his dialectic) as the only Athenian practicing the true art of politics. The *Republic* invests that authority in a class of specially trained philosophers possessed of the expert knowledge necessary to achieve the true vision of the Good. Even as it seeks to root politics in the truthful soil of Socratic dialectic, the *Gorgias* nevertheless acknowledges that philosophical ground as (in most places and at most times)

7. Cf. Guthrie, *Plato,* 298, who states that the *Republic* "is Plato's full and final answer to the question in the *Gorgias,* 'how to live' " (*pōs biōteon, Gorgias* 492d). The phrase at 500c, *hontina chrē tropon zēn,* occurs in identical form at *Republic* 352d.

unstable and shifting, subject to—and the subject of—struggle. The *Republic* would seem to reject this earlier Socratic ambivalence in its attempt to establish a secure foundation for a political order beyond politics.

If the Platonic search for stable foundations and pure origins bridles at Socratic ambivalence, it directly repudiates Sophocles' insight into the perplexing ironies of a mortal wisdom founded on ignorance. *Oedipus Tyrannos* dramatizes the difficulties involved in discovering pure origins and creating stable foundations through the sheer power of intellect alone. This impulse—to search out a single, unifying form that will unite a world experienced as irreducibly heterogeneous—although largely rejected by tragedy, is present as a possibility both in Oedipus's own search and in the structured (dis)order of the drama itself. With Sophocles' play, Plato's *Republic* contemplates the possibility (even necessity) of controlling the world, as well as the men and women in it, through the unifying power of human intelligence. Both Sophocles' king and Plato's philosopher search for a final, determinate form that will systematically encompass the whole of experience and render it intelligible to ambitious rational beings. Although of very different temperament and training than the impatient and unaided Oedipus (they have to be forced to rule), the philosophers of the *Republic*'s ideal city ultimately share his aim and quest. The Platonic philosopher's ability to think abstractly and ascend from the multiplicity and indeterminacy of lived life to the singularity of an intellectual "form" that comprehends unity beneath the diversity of the "seen particular" recalls Oedipus's own unifying mentality. Indeed, Oedipus's solution to the riddle of the Sphinx anticipates the philosopher's ability to discern the singular Form among its many embodiments, to uncover the permanent and unchanging amid the frustrating flux of worldly contingency.

The *Republic* also expresses a longing for the comfortable certainty of a stable identity that so tragically eluded Oedipus. In the ideal city, justice is doing what is one's own and knowing with certainty one's status and role in the city. Although that requires a lie for its legitimation, even the philosophers come to accept the myth of autochthony as an enabling fiction necessary for the establishment and maintenance of a stable and harmonious order. The *Republic* constructs its ideal city to provide a context in which certain knowledge is possible: thus does the Platonic theoretical imagination make the world safe for philosophy and philosophers. These philosophers are sure of what they know and certain that it is most worth knowing. Where Oedipus in the end came to understand that profound ignorance nourishes true wisdom, and where the play as a whole teaches that it is the best and most noble of us who are capable of the greatest tyranny, the *Republic* attempts a seemingly untainted vision of intellectual certainty and political stability that succeeds where Oedipus failed. Where Oedipus loses power the moment he gains knowledge, the *Republic* unites both in a paradigmatic embodiment that stands as a monument to the controlling power of human reason.

A text with a foundationalist epistemology in the sense already mentioned, the *Republic* also dramatizes a political "founding" as the central act of its performance. It thus anticipates my discussion of the themes of the *Oresteia* and joins that play as a form of cosmogony:[8] both Plato and Aeschylus are involved in nothing less than acts of world creation. In both dialogue and drama, worlds are defined through the ultimately creative power of the word. To this end, the *Republic* examines speech at the limits of coherence and, with the *Oresteia,* takes us to the edge of linguistic (and political) chaos. In Aeschylus's trilogy, we see language in the throes of breakdown: mishearing, misspeaking, and misanswering plague all attempts at communication on stage. Yet the play also brings us back from that edge in a number of ways. The fragmented world within the play regains its coherence when Athena ends the interminable cycle of blood vengeance that has plagued the house of Atreus. With the foundation of the law court that establishes *dikē* as legal justice, cosmic and civic order is restored. Orestes wins acquittal (although the jury's vote is tied), and Athens and Argos are allied. Moreover, Athena successfully persuades the Furies, now become Eumenides (Kindly Ones), to accept their new position as tutelary deities of the homicide court and so of the city's new democratic order. Moreover, the meaning of the words lost in the exchange between the protagonists onstage is regained by the audience watching the play. However much Clytemnestra succeeds in deceiving Agamemnon through manipulative persuasion, the spectators (or readers) see through the queen's deceitful game. Aeschylus here probes the limits of language and communication: the violent action of the drama pushes the world order to the limits of its intelligibility, but that order is restored for both characters and spectators alike when Athena's newly established civic

8. On Aeschylus's use of the cosmogonic myth, see Froma I. Zeitlin, "The Dynamics of Misogyny: Myth and Mythmaking in the *Oresteia,*" *Arethusa* 11, 1–2 (Spring/Fall 1978): esp. 162–63.

discourse merges with the democratic discourse of the city watching the performance.

Plato addresses a similar problem: the *Republic* portrays a world dislocated by misunderstanding, duplicity, and domination no less desperate than that dramatized in the *Oresteia*. Meanings multiply precipitously in the *Oresteia* as characters all appropriate the language of justice for their own purposes and interests; similarly, book 1 of the *Republic* portrays Athenian citizens as so factionalized that every interlocutor offers his own private definition of justice. Thrasymachus articulates the limit case when he defines and defends power as the only arbiter of meaning. Part of the dialogue's task will be to found a just city in speech and so mediate between these competing and conflicting claims, reconciling them while respecting their integrity as far as possible. So, while Socrates offers "tending to one's own affairs" as a definition of justice in book 4, Cephalus's "paying back what one owes" and Polemarchus's "helping friends and harming enemies" constitute suitable definitions of justice for the classes of moneymakers and warriors. Where Socrates' act of founding and attempt to define the meaning of justice once and for all recall the trial scene of the *Eumenides* and Athena's own contest with the Furies to establish *dikē* as legal justice, both dialogue and trilogy share a broader concern with the linguistic conditions necessary for a successful speech community and viable political life. The result of that concern is the foundation of a second community or "city," the community of interlocutors within the dialogue led by Socrates. Book 1 is thus occupied with the obstacles that confront the establishment of a secure civic discourse and so a settled political order. The commonality of speech that such stability requires, however, threatens to become an excessive unity, in which all citizens say either "mine" or "not mine" simultaneously and agree all too complacently with every argument Socrates offers. While excessive unity may not be the appropriate response to excessive diversity, the *Republic* does dramatize the difficulties involved in establishing a common linguistic ground among the interlocutors and articulates the necessity of gaining just enough agreement to make their disagreements intelligible.

The *Republic* also shares another fundamental concern with Greek tragedy: the constitution of a community outside the dialogue or play. A tragedy like the *Oresteia* safely dramatized the breakdown of linguistic and political coherence because it assumed the context of a relatively cohesive and specific audience. But where Aeschylean drama explores the limits of order and chaos within the structured confines of ritual performance and before an already-constituted citizen-audience, Platonic dialogue lacks an institutional form and (beyond the members of the Academy) addresses an unspecified audience of readers. The *Republic* aims to constitute a community, not of citizen-spectators, but of citizen-theorists, or philosophers, and it does so in at least two ways. The dialogue offers its own model of what a political and philosophical community looks like, or rather it offers its readers a choice between two very distinct forms of community: one modeled on the dialogic community of interlocutors, the other on the theoretically imagined ideal city. In either case, the foundation of a rightly ordered community becomes an explicit theme and a controlling aim of the dialogue, both the subject and the intent of Platonic political theory. Since that foundation itself relies on a foundationalist ontology and epistemology, it is to the *Republic* as an example of "founding" theory that I now turn.

I

Countless and diverse readings of Plato's *Republic* abound, no doubt a testimony to the complexity and multivocity of the work, to its seemingly inexhaustible power to generate meaning.[9] What else could account for so many different appropriations of the same book? As an ideal utopia, as a critique of idealism, as a blueprint for totalitarian politics, as a comedy and as a tragedy: there are almost as many *Republics*

9. The literature on the *Republic* is vast. Particularly useful are Paul Friedländer, *Plato,* trans. Hans Meyerhoff (New York: Pantheon Books, 1958); Werner Jaeger, *Paideia: The Ideals of Greek Culture,* vol. 2 (New York: Oxford University Press, 1943); A. E. Taylor, *Plato: The Man and His Work,* 3d ed. (1926; New York: Dial Press, 1929); Guthrie, *Plato;* F. M. Cornford, *The Unwritten Philosophy and Other Essays* (Cambridge: Cambridge University Press, 1950) T. H. Irwin, *Plato's Moral Theory* (Oxford: Oxford University Press, 1977); Martha Nussbaum, *The Fragility of Goodness: Luck and Ethics in Greek Literature and Philosophy* (Cambridge: Cambridge University Press, 1986); Hans-Georg Gadamer, *Dialogue and Dialectic: Eight Hermeneutical Studies on Plato,* trans. Christopher P. Smith (New Haven, Conn.: Yale University Press, 1980); and Charles Griswold, ed., *Platonic Writings / Platonic Readings* (New York: Routledge, 1988). Among political theorists, see Sheldon Wolin, *Politics and Vision: Continuity and Innovation in Western Political Thought* (Boston: Little, Brown, 1961); Hannah Arendt, *The Human Condition* (Chicago: University of Chicago Press, 1958), and *Between Past and Future* (New York: Viking Press, 1958); Leo Strauss, *The City and Man* (New York: Rand McNally, 1964), J. Peter Euben, *The Tragedy of Political Theory: The Road Not Taken* (Princeton, N.J.: Princeton University Press, 1990); Mary P. Nichols, "The *Republic*'s Two Alternatives: Philosopher-Kings and Socrates," *Political Theory* 12, 2 (May 1984): 252–74; and Alexander Sesonske, *Plato's Republic: Interpretation and Criticism* (Belmont, Calif.: Wadsworth Publishing, 1966).

as there are interpreters. I want to explore the *Republic,* at least initially, for what it has to say about theory as a founding activity, where such theory also implies a "foundationalist" epistemology. This means reading Plato as both a "heroic" and a "critical" theorist: heroic because he delineates the epic proportions of great political theory in a way that usefully describes the work of founding in the *Republic;* critical because the means of explanation and the standards of evaluation Plato employs share affinities with the tasks of a critical social theory outlined by Habermas and introduced in chapter 1.

The dialogue is pervaded by the appropriately theoretical images and metaphors of sight, light, and vision. Socrates begins his famous narrative by recounting a visit to the Piraeus to see (*theasthai*) an inaugural festival of the Thracian goddess Bendis. This journey to see the sights and Socrates' assessment of the spectacle invoke and transform an earlier meaning of the word *theory* and the vocation of the *theōros.* Originally, a *theōros* was an official envoy sent by the city to a strange or unfamiliar land to observe, and then report upon, the sacred events he had witnessed. But Socrates' journey down into the Piraeus, Athens's port and stronghold of radical democracy, does not conclude with his appraisal of the procession, nor does Socrates waste much time on the festival itself. He quickly moves on to describe the more important theoretical vision the *Republic* itself proposes. That initial journey, then, serves as both pretext and context for the prisoner's journey up and out of the cave into the light of day, a journey that culminates in the upward ascent of the philosopher to the vision of the Good and ends with the mythical descent of Er into the underworld at the dialogue's conclusion.

Of course, vision or sight as a controlling metaphor is nothing new in Greek literature. We have already encountered it in Sophoclean tragedy and know that the Greeks registered sight as a commonplace trope for knowledge in their literary and philosophical lexicons.[10] We have

10. The etymological beginnings of *theory* and *theorist* are to be found in the post-Homeric vocabulary. The verb *theōrein,* originally derived from the noun signifying a spectator (*theōros*), came specifically to mean "to look on, contemplate or observe." It differs significantly from the Homeric panoply of "sight" verbs because, as Bruno Snell has remarked, "it does not reflect an attitude or an emotion linked with sight, nor the viewing of a particular object: instead it represents an intensification of the normal and essential function of the eyes" (Snell, *The Discovery of the Mind: The Greek Origins of European Thought,* trans. T. G. Rosenmeyer [Cambridge: Cambridge University Press, 1953], p. 4). *Theōrein* thus emphasizes the object seen and the intensity of the viewer's

also seen the themes the *Republic* shares with Sophocles' *Oedipus Tyrannos:* the will to knowledge, a certain impatience with the constraints of tradition, the insistence on exposing underlying patterns of unity beneath the phenomenal world. Yet the *Republic* articulates a vision and transforms the tropics of "visual" discourse in a way that Oedipus only dreamed of and Sophocles perhaps feared to imagine. Where Oedipus seeks merely to master his own destiny (and perhaps the destiny of Thebes), Plato's *Republic* would reimagine an entire world in order to master the destiny of mankind. Neither oracles nor curses, nor seemingly much else, limit the capaciousness of the *Republic*'s theoretical imagination: its vision is breathtaking, not only for its vast scope, but for its utter innovation, its radical break with all previous standards of thought and judgment. In a heroic act of thought, Plato sought to re-

---

experiences rather than the "palpable aspects, the external qualifications, of the act of seeing" (ibid.). The Homeric attributes of manner do not cling to this verb, which in the classical period meant "to contemplate." Theory thus comes to signify mental activity, not the function of the eyes, although Plato uses the expression "to see with the mind's eye" (*Republic* 582c) to denote mental vision. The turn away from the Homeric conception of vision is both a turn outward, toward the object of perception, and a turn inward, toward the intensity or depth of the experience.

A *theōros* was originally a spectator of a sacred event or a public performance, an emissary sent to the oracle at Delphi, a witness of religious rituals, rites of purification, or the sacred games at Olympia. The *theōros* also traveled to other poleis in an official capacity to observe an event and then returned home to report on what he had witnessed. Theory became an activity that entailed watching and observing a spectacle related to things divine and recounting the essentials of the witnessed event clearly, accurately, and with discernment. This means that only those citizens were sent who could "see" with discrimination. Since theory required embarking upon a journey to foreign lands, the theorist acquired the connotation of a traveler, someone who had experienced the world beyond the parochial confines of the polis and even beyond the Hellenic civilizational area. Theory subsequently entailed "seeing with an eye toward learning about different lands and institutions, alien practices and experiences, distilling and comparing the pattern of things seen while engaged in travel" (J. Peter Euben, "Creatures of a Day: Thought and Action in Thucydides," in *Political Theory and Praxis: New Perspectives,* ed. Terence Ball [Minneapolis: University of Minnesota Press, 1977], p. 34). The etymology of *theater* also bears out a relation to philosophy and theory. The theater (*theatrōn*) is a place for seeing or beholding a spectacle, especially dramatic representations; it is also a place of assembly and a collective noun for *hoi theatai,* the spectators. The Greek *theatrōn* originates in the feminine noun *thea,* which signifies "see, sight, gaze, look upon, behold admire and contemplate." From it, Greek derived a field of words having to do with seeing, sight, and spectacle, e.g, *to theama* (sight, spectacle, play), *hē theama* (spectacle), and the verb *theaomai* meaning "to gaze at or behold, to see clearly and with a sense of wonder or admiration." *Theaomai* not only designates physical vision (*Rep.* 327a), but mental activity as well, especially in the sense of contemplation or a "vision of the mind" (*Rep.* 582c, *Phd.* 84b). On the etymology of *thauma, thea,* and *theōros,* see Pierre Chantraine, *Dictionnaire etymologique de la langue grecque* (Paris: Editions Klincksieck, 1970), pp. 424–25, 433, as well as Hjalmar Frisk, *Griechisches Etymologisches Wörterbuch* (Heidelberg: C. Winter, 1960), p. 669.

construct his entire political world by grasping present structures and relationships in order to represent them in a new and unfamiliar way.[11] But Plato's efforts involve more than a mere reassembling of the familiar world in a novel way. For the *Republic* does not merely—and fancifully—redescribe that world to us. Rather, it recreates the world as we know it, for the Platonic act of thought is in an important sense an act of creation, and the political theorist is also something of a political craftsman. In a crucial way, Platonic theory does not so much rearrange the old world as invents a new one. Such is the heroic task that the Platonic theoretical imagination sets for itself.

Plato exercises the creative powers of the theoretical vocation through the device of a foundation play. After the aporetic discussion of justice in book 1, Socrates must make a new start. He proposes the famous analogy between the city and the soul as a way to capture the truth about justice. Plato has Socrates cast himself and the company as founders (*oikistēs*) who will watch justice and injustice come into being with the growth of their city. The founding drama assumes the form of a political "cosmogony" as the founders create and order their successive cities and rank them in an ascending hierarchy, from Glaucon's primitive "city for pigs" to the callipolis of book 7.

That final city most perfectly embodies the nature of justice. Comprised of three classes, which parallel the three corresponding parts of the soul and character types, the best city is ordered on the principle of "one person, one task." This Platonic division of labor reconciles conflicting interests and conflicting classes: everyone and every class does what he, she, or it is best suited by nature to do. Justice becomes doing one's own rather than paying one's debts (Cephalus), helping friends and harming enemies (Polemarchus), or wanting or having more than one ought (Thrasymachus).[12] All three classes and parts of the soul are thus ordered by justice in conjunction with temperance. In this ordering, the good of each individual and of each class is identical with the

11. I draw this account from Sheldon Wolin, "Political Theory as a Vocation," *APSR* 63, 4 (Dec. 1969): 1078.

12. Though I should add parenthetically that both Cephalus's and Polemarchus's definitions of justice are encompassed in the class structure of the ideal city: the members of the moneymaking class pay their debts; the members of the warrior class are like well-bred dogs, kind to their friends, fierce to their enemies. Thrasymachus and the justice of tyrants remains unexplained in this schema. Perhaps that is owing to the difficulty of successfully uniting philosophical knowledge and political power. In terms of the drama of the dialogue, can Thrasymachus's desire for power be tamed and his soul turned toward the love of wisdom? Or, conversely, is the philosopher's will to knowledge really a will to power, and Socrates' desire not for wisdom but for rule and control?

good of the whole. Class relations, far from being antagonistic, are complementary and reciprocal. Under the principle of specialization, each class (and individual) contributes its proper share necessary for the successful functioning of the city. The result is a unified social and political order in which natural ability and social status are reconciled and harmonized. Certainly, there is hierarchy in this integrated order: some classes, some jobs, and some souls are indeed understood as more virtuous or valuable than others. Yet all are equally necessary to the just functioning of the city, no class or individual is demeaned, and in fact difference is cultivated and allowed to flourish. Moreover, that difference does not turn invidious, and the hierarchy that results in no way entails domination. In addition, advantages and rewards seem rather evenly distributed: for example, members of the ruling classes have access to political power, but they own no private property and hold all in common, while members of the working class may accumulate fortunes but are excluded from the workings of power. The rightly ordered city, the analogue of the rightly ordered soul, is thus in harmony with itself, and the *Republic* shows us how (and why) this order comes into being.

This rather schematic, truncated, and celebratory sketch of the just city's political architecture and founding vision indicates that the *Republic* is no mere intellectual exercise, but rather the willed creation of an entirely new political order. This raises a crucial question: why does the discussion of justice assume the form of a founding and Socrates the identity of a founder or lawgiver (*oikistēs*)? One ready response has to do with the analogous structures of city and soul and the comparative ease of discerning justice in the former as opposed to the latter. On this account, the *Republic* concerns only the justice of the individual, a reading that finds support in the initial motivation of the search, as well as in the more pessimistic pronouncements about the possibility of actually founding the just regime later in the dialogue (592b). But that answer is too easy, for it fails to recognize the claim that "justice can belong to a single man and to a whole city" (368e), and so account for the centrality of the foundation play. A better explanation, to my mind, rests with the inseparability, for the Greeks, of ethics and politics. The distinction we moderns might make between the two would have made no sense to Plato, for whom "the goodness of individuals was closely related to the goodness of the state in which they lived; the good life demanded the good society in which to express itself and the good society promoted and made possible the good life."[13] Yet even this Platonic expression of the "organic state" fails to confront the contending forces within the dialogue that drive Plato to confound the visual vocation of the theorist with the plastic craft of the political founder. A final reason for insisting that justice in the individual and justice in the city are coterminous has to do with Plato's obvious concern for the quality of public life and his radical critique of Athenian democracy. If we are to believe the "Seventh Letter," Plato never lost that concern for the politics of his native city, and ironically it was precisely that care for public things that turned him toward theory and makes his philosophy *political* philosophy.

As this latter remark implies, the *Republic* comprises a "structure of intentions" or set of controlling political purposes. The motivation behind its theoretical reformulation is a deep concern for public life. Although it may be a cliché that political theory emerges as a response to a crisis in politics, it is certainly true that without this concern, the *Republic* would not be *political* theory. If Plato indeed wrote the *Republic* in response to an experienced crisis in Athenian democracy, what was the nature of that crisis and why did it require a response of such extraordinary scope and so radical a nature? To be sure, Plato was not responding to this or that discrete failure in Athenian law, policy, or institutional arrangements, a failure that could be solved by other, less radical means. Rather, the *Republic* bears witness to a state of systematic distortion in the entire Athenian polity, a disorder in the fundamental structures, meanings, and purposes of the city, which, in Plato's estimation, calls forth from the theorist a distinctly theoretical response. As Plato diagnoses it, systematic disorder requires an equally systematic reordering of a polity's most fundamental principles.

Plato's politics, then, are foundational, because his theoretical vision is foundationalist: nothing less than the complete reform of both soul and city, self and order, according to the dictates of an absolutist epistemology will suffice (that Plato has Socrates give up political reform in favor of the individual goodness of the philosopher at the end of book 9 in no way diminishes the Platonic will to order, but rather indicates the frailty and imperfection of the human world). The presentation of soul and city as analogues, then, and their subsequent reordering ac-

13. J. H. Jacques, *Plato's "Republic": A Beginner's Guide* (Derby, Eng.: Citadel Press; London: Tom Stacey, 1971), p. 51, cited in Guthrie, *Plato,* p. 444–45.

cording to the form of the Good, is more than an aesthetic device that confers a certain level of satisfying symmetry to the construction (although it is that too). Rather, that presentation and reordering are driven by currents that run deep within the book (and perhaps within Plato himself): the almost obsessive impulse to place the unruly, disorderly, and disturbing matters of politics beyond contest and contestability. For these reasons, the *Republic* necessarily works from the ground up.

The *Republic* that has emerged so far is a work of heroic and critical theory. It is heroic because of the immensity and impossibility of its task. It is critical because its means of explanation and its standards of evaluation cohere in a single concept: to explain the systematic disorder of a polity is, in Platonic terms, also to judge that order from a critical vantage point. Explanation and judgment are necessarily "total," and the Platonic theoretical critique is radical: Plato goes to the root of things. There is no piecemeal social engineering here, but rather the radical transformation of the foundations of the social and psychic totality. As an act of radical theory, the *Republic* reimagines that totality; as an act of radical politics, the *Republic* replaces it with the creation of its own theoretical labors. Plato does not merely offer a new vision or version of the world; he would transform the world itself and in that transformation "validate" his theory. Nowhere does Plato suggest that theory ought to yield the role of arbiter to the facts of the world: if the theory does not conform to the facts, then the conclusion we must draw (certainly the one Plato draws) is that the fault lies in our world, not in our theory. "Is our theory any the less true," asks Socrates, "if a state so organized should not actually be founded?" (472e). On this telling, Platonic theory is both critical and radical, and the acts of the Platonic theoretical imagination are acts of radical politics. Plato barely leaves implicit what Marx would later make explicit in his eleventh thesis on Feuerbach: "The philosophers have only *interpreted* the world in various ways; the point, however, is to *change* it."[14]

The political dimensions of the *Republic* are hardly exhausted by this deliberately anachronistic, although I think rather telling, mapping of Marx's revolutionary rhetoric onto Plato. There is another, considerably less obvious, way in which the *Republic* intends a politics. The *Re-*

14. *The Marx-Engels Reader,* ed. Robert C. Tucker, 2d ed. (New York: Norton, 1978), p. 145.

public described thus far has been a text with theoretical designs on the political world. But perhaps the *Republic* has other designs in other directions as well. Here, I wish to mention briefly what I shall later develop in more detail. I want to suggest that the *Republic* comprises a complex set of strategies with political designs on its *readers.* At the level of its rhetoric and through its textual practice, the *Republic* deploys various and subtle strategies of persuasion: through the choice of its images and metaphors and in the tone, texture, and shades of meaning it gives words, the dialogue aims to draw us in and on, to bring us up short, to start our thinking anew, or to convince us of an argument we do not really believe. A book of diverse moods, the dialogue is now hopeful, now resigned, both confident and doubtful, at once conciliatory and combative, first comic, then tragic. A book of many rhetorical devices, the *Republic* deploys them to keep its readers off balance: we feel by turns provoked, seduced, repulsed, persuaded, or incited, but certainly never bored or disinterested. Judged in terms of communicative rationality, the *Republic* deploys an array of strategies and tactics meant to bring about perlocutionary effects—that is, effects of power—even as it states its illocutionary intent, its disavowal of power. But before I pursue a reading of the *Republic* as a complex set of rhetorical (and political) strategies, I should pause to take stock of my present position, survey the terrain I have covered, and chart the next stage of the journey.

II

The *Republic* considered so far, is, while critical and activist, also monolithic, unified, and hierarchical, a paradigmatic global discourse that values the Platonic virtues of order, harmony, and stability over the Athenian—and democratic—political virtues of contest, struggle, and liberty. Yet this gloss on the *Republic* hardly does justice to so complex, and at times contradictory, a work. Despite its smooth façade, the *Republic* remains an ambivalent book, no less fragmented by internal tensions, ambiguities, and paradoxes than the tragedy it rejects. It is now time to confront these fragments, to tease out of Plato a theory (and a politics) less total, less singular in form and less sure of itself than my reading has so far indicated. Paradoxical and disturbing book that it is, perhaps we should not be too surprised to learn that the *Republic* struggles against its own unitary, hierarchical, and, if I am right, ultimately disciplinary account of selves, citizens, and society. It is to that internally subversive narrative—as a countertext that interrogates and challenges the established authority of Platonic philosophy—that I now turn.

The dialogue form of the *Republic* comprises one challenge to the book's unitary narrative, a challenge that pushes back and against its imposing theoretical mass to open up cracks and fissures in an otherwise smooth and seamless surface. Written as a dialogue, the *Republic* is philosophy, although its form is in an important sense dramatic, not discursive. As such, Plato's work contains not one, but many, voices. While Socrates has the largest part in the dialogue, other speakers play important, even necessary, roles. Ten characters comprise the cast assembled in the house of Cephalus, and of these, seven speak, some at length, others quite briefly. This polyphonic form lends the *Republic* a certain complex multidimensionality and indeterminacy uncharacteristic of foundationalist philosophy: while several characters speak, Plato—as author(ity)—remains anonymous. This is especially true of book 1 (although not unique to it), where Plato represents a plurality of positions, viewpoints, and arguments, all expressed through the responsiveness of dialectical interactions. Dialogue thus offers an open-ended, ongoing discussion, rather than an authoritative pronouncement, proclamation, or prepackaged truth. As Paul Friedländer has justly remarked, "The dialogue is the only form of book that suspends the book form itself."[15] Moreover, by presenting multiple positions, and so multiple points of possible engagement, dialogue forces the reader "to enter critically and actively into the give and take" of the debate.[16] And, as we shall see, the challenges put to Socrates in book 1 recur periodically throughout the *Republic*. Dialogue thus asks the reader to take sides and make judgments, something a global theory or treatise is structurally incapable of doing. Yet my characterization of the *Republic*'s dialogue form begs an important question: how can one justly consider a book a dialogue in which most characters remain silent and Socrates does all the talking? Must we not look to other—less obvious, but still subversive—structures in the *Republic* to make Plato speak against himself?

One such structure upon which the *Republic* relies is the form of tragic elenchus. This point becomes most obvious when one compares

15. Friedländer, *Plato*, 1: 143.
16. Nussbaum, *Fragility of Goodness*, p. 126.

a play like Sophocles' *Oedipus Tyrannos* to a Socratic conversation. Sophoclean drama, like the Socratic dialogue that followed it, charts the course of confidently asserted claims that further developments and subsequent questioning prove wrong. Oedipus resembles a character in a dialogue who, blind to the dimensions of his decidedly self-serving beliefs, discovers that his grasp of, and control over, practical problems is irreversibly lost. As does the outcome of the play, individual scenes make this clear—he misinterprets oracles, misunderstands Jocasta, and falsely accuses both Creon and Tiresias. Oedipus's quest and the entire structure of action in fact parallel the structure of a Socratic elenchus. The king's certain belief that he knows who he is, who his parents are, and with whom he lives is permanently subverted. Here, drama most clearly reveals its influence on Socratic philosophical inquiry: the elenchic cross-examination that leads to Oedipus's discovery is not merely part of the drama, it is the whole of it, both the structure of the action and the substance of the plot.[17]

Again, book 1 of the *Republic* proves instructive. The dialogue opens with a Socratic cross-examination of three characters: Cephalus, Polemarchus, and Thrasymachus. Each conversation, however, plays a variation on the classical theme of tragic elenchus. Altthough Cephalus withdraws from the conversation before philosophy can affect him (a withdrawal that short-circuits the cross-examination), the subsequent debate with the spirited Polemarchus dramatizes an exemplary Socratic performance. Socrates successfully refutes the traditional definition of justice as helping friends and harming enemies, persuading Polemarchus to join him as an ally in the further search for justice. Thrasymachus, too, suffers defeat, but, like Callicles in *Gorgias,* and despite his blush of shame, answers merely to please the company, not from the conviction that justice is indeed more profitable than injustice.[18] As the three divergent responses of indifference, genuine conviction, and hostile denial indicate, Socratic elenchus—the central structural component of the dialogue—intends, although not always successfully, to effect a reversal at the level of both belief and action.

The force of the dialogue form, then, lies in its warning about the

17. Alister Cameron, *The Identity of Oedipus the King* (New York: New York University Press, 1968), pp. 50–51.

18. Not all dialogues idealize the experience of conversion. Polemarchus hints at this when he asks, "How can you persuade us if we won't listen?" and in *Gorgias,* Callicles refuses to listen.

dangers inherent in all searches for a single or unitary form of truth. Dramatic dialogue, with its portrayal of diverse characters, motivations, and points of view, is relentlessly multivocal, even multiperspectival, and heterogeneous. Against the singularity and simplicity of the pure Platonic Form, dialogue—following tragedy—"continually displays to us the irreducible richness of human value, the complexity and indeterminacy of the lived practical situation."[19] Socratic dialogue's primary responsibility lies with the particular individual's response to an immediate and complex ethical situation, rather than with general, abstract, or determinate accounts that simplify or otherwise reduce an unavoidably ironic and contradictory world. Socratic elenchus warns against such reductionism in thought and action by demonstrating the dangers of clinging to an overly narrow and excessively rigid conception of oneself and one's world.[20]

But Socratic elenchus is not just at work in this or that exchange between Socrates and his hapless interlocutor. As in tragedy, elenchus also defines the larger dramatic structure or form of the *Republic.* By *form,* I mean not only drama, dialogue, or treatise as a characteristic literary genre, but the architecture of a work's composition, the arrangement of its formal elements, including the structural articulation of both the action and the argument. This elenchic structure poses a further challenge to the book's intended theoretical unity, for the *Republic* disturbs expectations and sensibilities by reversing the direction of travel of its

19. Nussbaum, *Fragility of Goodness,* p. 134.

20. I have here taken certain liberties with Martha Nussbaum's account of philosophical dialogue. I should say something about her claim that dialogue moves from particular to general accounts and judgments, and that "tragedy warns us of the dangers inherent in the search for one form by continually displaying to us the irreducible richness of human value, the complexity and indeterminacy of the lived practical situation," while Socratic dialogue does not. As I have indicated, that warning might come from Socratic philosophy as well. I certainly argue that philosophical dialogue attends to the particular: Socrates treats his interlocutors as particular individuals with different and distinct needs. He treats his fellow citizens, not as abstract equals before the law, but as a father or older brother would treat his sons or younger brothers. At the same time, we should not neglect the philosophical elements in tragedy: Socrates does show us how to rise above the particularities of tragedy to inquiry, yet conversely, Oedipus and Socrates show us that inquiry can be tragic. I therefore think that Nussbaum understates tragedy's search for truth. Tragic theater indeed displays "the complexity and indeterminacy of the lived practical situation," yet it does so in a highly ordered and structured way. Tragedy might not ultimately find a "single or unitary form of truth," yet the impulse to search it out resides in the fabric and organization of the text, even as the play itself warns against such searches. Nussbaum both underplays the intellectual aspects of tragedy and overstates her case against philosophical dialogue when she argues that tragedy is antiphilosophical and dialogue overly abstract, determinate, ultimately reductionist, and so antitragic.

own narrative.[21] Like the unexpected reversal of action in *Oedipus Tyrannos,* and like Socrates' reversal of judgment on the great Athenian statesmen in *Gorgias,* the *Republic* unexpectedly changes course. Socrates literally reverses his initial direction of travel, up from and out of the Piraeus, to go back down to the harbor for an all-night festival. The peripetetic reversal of this opening scene certainly reflects through dramatic means the change of mind so essential to a successful Socratic elenchus. It also anticipates the "turning around," subsequent enlightenment, and grudging descent back into the shadows central to the parable of the cave and the dialectical education of the philosopher. That education is itself structured by a reversal, for a moral understanding of the world—an understanding that results in a just citizen—requires more than the dialectical sharpening of wits. The "turning around" that describes the philosopher's education reflects a change of heart, a metaphorical reorientation or reversal of one's life. Such reversal also structures the all-consuming task of the interlocutors, provides the *Republic* with a tragic sense of loss, and balances the central, hopeful ascent to the Forms with a concluding descent: after the long and exhausting upward journey that culminates in the polis of the idea, the ideal city proves as fragile and vulnerable as any finite human life. No sooner is the city in words completed than it begins to unravel in a downward spiral of decay and decomposition. From the optimism of books 5 to 7, where philosophers sought to remake the world in the image of the transcendent idea, the *Republic* gives way to the pessimism of book 9, where Socrates hopes that at least the polis of the idea could be realized in the soul of the individual (592b). These reversals at the level of the dialogue's dramatic structure subvert even the most confidently self-contained theoretical account, alerting us to its attendant insufficiencies and inconsistencies.

The *Republic* unpredictably changes its course to violate its own assumptions, prejudices, and expectations, not only by means of reversal but also through the use of interruptions, paradox, and the juxtaposition of opposites. A series of interruptions, false closures, and new beginnings disrupts the forward (and upward) movement of the *Republic*'s narrative, further subverting the "tyranny" of its foundational discourse with discrete acts of resistance directed against any final closure.

21. This is as true for Plato's contemporaries as it is for us. See Julia Annas, *An Introduction to Plato's Republic* (Oxford: Clarendon Press, 1981), p. 2.

Book 1 ends in typical and well-known Socratic confusion, so that many have considered "Thrasymachus" a self-contained example of the early and aporetic type of dialogue in which Socrates himself admits ignorance (354c).[22] Yet while parallels to this inconclusive conclusion abound in the Platonic corpus, no other dialogue offers anything like the beginning of book 2, where Socrates reopens the problem of justice. The aporetic closure of book 1 thus proves deceptive and disruptive: against our expectations (and against those of Socrates), Glaucon and Adeimantus force Socrates to renew the argument.[23] The dialogue begins anew. Still other examples of inconclusion in a dialogue that refuses to conclude indicate the *Republic*'s resistance to its own impulse toward theoretical closure. First, there is Adeimantus's challenge to Socrates' description of the guardian class at the beginning of book 4, when he asks: "What would you say in your defense, Socrates, if someone were to say you don't make these men very happy?" (419a) Adeimantus is satisfied with Socrates' defense, but others, either inside or outside the dialogue, may not be. Perhaps this overture, and others like it in the dialogue, are invitations to interrupt the flow of Socratic discourse from the outside and so interrogate its adequacy, as do the interlocutors from the inside. Or consider the digressionary nature of the *Republic*'s central books, books that introduce the most controversial themes in the dialogue. If Socrates had his way, that conversation would never have occurred. For once Socrates has completed founding the "city in words," he turns, at the start of book 5, to discuss the types of cities and characters that are inferior to the best regime and lack its degree of perfection. This would seem the next step in a logical argument, but Socrates is interrupted in mid-sentence by Polemarchus, who asks Adeimantus: "Shall we let him go on, or what?" (449b) With this interruption, Plato has Socrates introduce the three waves of paradox that we most associate with the city of the idea: the equality of the sexes, the community of women and children, and rule by philosopher-kings. It is not until the beginning of book 8 that the narrative resumes its interrupted course, when it takes up, once again, the cycle of political decay and decline.

This series of interruptions fragments the totality of the book's theo-

22. Friedländer, *Plato,* 2: 50–56.

23. Diskin Clay, "On Reading the *Republic,*" in *Platonic Writings / Platonic Readings,* ed. Charles Griswold (Routledge: New York, 1988), p. 22.

retical discourse, forcing the reader to consider a *Republic* of one book (the aporetic "Thrasymachus"), three books (1–3), six books (1–4, 8–9), and finally of ten books. But how complete, one may ask, is a *Republic* of ten books, given repeated interruptions in which Plato has radically qualified a founding discourse that could easily be self-content and self-contained?[24] It is not merely the aporetic book 1 that resists closure. The entire *Republic* is structured by a series of interruptions, false closures, and reopened or contested arguments.

The *Republic*'s deployment of startling oppositions and paradoxical contradictions further disturbs its apparently settled order and mar(k)s an apparently flawless and seamless text. The *Republic* conjoins opposites in uneasy and paradoxical tension: it juxtaposes the novel and innovative to the ancient and traditional, it joins poetry to philosophy, and suggests that justice requires an essential equality between men and women, the community of women and children, and the unity of political power and theoretical knowledge. This last paradox—the third wave that threatens to engulf Socrates—unites power and knowledge and indicates a paradox central not only to the *Republic* but to the vocation and phrase "political theory" itself. On one hand, politics concerns the vicissitudes of human affairs in the city and has to do with particularities of time and place, the indeterminacy and unpredictability of chance in human action and decision; in short, with all that is mutable, changeable, and fluid. Theory, on the other hand, concerns the fixed, the necessary, the eternal and unchanging order of the cosmos, those things that exist by nature and admit of certainty as independent objects of contemplation. "Political theory" thus joins two separate realms of knowledge and its objects and two distinct sensibilities or styles. In the *Nicomachean Ethics,* Aristotle expresses his own astonishment at the attempted unification of politics and theory when he remarks that only an uneducated man would expect the same amount of precision from the human sciences as from the theoretical sciences. By joining two activities and modes of knowing traditionally in opposition to each other in the paradoxical unity of philosophy and politics, the *Republic* invites its readers to question now-established categories and

24. Ibid., p. 23. I agree with Clay that the *Republic* is structured by interruptions and questions, but where he argues that the book is ultimately "an open dialogue," I maintain that the text subverts itself, undermines its drive toward closure, and questions its conclusions. This is to recognize contending forces at work in the text that make it an ambivalent book, but not to settle for a "single" reading, either "open" or "closed."

divisions as each term in the phrase "political theory" interrogates its counterpart. Here is one more example of elenchus at work in the *Republic.*

The architecture of the *Republic* presents another paradox, different from, although related to, the paradox of "political theory" I have just mentioned. In chapter 3, I argued that the dramatic form or structure of a play often reflected its substantive teachings. For example, in Sophocles' *Oedipus Tyrannos,* form rearticulates content in the complex interplay and interpenetration of language, action, and plot. The ambiguity of the play's language (its duality) reflects the ambiguity of Oedipus's actions and self. Thus the paradoxes of idiom and speech that characterize the language of the play also characterize Oedipus. The play unfolds on two distinct and separate levels of meaning, until the final revelation unites word with deed, character with fate, and Oedipus with himself. The tensions and ambiguities—of action, knowledge, and meaning—lived by Oedipus are thus reflected in the formal structure and language of the play.

Something similar happens in a Socratic dialogue. Socratic question-and-answer is the most appropriate form for imparting the substantive philosophical teaching that true knowledge is rooted in an awareness of one's ignorance. Socratic wisdom recognizes itself to be partial, one-sided, incomplete, and so in need of others: the dialogue form recognizes these deficiencies as the necessary conditions for the collaborative pursuit of wisdom. The Socratic search is thus a collective endeavor, and Socratic philosophy an ongoing activity of debate and deliberation, of vision and revision. Since the dialogue form also invites interlocution, as auditors we are welcomed into the human community of the dialogue and encouraged to explore its substantive arguments and conclusions for ourselves. Socrates' teaching about wisdom's reliance on ignorance is thus reiterated by the partial, incomplete, and fragmentary character of the human conversation and quest the dialogue embodies, represents, and at its best attempts to mitigate.

The parallel relationship between philosophical substance and dramatic structure that characterizes Socratic dialogue does not, however, adequately describe the *Republic.* The *Republic*'s dramatic form does not so much reflect its explicit teaching as subvert it. Where the tensions and ambiguities of form reflect the tensions and ambiguities of content in Sophoclean drama and Socratic philosophy, the architecture of the *Republic* presents a paradox of its own. There is a disjunction or dissonance, if not a contradiction, between *what* Socrates and the interlocutors say, and the *way* they say it. The practice of Socratic philosophy, which displays justice in the activity of the search for it, subtly subverts the substantive definition achieved by that practice. I want to conclude this present discussion by suggesting one last way in which the dramatic form of the dialogue struggles against the *Republic*'s pretensions to foundationalist theory.

This struggle points to an ambiguity, if not an outright opposition, between the kind of philosophy Socrates and the interlocutors practice *in* the dialogue and the kind of philosophy they come to recommend *through* the dialogue.[25] The familiar interpretation evaluates the *Republic* as radically discontinuous with the Socratic philosophy of the *Apology*.[26] This *Republic* proffers as rationalist construct an ideal city intended to be embodied in the world. Objective knowledge of justice, apprehensible by properly initiated and trained philosophers, is possible given favorable circumstances and a few citizens with suitably philosophical inclinations. The *Republic* is a work of utopian philosophy that manifests the will to power of the philosopher who would remake society in the image of the transcendent idea. Plato's radical reform of the social order requires the judicious use of philosophical technique on political matter in order to banish art and poetry, institute communism, enforce strict educational practices, and pacify the inhabitants with a calculated lie. The result is a harmonious and well-ordered polis, in which the rational part rules the whole as it does in the well-ordered soul. Less generously, the society of the *Republic* is, to use Karl Popper's phrase, a closed one. In the closed society of the *Republic*'s best regime, philosophy tends toward tyranny and the dogmatic closure of the mind one associates with the possession of truth, rather than with the open and pious quest for wisdom, knowledge, and justice.

But I have pointed to ample evidence that the *Republic* is, if not con-

25. For a recent statement of these two positions, see Dale Hall, "The Republic and the Limits of Politics," *Political Theory* 5, 3 (Aug. 1977), and the response by Allan Bloom that follows. Nichols, "The *Republic*'s Two Alternatives," pp. 252–74, finds a discrepancy in the *Republic* as to what philosophy means, although she finally concludes that "Plato obviously prefers Socrates, whose way of life he immortalizes in his dialogues, to the philosopher-kings of the *Republic*" (270). For Nichols, the most telling way in which Plato distinguishes himself from Socrates is by writing. For an extended treatment of this position, see her *Socrates and the Political Community: An Ancient Debate* (Albany, N.Y.: State University of New York Press, 1987).

26. This is Cornford's position in *Unwritten Philosophy*, pp. 58–59, as well as Karl Popper's in *The Open Society and Its Enemies*, vol. 1: *The Spell of Plato* (1949), 5th ed. (Princeton, N.J.: Princeton University Press, 1966). R. S. Bluck defends Plato against some of Popper's more outrageous allegations in "Is Plato's *Republic* a Theocracy?" *Philosophical Quarterly* 5, 18 (Jan. 1955): 69–73.

sistent with Socrates' self-interpretation in the *Apology* or *Gorgias,* certainly more ambivalent and ambiguous than a "Platonic" reading allows. Its dramatic form as dialogue and structured elenchus and the patterns of reversal, interruption, and paradox are all tactics and strategies the dialogue deploys to fragment the global theoretical (and political) totality Socrates constructs, tactics and strategies that resist the disciplinary closure we most associate with Plato's *Republic.* In these terms, the *Republic*'s countertext approximates an aporetic dialogue, and philosophy the open-ended quest for knowledge, wisdom, and justice, unpretentious and conscious of its mortal limits. This *Republic,* no less than the early "Socratic" dialogues, obeys the Delphic maxims "Know thyself" and "Nothing in excess." Socrates and his partners search for the nature of justice, but they never find it. They do, however, embody it in the just community they create among themselves during their search. Justice, like the other virtues, may not prove definable, nor may absolute knowledge of it be possessed, but it can be practiced. The *Republic* thus illustrates justice indirectly in the action of the quest. The activity of philosophical speech that the interlocutors undertake in the dialogue, rather than any definitive or final possession of knowledge, is justice.

On this "aporetic" reading, the *Republic* neither presents a plan for political action nor constructs an ideal utopia to be realized in the world. The practice of Socratic philosophy demonstrates, rather, the impossibility (and undesirability) of such plans and constructions. By showing the interlocutors (and readers) the limits of philosophical discourse in the uncompleted task of defining justice, Socrates also shows us its limited application to politics. The *Republic* issues a call, not for the radical transformation of the social and political order administered by a philosophical elite, but for the moral reform of the individual in its call to practice philosophy.[27] Such a reading also finds its justification in the pessimism of book 9, where Glaucon despairs of the possibility of ever founding a just city: "If this [harmony of the soul] is his deepest concern, he will not willingly become involved in politics" (592a), for

27. For a similarly dramatic reading of Plato's dialogues, besides the works of Strauss, Sesonske, and Friedländer cited in n. 9 above, see Eric Voegelin, *Plato and Aristotle* (Baton Rouge: Louisiana State University Press, 1957); Jacob Klein, *A Commentary on Plato's Meno* (Chapel Hill: University of North Carolina Press, 1965); Paul Plass, "Philosophical Anonymity and Irony in the Platonic Dialogues," *American Journal of Philology* 85, 3 (1964): 254–78; and J. H. Randall, *Plato: Dramatist of the Life of Reason* (New York: Columbia University Press, 1970).

the city they have just founded in words "exists nowhere on earth" (592b). Socrates then qualifies this statement by adding: "Yet perhaps there is a pattern for this laid up in heaven for the man who wants to observe it and, holding it in his sight, to found this city within himself [*heaton katoikizein*]. It makes no difference whether it exists now or ever will. It is in the life of this city that he would be active and in no other" (592b). If the *Republic* can be said to be "foundational" in any meaningful sense, that foundation is now restricted to the "inner polity" within the just individual. That justice is not possible in the city, but only in the soul of the individual is further indicated in the myth of Er, which concludes the dialogue. Given a choice between a life of ambition and that of an ordinary citizen who minds his own business, the soul of Odysseus chose the latter life, saying that had he been given first choice rather than last, he would not have chosen differently (620c).[28] With these pronouncements, it seems that philosophy has bid farewell to the heroic impulses that structured the earlier books and taken leave of politics altogether.

Each conception of philosophy also implies a corresponding form of political community and a corresponding relationship between them. The first community, constructed in speech by Socrates with the help of the assembled company, is an ordered hierarchy of three classes, which corresponds to the appetitive, spirited, and rational parts of the soul. In this community, led by the philosopher-kings, the rulers do not so much respond to the individual needs of their subjects as create and limit those needs through various manipulative mechanisms: the myth of the metals, or "noble lie," and poetic and gymnastic education. Rather than being grounded in dialogue, this community is remarkably silent and philosophy the privileged and private activity of a few, which consists of the pursuit of a pristine knowledge purged of the particularities of those individuals who pursue it. Such knowledge entitles the philosopher to rule the city as a captain rules a ship: with absolute authority.

The second community, composed of the interlocutors and led by Socrates is, if not democratic, certainly not authoritarian. It relies on the art of dialogue and debate, and resembles the deliberative community Socrates sought to establish as a paradigm for politics in *Gorgias*.[29]

28. On this issue of pessimism and the renunciation of politics, see Clay, "On Reading the *Republic*," pp. 32–33.

29. Arlene Saxonhouse characterizes Socratic philosophy this way in "The Philosophy of the Particular and the Universality of the City: Socrates' Education of Euthyphro," *Political Theory* 16, 2 (May 1988).

Socrates here leads the philosophical community he has helped establish, ever responsive to the particular needs of his partners in conversation. He originally let himself be persuaded by Polemarchus to return to the Piraeus, and it is evident that he treats each interlocutor differently according to differences in character. At the end of book 5, when Socrates is about to begin an account of the best regime's decline, he responds courageously to the spirited entreaties of Glaucon and Polemarchus to render a full account of the philosopher's education and so of justice. In the give-and-take of dialogue, the community is "ruled" as much by the collectivity of interlocutors as it is by Socrates. In that collectivity, individual needs, viewpoints, and characteristics are honored as irreplaceable parts of a larger whole: Thrasymachus's passion for power is just as necessary to the community of the dialogue as Glaucon's and Adeimantus's passion for justice.

Such ambiguities and oppositions concerning the nature of philosophy and its relation to politics complicate any interpretation that understands the *Republic* as either a utopian ideal or an anti-utopia intended as a critique of idealism.[30] To maintain that it is simply one or the other means to mistake a part for the whole, that is, to do what Oedipus did when he "solved" the riddle of the Sphinx, what Gorgias did when he claimed for the craft of rhetoric more than was its due, and what the interlocutors in book 1 of the *Republic* do when they claim a partial and self-serving understanding of justice to be the whole of it. But the *Republic* is neither simply a utopia nor an anti-utopia. Nor does it ultimately resolve its contending parts into a grand synthesis that contravenes the dialectical tensions that drive it. To think that it does ignores the dialogue's warning against the dangers of attaining a single or unitary account of anything, about gaining unity, consistency, coherency, and order at the expense of individuality, particularity, and diversity. It also fails to account for the varied strategies by which the dialogue struggles against its drive toward final narrative closure.

Despite the fact that the dialogue internally subverts its own foundationalist impulses, the *Republic* does make explicit what remained largely implicit in *Gorgias*. Plato's repudiation of Socrates and Socratic political philosophy—his triumphant announcement of political knowledge beyond contest—indicates that however useful radical philosophical questioning may be, it does reach a point of diminishing

30. Strauss, *City and Man*, p. 127; Allan Bloom, *The Republic of Plato* (New York: Basic Books, 1968), "Interpretive Essay."

returns. Socratic philosophy, or so Plato indicates in the *Republic,* is unable to provide the foundations necessary to secure a stable political community. Criticism is certainly necessary, but so too are the visions of unity, wholeness, and harmony that make it possible and that the *Republic* provides. The *Republic* is thus a perfect example of what Foucault terms a global theoretical discourse. In its diagnosis of political problems in systemic and structural terms, in its elaboration of an analogy between city and soul, in its creation of a center and a hierarchy, and in its derivation of a comprehensive theoretical and political order from an epistemological absolute, the *Republic* indeed assumes global aims and proportions. None of this means that Plato escapes the contradictions of political and theoretical foundings. I have been arguing that the dialogue subverts its own tendency toward such theorizing and the disciplinary regime that accompanies it. As necessary as it is to think in both systemic or structural terms and provide visions of unity, reconciliation, and fulfillment, such terms and visions tend to turn into closed systems. Even the most inclusive of systems excludes what necessarily falls outside or below the threshold of its cognition, forecloses some aspects of the world even as it discloses others, and enslaves the subjects it intends to liberate. From one perspective, the *Republic* seems to offer just such an inclusive, self-confident, and self-contained vision of the whole. From another—simultaneous—perspective, it invites its readers to wonder if Socrates would not be the first banished from the ideal city, Socratic philosophy purged from it along with poetry, and philosophical discussions of justice (like the one in the *Republic*) outlawed.

The *Republic* is neither simply continuous nor discontinuous with the Socrates of the early dialogues. Although it presents the activities of Socrates familiar from those dialogues, it also contains an account of philosophers that does not describe Socrates himself. Two modes of philosophy and two models of political community contend with one another for authority in the *Republic.* To the extent that it is cast in the form of a dialogue in which these two opposing conceptions interrogate each other, the *Republic* is an extension of Socratic philosophy. But to the extent that the *Republic* agrees with Socrates' Athenian accusers and questions the practice of Socratic questioning,[31] rejects his ironic stance for an altogether unironic conclusion, and entertains the idea

31. On Plato's questioning of Socratic questioning, see John Sallis *Being and Logos: The Way of the Platonic Dialogue* (Pittsburgh, Pa.: Duquesne University Press, 1978), p. 27.

that objective knowledge of the Good is possible and perhaps necessary for establishing a well-ordered city and soul, the *Republic* betrays both the practice and the intention of a Socratic philosophy based on the ironic knowledge of ignorance.

These ambivalences and oppositions, the contending forces and competing claims that struggle against each other, leave us with no easy conclusion about the kind of theory and politics the *Republic* recommends. To reduce the *Republic* to an "aporetic" dialogue means to miss Plato's warning (already registered in *Gorgias*) about the insufficiencies inherent in "pure" Socratic philosophy, and to ignore his caution against naively raising "dialogue" to a cult. To reduce it to a "dogmatic" dialogue ignores Socrates' warning about the tyrannical closure of mind to which even the best-intentioned intellects—and theories—fall prey. The *Republic* is thus a paradigm, but not without its own internal tensions and ambiguities, which subtly disrupt the settled order the dialogue so powerfully projects. Such tensions and ambiguities recall the ambiguous status of Sophocles' paradigmatic hero, Oedipus. Like Oedipus, the *Republic* is both noble exemplar and object lesson, perhaps the greatest example of a global theoretical discourse *and* the greatest criticism of such globalized thinking, one of the finest examples of a systematic order of knowledge and a negation of the possibility of such an order.[32] I do not think, however, that the *Republic* successfully resolves the tensions, ambiguities, and ambivalences that mark its theoretical vision and textual practice. In its own terms, the *Republic* must be judged a failure: Plato's dialogue wavers between two contending and compelling modes of theory (or philosophy) and models of politics. Ambivalent book that it is, we are left contemplating a global theoretical discourse of epic proportions, the singular totality of which is fragmented by multiple points of view, fresh starts and false closures, reversals, interruptions, and tragic disappointments. Yet like the tragedy that it simultaneously criticizes and absorbs, the *Republic* asks us to render a judgment about its achievements and failures, a judgment it has helped educate its readers to make.

The tensions and ambiguities that pervade the *Republic* have enabled the search for those internal subversions that fragment the dialogue. I have argued that the *Republic* is as much philosophical fragment as self-contained theoretical totality. That fragmentation has allowed me

32. Timothy Reiss, in *Tragedy and Truth* (New Haven, Conn.: Yale University Press, 1980), pp. 21ff., describes Greek tragedy this way.

to turn the text against itself for the contemporary purpose of discovering that within its global discourse, the *Republic* deploys a variety of textual strategies and practices that struggle with and against totality in both theory and society. Against the systematic order of its identitarian discourse and the disciplinary regime it simultaneously creates and legitimates, the dialogue mounts something like a counterattack. The interruptions, reversals, and paradoxes that punctuate the *Republic* and disrupt the even flow and smooth functioning of its orderly narrative (and its projected political order) work like the strategies and tactics of those Foucauldian genealogies that disturb the hegemonic claims of globalizing discourse in the struggle against the forms of discipline such discourse engenders. Within and against its own orderly body of theory, the *Republic* gives subversive expression to disruptive experiences, knowledges, and selves that it would otherwise suppress or banish, much as genealogies excavate the local, discontinuous, disqualified, and illegitimate knowledges that have been buried and disguised within and beneath formal systems of knowledge. What I have been calling the *Republic*'s countertext—a "text" that is heterogeneous, dispersed, discontinuous, and fragmentary—resists the dialogue's unified narrative and so the closure that mar(k)s all theoretical and political foundations. That the *Republic* contains such a fragmentary countertext does not mean, however, that the dialogue is fragmented. The fragmentary character of the book is mediated by a thematic coherence (whether one reads the *Republic* as the answer to, or a continued search for, the solution to the problems generated by politics, justice is the common theme) that makes the book a whole, even as it subverts its own forcefully projected theoretical totality.

But strategies of disruption, fragmentation, and disturbance necessarily require a "center" against which to push, a suitable amount of law and order to make disturbing the peace worthwhile, a foundation stable and permanent enough to withstand seismic assault. That foundation is, of course, the philosopher's knowledge of the Good, a knowledge that enables a just ordering of the city. Such knowledge is in an important sense independent of power, interest, passion, and even argumentation—it is a knowledge beyond the contest of politics—and so beyond speech. The Platonic desire to escape politics, to settle once and for all the struggle and contest over meanings cultural, social, and theoretical, has always been a dream of critical theory. Since its inception, critical theory has sought a way to fix power's limit through an appeal to reason in order to distinguish between just and unjust regimes, between legitimate and illegitimate exercises of power.[33] That desire is no less present and operational in Habermas's latest iteration of the Frankfurt legacy.[34] Like the Platonic philosopher in the presence of the Forms, the subjects of communicative reason seek to be wholly transparent to themselves and to others, perfectly present in a context of communication the fundamental (and unperceived) irony of which is that its logic leads beyond speech to silence. Critical theory's temptation to transparency flees politics (and its own critical vocation) by failing to acknowledge that its linguistic grounds are also subject to contestation, that even the claims of reason conceal strategies and mechanisms of power—are political. Platonic dialogue alerts its readers to the need for, and the inadequacy of, its own theoretical foundations, so that even a "closed" book like the *Republic* keeps on talking. By contrast, critical theory tires of its labor and seeks a final resting spot beyond speech. It thus contravenes its own prohibition of silence. But there is a further irony here: the almost impenetrable discursive form of Habermas's critical theory unwittingly works against, rather than with, the theory's communicative intent. What are we to make of a theory founded, and grounded, in speech that positively discourages the give-and-take of moral communication and debate? Would not a form less willfully obtuse, one more akin to dialogue, prove more appropriate to a theory of *communicative* action purporting to be democratic?

Although I shall let these criticisms stand, I do not want to dismiss Habermas's project of a rationally grounded politics too readily. After all, the *Republic* is sometimes silent about its own origins, and Socrates, too, often seems ready to discourse at length rather than pursue a conversation. Moreover, what I am unwilling to relinquish in Plato—a standard (or paradigm) that is useful both for explaining *and* for criticizing systematically distorted social relations—is no less present in the critical theory of Habermas. But what other lessons might critical theory learn from Plato? How might the *Republic* instruct contemporary

33. See, e.g., Max Horkheimer, "Traditional and Critical Theory," in id., *Critical Theory: Selected Essays,* trans. Matthew J. O'Connell et al. (New York: Herder and Herder, 1972), p. 243. See also the "Postscript," p. 246, where Horkheimer compares critical theory with Greek philosophy: "Its goal is man's emancipation from slavery. In this it resembles Greek philosophy, not so much in the Hellenistic age of resignation as in the golden age of Plato and Aristotle."

34. See, e.g., the essays in Jürgen Habermas, *Toward a Rational Society,* trans. Jeremy J. Shapiro (Boston: Beacon Press, 1970); id., *Knowledge and Human Interests,* trans. Jeremy J. Shapiro (Boston: Beacon Press, 1971); and *The Theory of Communicative Action,* trans. Thomas McCarthy (Boston: Beacon Press, 1984, 1987).

theory committed to reason and enlightened thought today? One way has to do precisely with a theory's (or theorist's) relation to its own origins, a point the dialogue at least reveals to its readers, even if it does not in fact get it quite right. Critical theory would thus leave this staged encounter having learned both the attractions and dangers involved in constructing a self-contained and self-contented discourse. Such theory would also recognize the necessity of providing a *critical* account of its own activity by treating its theoretical foundations with proper genealogical suspicion, and in this manner keep the dialogue it seeks to establish alive. The *Republic* aids in the present task of imagining a postfoundationalist theoretical sensibility by balancing the quest for an orderly theoretical account of politics with the drive to subvert, interrupt, and interrogate all such comprehensive, "global" orders. Plato's dialogue helps articulate a theoretical sensibility that both founds and confounds the Western theoretical imagination and points toward an agonistic ethos that introduces heterogeneity, difference, and contest into our theoretical visions, while conserving those aspects of order—rule, authority, stability—as elements of a center against which to struggle. Because the dialogue (con)founds the theoretical imagination in this way, it is particularly useful for resisting the polarized terms of the present contest over the meaning of theory, for charting an alternative route through that unstable terrain. The usefulness of the *Republic* for contemporary theory lies precisely in its ability to think such apparently intractable contradictions in tension, to embody the very dilemmas it seeks to solve, to give voice to the very conflicts it would erase.

For these reasons, the *Republic* proves instructive as a model for contemporary theoretical critique, for the establishment of a "text" in tension with its margins provides the dialogue with a position from which to transform the "norms and forms" both of its inherited culture and of its own founding principles. That transformative capacity in the *Republic* is an instance of what I have been calling immanent critique. Two examples, one from tragedy, the other from Socratic dialogue, should prove sufficient to recall the context for this claim. A tragedy like Sophocles' *Oedipus Tyrannos* could question the present from within the tradition of a public festival by juxtaposing past and present in a way that would initiate a dialogue among the members of the citizen-audience and so promote collective self-examination. Rooted firmly in the conventions of civic tradition and religious ritual, tragic action nonetheless questioned the order in which it participated. Although Socratic philosophy was not anchored institutionally in any way, it performed its own critical work in a similar manner. Socrates appealed to such traditional Athenian values as justice, courage, temperance, and piety, and at the same time subjected these unexamined meanings to the most severe and critical scrutiny. Like tragedy, Socrates thought within and against the Athenian tradition in order to think beyond it. But what of the *Republic?* Does not Plato finally and decisively break with all inherited Athenian traditions, especially the poetic? How can I claim that Plato pursues a strategy of immanent critique similar to the practice of both tragedy and Socratic philosophy when the *Republic* proposes a form of civic education that emphatically rejects the two cornerstones of Athenian *paideia*—epic and tragic poetry? One response is that while the *Republic* rejects poetry, the dialogue itself is a profoundly poetic work, impossible without the epic and tragic tradition to give it substance, scope, and definition. The *Republic* positions itself within and against the poetic tradition in order to redefine and transform it.[35] Second, the *Republic* is a work of philosophy and philosophical education that, as I have indicated, seems to repudiate Socrates, its greatest exemplar and source of inspiration. Yet even as it suggests that Socratic elenchus is not enough to secure a stable political community, the *Republic* is a highly Socratic work by virtue of its dialectical form and self-critical stance: as a critique of Socratic philosophy, it refuses to abandon Socratic philosophy. Platonic philosophy, too—at least in the *Republic*—thinks with and against Athenian tradition in order to think beyond it.

IV

I want to end this chapter and prepare for the next by returning to the theme of founding with which I began, for Plato's *Republic* and Aeschylus's *Oresteia* are both "founding" texts.

Looking back over these reflections, I am not at all sure that the *Republic* successfully conceals its will to power—manifest in its global theoretical discourse and the disciplinary politics that follow—behind a metaphysical veil of pure knowledge and pristine origins. Indeed, I am not even sure it attempts such a philosophical sleight of hand, at least not in any simplistic way and not without making such an operation clear—almost transparent—to the reader. The interruptions, para-

35. On this point, see Martha Nussbaum, *Fragility of Goodness,* pp. 121–32, esp. p. 123.

doxes, and reversals that mark and mar the text invite the reader to question its founding constructions and interrogate its fundamental theoretical assumptions. Despite the seamless façade of its smooth surface, the *Republic* is a dialogue traversed by cracks and fissures, which provide critical purchase for the inquiring and adventuresome reader who remains skeptical of any author(ity)—textual, political, theoretical—constituted by pure forms and revealed essences. The *Republic* is a surprisingly permeable text. A dialogue that produces itself by generating diverse and contradictory meanings, it employs multiple strategies to resist the Platonic drive toward final political and theoretical closure. As the dialogue attempts to establish a psychic and social order securely grounded in foundations beyond the reach of political contest and contestability, that ground begins to shift and move, to fragment and fall away. Once stable terrain yields to fractures and fault lines, the depths of which I have here tried to plumb.

But does this permeability and impermanence mean the dialogue escapes the "paradox of founding"? Does not the *Republic,* too, violate its own precept of justice precisely at the moment of its origin, a violation it subsequently conceals in a series of retrospective justifications, standards, and judgments that amount to a pernicious politics of forgetting?[36] After all, is not the authority of the *Republic* derived from the philosopher's incontestable vision of the good, and is that authority—and the controversial social arrangements that support it—not precisely what the dialogue seeks to establish? Like all acts of foundation, the *Republic*'s is a supremely *political* act—an act of power—in spite of its sometime denials and evasions to the contrary. I say sometimes because Plato's dialogue is distinct (although not unique) for facing that beginning squarely and recognizing clearly—almost brutally—the violent excesses at its own origin. The *Republic* thereby acknowledges its reliance upon the violence and exclusion that attend every founding. We have only to recall the acts of "injustice" at the origin of the just city: the principle that the happiness of the guardians is secondary to the health of the whole, the radical purge of poetry, the forced exile of all those over ten years of age, the "noble lie" and the program of eugenics that accompanies it. Moreover, the dialogue reveals its own deployment of strategies and rhetorical devices that conceal the rifts they necessarily open. Consider the meaning of a book that

36. William Connolly, "Democracy and Territoriality," *Millenium: Journal of International Studies* 20, 3 (Winter 1991): 465.

excoriates mimetic representation, yet itself contains just such an imitation; or the fact that Socrates himself would not be allowed to practice philosophy in the city he founds; or, finally, the paradox of a text that radically rejects poetry yet is itself a poetic work. How to appropriate such ambiguities, inconsistencies, and ambivalences is a substantial burden of this chapter.

I have suggested that as a series of internal subversions, such paradoxes and inconsistencies struggle with and against the global narrative of the *Republic,* arresting its flow and fragmenting what appears to be a seamless totality flawed by neither conceptual, political, nor structural gaps. They thus force us to consider its act of founding—and the accompanying invention of a global theoretical discourse—as a *political* act, an act that is sui generis, unlegitimated by any prior agreement, consent, or author(ity). This further suggests that the norms of justice it subsequently inscribes are not derived epistemologically, but fabricated politically (perhaps punningly?) by that divine plastic artist (*ho theos plattōn* of 415a) who created them.[37] As a text that founds itself, the *Republic* is a supremely creative text, a text that initiates something for the first time. As a text that *con*founds itself, the *Republic* also disrupts its own bid for an absolutist epistemology from which it might derive ultimate political authority. Perplexing book that it is, the *Republic* both founds an order that (perhaps) satisfies our deeply felt longings for the certainties of community, solidarity, and identity by anchoring its politics in a knowledge of the Real that is beyond contest *and* confounds—by struggling against—the ordering, hierarchizing, and systematizing mentality it projects. The *Republic* thus helps us negotiate those theoretical foundings and foundations that living in an unstable postmodern world entails by exposing the reductions and violations such acts of founding (and foundationalist theory) necessarily engender.

The *Oresteia,* like the *Republic,* is also a "founding" text. To the extent that it is, the trilogy shares with Plato's dialogue all the characteristics of a globalizing discourse: the narrative steadily progresses from blood vengeance to legal justice and from myth to enlightenment, authoritatively distinguishes between legitimate and illegitimate regimes, decisively establishes stable social categories and triumphantly reconciles a previously fragmented world into a harmoniously ordered social totality. Competing forces and contending figures join in a whole that is larger than the sum of its parts: reason is reconciled with pas-

37. On this pun in Plato, see Clay, "On Reading the *Republic,*" p. 19.

sion, Olympian with chthonic divinities, the younger with the older generation, men with women. Such is the achievement of Athena's artful wisdom and Aeschylus's wise art. As a text about political beginnings, however, is the *Oresteia* any less immune to the paradox of founding than was the *Republic?* Does the triumphant celebration of the democratic polis that concludes the trilogy similarly conceal violations, exclusions, and subordinations that accompany its origin? Or are these questions merely the objections of an obsessive pedant unwilling to acknowledge the tremendous achievements Aeschylus dramatized onstage? While I agree that the twin accomplishments of restored cosmic order and the invention of democracy are hardly negligible, I must also ask at what price such achievements are purchased, and who underwrites their costs? The questions put to Plato must also be put to Aeschylus. For the *Oresteia* is no less ambivalent and no less (d)riven by contending currents and impulses than the *Republic.* To make sense of how those ambiguous impulses work themselves out over the course of the trilogy and to assess the disciplinary costs of democracy for the "subjects" of the social order are the appropriate tasks of the next chapter.

5

Democracy and Discipline in Aeschylus's *Oresteia*

Democratic ages are times of experiment, innovation and adventure.

—Alexis de Tocqueville,
Democracy in America

The subject is constituted through the force of exclusion and abjection, one which produces a constitutive outside to the subject, an abjected outside which is, after all, "inside" the subject as its own founding repudiation.

—Judith Butler, *Bodies That Matter*

The dispute between Habermas and Foucault sketched in chapter 1 leaves us with a choice between democratic politics and "normalizing" techniques, between the ideal of a rationally achieved consensus and the rejection of all democratic ideals as insidious strategies that aim to discipline selves and citizens. Democracy represents either our last, best hope of fulfilling the political promises of the Enlightenment or else is one more regulative ideal, a subtle strategy of disciplinary control that ironically extends the carceral archipelago.

Stated in terms as stark as these, critical theory and genealogy share little, if any, common ground on the terrain of democratic politics and theory. What to Habermas are merely the necessary preconditions for radical democratic will formation—the rational, autonomous, deliberative, consensus-oriented self—are for Foucault the prior effects of a power that produces the very subject it then controls. Only those selves that attain the critical threshold of rationality rightly take their places on the deliberative tribunal, yet the very requirements of rational deliberation serve to exclude, silence, or discipline those differential selves that democracy requires. Separated by this radical divergence between the need to maintain the prerequisites of democratic culture and practice and the determination to disrupt modern, democratic forms of normalization, these views construct mutually exclusive interpretations of contemporary democratic theory and politics. We are left with the unsatisfying dilemma of having to choose between a homogenizing democratic consensus and a perpetually agonistic politics of resistance. Is it possible, however, to envision a democratic sensibility that balances the quest to fulfill the democratic aspirations of critical theory with an attendant politics of resistance meant to disturb and otherwise unsettle the normalizing effects of a democratic order? Might we not yet articulate a "democratic politics of disturbance,"[1] a politics that resists the norms and forms of a democratically and consensually constituted self and order even as it provides a democratic identity and practice against which to struggle? Put another way, is it possible to sustain the tension between a democratic critical theory and a genealogy critical of democracy, between Habermas and Foucault, and so pursue the dream of a democratic politics while simultaneously avoiding the nightmare of disciplinary (en)closure?

I think it is, and this chapter considers the contribution Aeschylus's *Oresteia* makes to a democratic politics of disturbance, a politics that (like the trilogy) sustains and celebrates democratic norms even as it resists and otherwise disrupts democratic normalization. But why choose the *Oresteia,* and in what ways does Aeschylus's trilogy speak to the contemporary issues with which I am concerned?[2]

I

There are at least two reasons why Aeschylus's *Oresteia* is particularly well suited to help us think through the contemporary tension between democracy and the discipline it potentially engenders. It is by now a commonplace to note that Greek tragedy emerged when the old myths

1. William Connolly, "Democracy and Territoriality," *Millenium: Journal of International Studies* 20, 3 (1991): 477.

2. I have used the Oxford Classical Text of the *Oresteia,* ed. Denys Page (Oxford: Clarendon Press, 1972), and unless otherwise noted, I have used Richmond Lattimore's translation, vol. 1 of *The Complete Greek Tragedies,* ed. David Grene and Richmond Lattimore (Chicago: University of Chicago Press, 1953). Commentaries on Aeschylus that I have used include *Agamemnon,* ed. J. D. Denniston and D. L. Page (Oxford: Oxford University Press, 1957); *Oresteia,* ed. George Thomson (1938; rev. ed. Amsterdam and Prague, 1966); and *Eumenides,* ed. Anthony J. Podlecki (Warminster, Eng.: Aris & Phillips, 1989).

were for the first time considered from the point of view of a citizen. As Jean-Pierre Vernant has pointed out, all tragedies shared this concern with the city by virtue of their ritual status within the context of a popular and democratic civic festival.[3] The *Oresteia* is unique, however, because it alone of all extant tragedies is preoccupied with the newly emerging democratic order itself.[4] In the context of a democratic celebration, the *Oresteia* celebrates democracy.

All tragedians also reworked and expanded the traditional myths that supplied their material, and Aeschylus was certainly no exception to this.[5] What I find especially significant about the *Oresteia* is the specific way in which Aeschylus revised the ancient, mythic materials so that Athenian democracy provided the trilogy's content as well as its context. Athens's own recent, ongoing democratic transformations are surely reflected in the fact that the playwright chose Argos over the traditional settings of Sparta or Mycenae, transferred the action to Athens, alluded to a recently concluded treaty with the Argives, and employed the Areopagus as his instrument for disrupting the ancient chain of vengeance and countervengeance.[6] Athena's establishment of the law court, the acquittal of Orestes, the reconciliation of the Erinyes, their acceptance in Athens, and their transformation into the new cult of the Eumenides are also the inventions of the poet.[7] Finally, the pag-

3. "Tragedy is, properly speaking, a moment," Vernant writes. "For tragedy to appear in Greece, there must first be a distance established between the heroic past, between the religious thought proper to an earlier epoch and the juridical and political thought which is that of the city performing the tragedy" (Jean-Pierre Vernant, "Greek Tragedy: The Problems of Interpretation," in Richard Macksey and Eugenio Donato, *The Languages of Criticism and the Sciences of Man: The Structuralist Controversy* [Baltimore: The Johns Hopkins University Press, 1970], p. 138).

4. *The Suppliants* might be an exception, because it too concerns the use of persuasion (*peithō*), a theme that is certainly democratic, although it does not reflect on the democratic order itself.

5. In fact, a number of recent interpretations of the *Oresteia* take the structure of its mythic narrative as the most important element determining its meaning. I say more about this below.

6. These events in the play allude to the Ephialtic reforms of 462/461 B.C., when the power of the Areopagus was curtailed, the franchise was extended, and a treaty between Argos and Athens was concluded. For an attempt to sort out contemporary allusions and specific references, see Anthony J. Podlecki, *The Political Background of Aeschylean Tragedy* (Ann Arbor: University of Michigan Press, 1966), ch. 5 and esp. pp. 80–100. In *The Greek Discovery of Politics* (Cambridge, Mass: Harvard University Press, 1990), ch. 5, Christian Meier also sifts the evidence to assess the influence of contemporary events on the composition of the trilogy, but is more concerned with the political and historical context in which Aeschylus wrote, so as to demonstrate how the *Eumenides* for the first time took up the problem of democracy and the political.

7. A. Lesky, *Greek Tragic Poetry,* trans. M. Dillon (New Haven, Conn.: Yale University Press, 1983), p. 90. For a slightly different view, see *Oresteia,* ed. Thomson), rev.

eant that concludes the play and trilogy recalls the democratic festival of the Great Panathenaia, which, as the name suggests, was a celebration that included all Athens and culminated in a procession to the Acropolis, where a sacrifice was offered to Athena. As Athena leads the procession of Eumenides and citizens from the theater to the Acropolis, the legendary aristocratic past fuses with the city's contemporary democratic present.[8] The final play of the trilogy presents democratic Athens to itself.

The critics agree that the *Oresteia,* first performed in the spring of 458 B.C.—not more than three or four years after the momentous events that abolished the political power of the Areopagus in 462/461—is inextricably linked to contemporary Athenian politics. All cite the reforms, led by Ephialtes, that broke the traditional power of the Areopagus, the last aristocratic bulwark against a rising popular tide, the reorientation of foreign policy away from conservative Sparta and toward Argos, and the ostracism of Cimon, the respected leader of the conservative party, as influences on the trilogy. All power passed to the Assembly and the Council of 500—that is, to the demos of Athens—and the citizens effectively gained control over the constitution as a whole. To be sure, the great aristocratic families remained powers to be reckoned with, but birth alone no longer determined political position: every citizen was born a second time into an artificial order constituted and bounded by equality before the law (*isonomia*) embodied in a legal, constitutional order.[9] Although there is considerable controversy over the significance of allusions to contemporary political events, all are agreed that in the *Oresteia,* the playwright reflected on Athens's newly emerging democracy.[10]

---

ed., 1: 57. The mythical archetype was thus concerned with the destinies of great families, whereas Aeschylus places the city, the threat of civil war, and possible ways of meeting this conflict at the center of interest.

8. On the significance of the Panathenaia, see George Thomson, *Aeschylus and Athens* (New York: International Publishers, 1950), pp. 295–97. The fact that once Orestes leaves the stage, no heroic persons remain further underscores the democratic focus of the play.

9. For a slightly different interpretation, see Martin Ostwald, *From Popular Sovereignty to the Sovereignty of Law: Law, Society and Politics in Fifth-Century Athens* (Berkeley: University of California Press, 1986), pp. 28–42. While Ostwald does not deny that the reforms of 462/461 effectively "removed control over the magistrates from a once-powerful aristocratic body and handed it to agencies constituted by the people as a whole," he does argue that much of this process had already begun with the reforms of Solon. Ephialtes, on this account, merely completed what Solon had initiated by abolishing the political power of the Areopagus entirely (p. 42).

10. On the historical questions concerning the *Oresteia* and the emergence of Athe-

Viewed in retrospect, then, from the opening lines of *Agamemnon* to the final scenes of the *Eumenides,* the trilogy seems to lead in a significant sense toward a resolution in the democratic polis. The whole trilogy, but particularly the *Eumenides,* thus concerns itself primarily with "the city of Athens and its newly established civic order."[11] When Athena establishes the law court and calls upon her "best citizens" to render judgment in the first homicide case, she alludes to that event when, for the first time in Greek history—in world history—the civic order as a whole was placed at the disposal of the demos. The events of 462/461 were so far-reaching that the Athenian civic order itself, its very constitution, had become a matter of popular controversy, hence a democratic political issue in its own right. In the *Oresteia,* we see that democratic civic order established: conflict between tribal custom and aristocratic privilege finds its resolution in the legally constituted order of the democratic polis embodied in court of law. Within the context of the Ephialtic reforms, the *Oresteia* for the first time articulated a series of reflections on the newly established democratic order at Athens.[12] I am concerned here to show how that order is thought out, embodied, reflected, *and* challenged in and by the drama.

The second reason I find the *Oresteia* particularly well suited for my purposes has to do with the way in which the trilogy represents the "other" in gendered terms and so introduces the marginalization of the feminine directly into a civic context.[13] In the *Oresteia,* for the first

nian democracy, see Leslie Ann Jones, "The Role of Ephialtes in the Rise of Athenian Democracy," *Classical Antiquity* 6, 1 (Apr. 1987): 53–76; K. J. Dover, "The Political Aspect of Aeschylus's *Eumenides,*" *Journal of Hellenic Studies* 77, 1 (1957): 230–37; E. R. Dodds, "Morals and Politics in the *Oresteia,*" *Proceedings of the Cambridge Philological Society* 186, 6 (1960): 19–31; C. W. Macleod, "Politics and the *Oresteia,*" *Journal of Hellenic Studies* 102 (1982): 124–44.

11. Meier, *Greek Discovery of Politics,* p. 91.

12. I do not want to construe an exact correspondence between the reforms of Ephialtes and the solution achieved in the *Eumenides.* The references to the Argive alliance and the curtailment of the powers of the Areopagus to matters of homicide can be construed as Aeschylus's support of the radical democracy; likewise, the fact that Athena echoes the Furies' counsel to incorporate fear (*to deinon*) in the new order, to avoid both anarchy and despotism, and to seek the mean can be understood as a protest against the democratic reforms. I find it more useful to interpret the trilogy as a reflection on both the gains *and* losses that attend the establishment of democracy. This dissolves the question about the politics of Aeschylus, first by focusing on the trilogy, second, by understanding it in a broader context: the reforms of Ephialtes might provide an *occasion* for reflection, but they do not necessarily determine the course or outcome of that reflection.

13. I am aware, of course, that the conflict in the trilogy is not reducible to sexual difference. However, I agree with Froma Zeitlin, "The Dynamics of Misogyny: Myth and Mythmaking in the *Oresteia,*" *Arethusa* 11, 1–2 (Spring/Fall 1978): 149–81, that the conflict between the older and younger gods, between Greek and barbarian, is presented

time, women struggle forcibly against the boundaries of the masculine public world,[14] and the outcome of that struggle, as we shall see, is by no means certain. In retelling the Homeric myth, Aeschylus did more than simply transfer the action from Argos to Athens and provide the contemporary city with a founding myth for its nascent democratic order. Aeschylus implicates gender in his retelling in such a way that one cannot avoid the questions the trilogy raises regarding the status and role of women in a democratic civic order.[15]

For his part, Homer virtually ignores Clytemnestra. Aegisthus seduces the queen, plans the trap, kills Agamemnon, takes control of the house, and is finally killed in turn by Orestes, who successfully reclaims his patrimony.[16] The *Odyssey* thus focuses on the male struggle for control of the household, and that struggle is settled within its narrow framework. The transgressions that set in motion the narrative of return and revenge find both their location and their resolution in the order of the *oikos.*[17] In the return and triumph of Orestes, as well as in that of Odysseus and Telemachus, the *Odyssey* unproblematically defines the proper and controlled order of the patriarchal household.[18]

Aeschylus, by contrast, focuses all his attention directly on Clytemnestra's character, revenge, and plotting of reciprocal murder. *His* Clytemnestra moves to the center of the stage: she, not Aegisthus, sets the watchman, tricks Agamemnon, defeats him in combat, and takes control of house and city. Homer passes over Clytemnestra's death in

in terms of an opposition between male and female. On misogyny in Greek myth and society, see P. E. Slater, *The Glory of Hera: Greek Mythology and the Greek Family* (Boston: Beacon Press, 1968), and Sarah B. Pomeroy, *Goddesses, Whores, Wives and Slaves: Women in Classical Antiquity* (New York: Schocken Books, 1975).

14. Although Aeschylus's *Persae* does not explicitly challenge the masculine norms of public achievement and glory as does the *Oresteia,* it does describe the hardships suffered by women at home that attend the masculine pursuit of war. On this point, see Michael Gagarin, *Aeschylean Drama* (Berkeley: University of California Press, 1976), p. 91.

15. Christian Meier, in his otherwise rather astute interpretation of the trilogy, misses the importance of gender altogether when, commenting upon the significance of the role "accorded to the fundamental division between man and woman, which is so starkly emphasized in certain passages in the first part of the *Eumenides,*" he states that "in view of the fact that the problem of man versus woman was not one that much exercised the Greeks, it is hardly likely to have constituted a central theme of the play." The real theme of the *Oresteia* is, rather, "the conflict of the *Eumenides* and its resolution as an expression of political thought" (*Greek Discovery of Politics,* p. 98).

16. *Oresteia,* trans. Lattimore, pp. 8–9.

17. Simon Goldhill, *Aeschylus: The Oresteia* (Cambridge: Cambridge University Press, 1992), p. 50.

18. Homer tells the story of Orestes piecemeal and by way of positive example for Odysseus and Telemachus. The relevant passages are *Odyssey* 1.29–43; 1.298–300; 3.254–312; 4.514–37; 11.405–34.

silence,[19] but she becomes the object of further revenge in the *Choephoroi,* her murder the central enacted confrontation in the central play of the trilogy. Moreover, the "feminine" Aegisthus contrasts sharply with the "masculine" Clytemnestra, thereby heightening our awareness of the dramatic reversal of sexual roles. The deaths of Aegisthus and Clytemnestra do not, however, return Orestes to his patrimony. Clytemnestra may be dead, but her Furies, the archaic goddesses of the underworld, prosecute her claim against Orestes, a claim that can only be redeemed in blood. Finally, in the trial of the *Eumenides,* the arguments proffered by both sides turn in a significant way on Clytemnestra's biological relation to Orestes, while the paradoxical figure of Athena reopens the question of a woman's civic role and status precisely at the moment of its intended resolution.

Throughout the trilogy, then, men and women are at odds: women aim directly at power and domination, while men aim to return them to their "normal" places. In the final confrontation, we are asked to choose between our obligation to blood ties and our obligation to the city. Homer's heroes could hardly conceive of such a choice, much less confront it. The transgressions that motivate the archaic narrative of return and revenge find both their expression and their resolution in the patriarchal order of the household. Aeschylus clearly indicates, however, that the oikos of the noble *genos* is no longer adequate to contain and resolve the sexual conflict unleashed within the house of Atreus. This is in part because the household is not merely the site, but also the cause, of the conflict between men and women. Only the polis, with its more inclusive and more encompassing view, will prove adequate to the larger task of reconciliation Aeschylus sets himself. But can we say that Aeschylus finds even the expanded framework of the democratic polis sufficient to contain the conflicts generated in the trilogy? The conclusion of the *Oresteia* certainly leaves no doubt that the more impartial and inclusive legal and political institutions of Athens constitute an advance over the particularity of the household and clan, but as the persistent presence of the Furies, the unannounced departure of Apollo, and the displacement of the solution onto the divine agency of Athena all indicate, the conflict between genders is larger than the polis itself. That the citizen-jurors probably vote *against* Orestes (Athena breaks the tie in favor of the city) also suggests that perhaps the framework of the polis is itself neither adequate nor any too secure.

19. Homer *Odyssey* 3.304–10.

That Aeschylus departs in significant ways from the myth as it appears in Homer and the other traditional sources is agreed,[20] yet the nature and purpose of that departure remains contested. A lively controversy over this issue has sprung up recently among classical scholars,[21] a controversy that illuminates, if not anticipates, my own attempt to insert the ancient text into a contemporary theoretical debate. Not surprisingly, it turns on the way in which the *Oresteia* "integrates" women into the newly founded civic order.

The usual interpretation of the play celebrates the transition from chaos to order, darkness to light, perversion to "normalcy."[22] This movement of progress occurs in the medium of a mythic structure that reconciles conflict with harmony, the chthonic with the Olympian divinities, female with male, old with new, clan-based blood vengeance with civic justice. John H. Finley, Jr., in an influential treatment as broad and inclusive as the *Oresteia* itself, argues that the trilogy traces the emergence of democracy, an order based on reason and consent, from its troubled beginnings in the archaic past to its triumph in the contemporary Athenian regime.[23] The rational and creative male principle of freely chosen compacts (represented by Apollo and the marriage bond) triumphs over what is female, inherited from the past, natural, and local. Aeschylus thus resolves the tension between place and creativity, scope and commitment, feminine and masculine values, earth-born and Olympian gods, Agamemnon and Clytemnestra, through his faith in the moral cogency of reason, a reason that resolves conflicts, not through assertive will, but through a generous and inclusive understanding.[24] Finley concludes his reading of the *Oresteia* with the judg-

20. For example, Stesichorus, Simonides, and Pindar. See Macleod, "Politics and the *Oresteia.*"

21. This debate is largely animated by feminist scholars who challenge the traditional interpretations of the trilogy. Their work centers on the themes of narrative and sexuality. See Zeitlin, "Dynamics of Misogyny"; Aya Betensky, "Aeschylus' *Oresteia:* The Power of Clytemnestra," *Ramus* 7, 1 (1978): 11–25; Nancy Rabinowitz, "From Force to Persuasion: Aeschylus' *Oresteia* as Cosmogonic Myth," *Ramus* 10, 2 (1981):159–91; and Simon Goldhill, *Language, Sexuality, Narrative: The Oresteia* (Cambridge: Cambridge University Press, 1984).

22. See, e.g., Brian Vickers, "Nature versus perversion: The *Oresteia,*" in id., *Towards Greek Tragedy: Drama, Myth, Society* (1973; New York: Longman, 1979).

23. John H. Finley, Jr., *Pindar and Aeschylus* (Cambridge, Mass.: Harvard University Press, 1966). In *Aeschylus and Athens,* Thomson argues similarly, as do H. D. F. Kitto, *Form and Meaning in Greek Drama* (London: Methuen, 1956), Dodds, "Morals and Politics in the *Oresteia,*" pp. 19–21, and Podlecki, *Political Background of Aeschylean Tragedy,* pp. 75–78, 80–82. Hugh Lloyd-Jones, *The Justice of Zeus* (1971; 2d ed., Berkeley: University of California Press, 1983), is an exception.

24. Finley, *Pindar and Aeschylus,* p. 277.

ment that Aeschylus was a prophet of democracy and reason. His trilogy is more than merely a charter for the democratic polis: it is nothing less than a founding document of Western civilization.

Some feminist accounts of the *Oresteia* protest that while Aeschylus may depart from the traditional narrative, he does so only to install a new myth in place of the old, and one that is, from the point of view of women, not an appreciable advance over the original. Froma Zeitlin argues, for example, that a cosmogonic myth indeed structures the *Oresteia*'s narrative, that it creates a world, traces the evolution of civilization, and culminates in the triumph of the democratic polis, an institution endowed with "the creative power to coordinate human, natural and divine forces."[25] The trial scene in the *Eumenides* certainly brings to an end the conflict between opposing interests and forces that has driven the action of the trilogy from the start. The solution, as we have seen, reconciles Olympian with chthonic deities on the divine level, Greek and barbarian on the cultural level, male and female on the social level. But Zeitlin does not see this solution as a true reconciliation in which opposing forces come to abide in a "just" state of respectful mutuality and reciprocity.[26] Rather, the "solution" of the *Eumenides* is achieved through the hierarchization of values: the subordination of the Erinyes to the Olympians, of barbarian to Greek, of female to male. Through the democratic rhetoric of equality, reason and consent legitimate the institutionalization of exclusionary polarities into systematized hierarchies, rather than creating a truly democratic order.[27] The *Oresteia* may well be a founding document of Western civilization, but what it founds is a tradition of misogynistic exclusion: "By integrating the issue into a coherent system of new values, by formulating it in new abstact terms, and by shifting to a new form of argumentation, it provides the decisive model for the future legitimation of this attitude in Western thought."[28] In these terms, the Athenian culture and practice of democratic citizenship prove to be one more strategy for disciplining the "feminine other" and constructing a normal and normalizing order.

25. Zeitlin, "Dynamics of Misogyny," p. 149. For other feminist accounts, see, e.g., Kate Millett, *Sexual Politics* (Garden City, N.Y.: Doubleday, 1971), and L. Bamberger, "The Myth of Matriarchy: Why Men Rule in Primitive Society," in *Women, Culture and Society*, ed. Michelle Rosaldo and Louise Lamphere, 263–80 (Stanford: Stanford University Press, 1974).

26. Cf. Kitto, *Form and Meaning*, who claims that the problem of *dikē* is solved.

27. Zeitlin, "Dynamics of Misogyny," does not, however, put it in precisely these terms.

28. Ibid., p. 150.

The *Oresteia,* on this reading, replaces a dynastic myth with a myth of wide-ranging origins in which the democratic city is founded on the defeat and subordination of women. For these critics, the *Oresteia* as origin myth creates a center, establishes a hierarchy of values based on difference, and legitimates an effective system of gender domination. While I find this criticism persuasive, and especially helpful for the argument I am going to develop, it shares one crucial element with the "progressivist" reading it rejects. Both uncritically accept a linear development in the narrative that culminates in a final resolution of the conflicts and oppositions that mark the trilogy. Both impute a well-defined telos to the structure of the *Oresteia*'s narrative: where the progressivist sees harmony and reconciliation, the feminist critic sees hierarchy and subordination. In these terms, the *Oresteia* either contributes to our understanding of the rational and consensual preconditions of democratic politics *or* else participates in the hierarchical and exclusionary order democracy purportedly rejects.

To break this interpretive impasse, I suggest adopting a reading of the *Oresteia* informed by the recent structuralist interpretations of Charles Segal.[29] Such an analysis suspects the too-easy identification of tragic "message" with mythologized narrative structure, whether that narrative culminates in reconciliation and inclusion or in hierarchy and subordination. This is so for two reasons. First, where a structural analysis treats the coded patterns of a myth as a microcosm of the social order and reads that order off the myth it analyzes, the "literary work imposes a secondary structure of language and meanings upon the given structures of the society."[30] A structuralist interpretation applied to a literary work thus proceeds differently than when applied to a myth. By necessity, the playwright uses the accepted, normative codes that constitute the mental patterns of society, and one could analyze a tragedy solely in terms of those codes. At the same time, however, tragedy deliberately manipulates, distorts, or transforms the given linguistic, intellectual and political codes in the self-conscious structure created by its own internal, aesthetic coherence.[31] In tragedy, unlike in myth, the codes of narrative and society do not cohere. The *Oresteia* is particularly notable for such a deliberate destructuring of the familiar coded

29. Charles Segal, "Greek Tragedy and Society: A Structuralist Perspective," in id., *Interpreting Greek Tragedy: Myth, Poetry, Text* (Ithaca, N.Y.: Cornell University Press, 1986).

30. Ibid., p. 24.

31. Ibid.

patterns of social order: the perversion of ritual sacrifice, the inversion of sexual roles, and the strained diction of failed communication all express the violence done to the ritual, familial, and linguistic codes.

Second, a structural analysis of tragedy places as much emphasis on a work's synchronic structure of polarities as it does on its "syntagmatic" progression of a linearly developing plot. It is precisely this neglect of tragedy's synchronic structure that allows the critics to overlook the radical destructuring and distortion of the familiar codes that mark tragedy. If Segal is right in observing a preoccupation with the "linear progression of the plot" to the neglect of the "synchronic structure of polarities which underlies the cultural values" that operate in the text, then a shift of focus toward the latter will disentangle tragic "message" from mythologized narrative structure and illuminate those decentering, distorting, and transformative moments in the text as present *simultaneously* with, and perhaps arresting, the forward progress of the narrative.

I appropriate this interpretive strategy to examine two related themes in the trilogy in a way that will undermine the secure sense of final narrative closure assumed by most readers of the *Oresteia.* In what follows, I am concerned broadly with the themes of language and sexuality, but specifically with the ways in which the *Oresteia* dramatizes the difficulty of establishing a secure civic discourse and a stable sexual order for a democratic Athens. Even though the linguistic and sexual transgressions that mark the trilogy find their resolutions in the trial scene and its aftermath in the *Eumenides,* I have reason to believe that the solution Aeschylus proposes (imposes?) is neither as stable nor as permanent as it appears. My argument turns on the crucial figure of Athena, that architect of the "solution" to the violence and chaos unleashed, at least in part, by Clytemnestra. For surely it is a mistake to interpret Athena's decisive role without reference to Clytemnestra, not least because the disturbing transgressions of the linguistic, ritual, and sexual order that characterize the *Agamemnon* run right through the entire trilogy to its very end. If this is indeed the case, then even the tragic performance itself will not prove immune to the disturbing transgressions it purportedly ends.

II

The world of the trilogy is riven by violent trespasses against the linguistic and sexual order of the city, trespasses that seek to thwart any final accommodation between the hostile characters and forces. As the *Oresteia* moves closer, at least on the surface, to the generous reconciliation that culminates in the grand procession of the *Eumenides*, trespasses against a stable civic and sexual order multiply precipitously and implicate one another. It is not possible to discuss them all. Two examples that demonstrate the difficulties involved in establishing a secure civic discourse and a stable sexual order for the new democracy should prove adequate to make my point.

Throughout the trilogy, language is in flux. The *Oresteia* is replete with instances of deceit, manipulative persuasion, and miscommunication in the exchange of language. Yet the trilogy makes a coherent point about the ambiguities and ironies of language and so articulates the dangers, difficulties, and violations that attend the founding of an effectively functioning civic discourse. Clytemnestra's manipulative use of persuasive language enables her to overthrow order and illustrates the way in which the trilogy dramatizes the radical instability of the very discourse it aims to establish.

The difficulties that hamper clear human communication are announced by the watchman's last words at the very beginning of the trilogy (33ff.):

> May it only happen. May my king come home, and I
> take up within this hand the hand I love. The rest
> I leave to silence; for an ox stands huge upon
> my tongue. The house itself, could it take voice, might speak
> aloud and plain. I speak to those who understand,
> but if they fail, I have forgotten everything.

The watchman's parting words are significant for more than their tone of foreboding,[32] for more than their warning about what has transpired in the king's absence: the passage is remarkable for the way its juxtaposition of speech and silence, clarity and obscurity, prefigures the play's preoccupation with the exchange of words on stage. Like Heraclitus's description of the oracle, the watchman neither speaks out nor conceals, but gives a sign to be interpreted,[33] while the contrast between *saphestat'* and *lēthomai,* clarity and obscurity, alerts us to a discrepancy between what is said and what is meant. The watchman is here offering

32. Vickers, *Towards Greek Tragedy,* p. 379, notes that the use of the optative in these lines comes to have the reverse effect intended.

33. Since the word the watchman uses, *audō,* means "to speak" or "to say" in connection with the utterance of an oracle, Aeschylus here places us immediately in the midst of the enigmatic and oracular, something in need of interpretation.

us an interpretive principle: silence often speaks volumes, while what needs saying is often left unsaid, and what is said is not always what is meant.

We can use this principle to interpret the ambiguous speeches and their meanings in the play. Clytemnestra exploits it to create a discrepancy between what she says and what she means. She is adept at meaning both more and less than she says. Her purposeful deceit resides in her ability to dissociate what she means from what she says, and her chain of beacon fires demonstrates this skill. While the ingenious signal system serves severally to warn her of Agamemnon's return, display her command of technological resources,[34] and disclose her masculine character (a woman of man-counseling heart), it also demonstrates Clytemnestra's control over the process of communication.[35] Clytemnestra gives two proofs of Troy's fall to the chorus, two speeches that, viewed in the context of communication and exchange, could not be more different. The first speech is a purely technical description of how the message traveled from Troy to Argos, proving Clytemnestra's familiarity with geography,[36] while the content of the second speech is almost oracular in its images and prophetic truth. This juxtaposition of form and content, of message and meaning, amply reveals Clytemnestra's ability to control the process of communication to her advantage. The beacon signal in itself means nothing, it only gains significance in the context of a prearranged system, a code. By explaining her coding system to the chorus, Clytemnestra establishes her skill and knowledge. It is only in the second speech that she reveals to the chorus the signal light's meaning, where she gives a detailed, prophetic account of the destruction and violation at Troy. The separation of the two proofs in two separate speeches, and the separation of form from content, emphasizes the arbitrary connection between what is said and what is meant, the code and its content, that marks the verbal exchanges in the trilogy.[37]

The beacon speeches scene thus serves as both preface and prelude to Clytemnestra's deception of the returning Agamemnon. If the queen "renowned for skill"[38] revealed the principle of her method in the first

34. Betensky, "Aeschylus' *Oresteia,*" pp. 13–14.

35. Simon Goldhill, *Reading Greek Tragedy* (Cambridge: Cambridge University Press, 1986), p. 9.

36. Ibid., p. 14.

37. See ibid., p. 10.

38. One way to etymologize Clytemnestra is as *hē kluta mēdomenē,* an etymology that points to her skill or cunning in plots and deception. See *Etymologicum Magnum,* ed. Thomas Gaisford (1848: Amsterdam: Adolf M. Hakkert, 1967), 521, 17–20.

two speeches, she is now prepared to put that method into practice upon the return of the king. In defending her fidelity and deceiving Agamemnon, Clytemnestra will demonstrate her formidable power to manipulate language through rhetorical persuasion. In her first speech, addressed to the chorus, she reflects on the king's homecoming:

> But now how best to speed my preparation to
> receive my honored lord come home again—what else
> is light more sweet for woman to behold than this,
> to spread the gates before her husband home from war
> and saved by god's hand? (600–604)

A conventional enough sentiment for a wife who anticipates the return of a husband after a ten-year absence. Yet we know the sinister intent behind the queen's haste, that she longs for the sweetness of revenge, secretly glad that Agamemnon has been delivered by the hand of a god into her own hands.

The remainder of this speech is significant for at least two reasons. First, it continues to play out the ironic deception, intending the opposite of what is said, while at the same time it reveals a deeper and more complex layer in Clytemnestra's manipulation of Agamemnon. When she wishes that her husband find her as faithful to the house as on the day he left, she is not lying. When she describes herself as a *gunaika pistēn d' en domois*[39] (a woman faithful to the house) and a *dōmatōn kuna* (a watchdog of the house), she in fact professes fidelity to the house, not to Agamemnon.[40] Clytemnestra's words ring true because there is some truth in them. But this speech is also significant because it sends a message, and we have seen how important the context of message sending and receiving is. "Take this message to the king" looks backward to the "coded message" (*paraggeilantos*) sent forth from Troy to Argos (and forward to another false message (*hupangelos, Choephoroi* 838) that will summon Aegisthus without his bodyguard). Clytemnestra's skill lies in her ability to encode messages the chorus and Agamemnon do not understand, messages, however, that the spectator successfully decodes. From this vantage point, we are able to restore to language "the full function of communication that it has lost on the stage between the protagonists in the drama" and so experience in this process

39. A slight modification in the pronunciation of this phrase yields *gunaik' apistein* (a faithless wife), a pun that any actor, and no doubt the audience, would appreciate.

40. I do not want to push this too far: she then continues to employ the watchdog metaphor in direct relation to Agamemnon, so that when she professes kindness to the king and fierceness to his enemies, we know she means the contrary.

those zones of incommunicability that successful communication requires.

Clytemnestra's second speech reasserts her fidelity to Agamemnon in even stronger terms, and once again expresses sentiments more complex than they at first appear. She recounts to the chorus the pangs of a wife left alone while her husband is gone to war: her anxiety at the outbreak of groundless rumors, her attempt to hang herself and her dreams of his death. Once again, Clytemnestra speaks duplicitously in order to further her plot and deceive Agamemnon, yet she ironically tells the truth. There is no reason to doubt that she has longed for his return, although if at first this longing fed on love, now it surely feeds on hatred: she longs for Agamemnon in order to kill him. Her speech is all the more deceptive because of this core element of truth in it.[41] The queen's speech, so full of allusions to her past anguish, is also full of the vocabulary of rumor, false tales, and lying speeches. As she dwells on the long years of misinformation, false reports, and deceptive messages, we realize that Clytemnestra not only weaves a net of deception around Agamemnon, but that her false language describes itself in the account she constructs of her past experience. The queen's speech refers to itself: it is a deceptive speech about deceptive speeches.[42]

All this prepares for Agamemnon's entry into the house across the purple tapestries.

> Now, my beloved one,
> step from your chariot; yet let not your foot, my lord,
> sacker of Ilium, touch the earth. My maidens there!
> Why this delay? Your task has been appointed you,
> to strew the ground before his feet with tapestries.
> Let there spring up into the house he never hoped
> to see, where justice leads him in, a crimson path.
> In all things else, my heart's unsleeping care shall act
> with the gods' aid to set aright what fate ordained. (905–11)

The image is that of a spider at the center of a web, who will entangle its hapless victim as Clytemnestra will entangle Agamemnon in the robes upon which he treads.[43] The spectators, although perhaps not the chorus, cannot mistake the menace in Clytemnestra's welcome. Yet

41. Betensky, "Aeschylus' *Oresteia*," pp. 15–17, elaborates this interpretation concerning the core of Clytemnestra's past experience, which she now truthfully puts into speech, although to a devious end.

42. Goldhill, *Reading Greek Tragedy*, p. 11.

43. On the spider image and use of nets, see Rabinowitz, "From Force to Persuasion."

Agamemnon is characteristically unconscious of her irony and must feel that as the conquering hero returning home, he well deserves the right to walk on the tapestries. Why, then, does he at first refuse to tread upon the crimson path? Certainly, his refusal heightens the tension in the scene, for once Agamemnon steps upon the tapestries, his fate is sealed. There is good dramatic sense here. But Agamemnon demurs for some very good reasons of his own: he fears being made effeminate; he recoils from such profligate wastage of the substance of his house, and he fears the envy of the gods. It is not his place as a mortal, Greek male to tread upon such wealth. Of course, no such scruples hindered him from sacrificing Iphigeneia, described as the delight of his house, nor did fear of the gods restrain him from trampling upon the altars at Troy. This scene surely recalls those earlier transgressions, yet Agamemnon is again characteristically blind to the meaning of his own deeds and impermeable to Clytemnestra's brilliant indirection and deception. The queen predictably exploits Agamemnon's one-sidedness to her advantage: he fears the gods where he ought to fear his wife. His refusal also prefaces a short, complex, and highly significant exchange that demonstrates the power of Clytemnestra's ability to manipulate language.

Clytemnestra draws Agamemnon out by simply asking him not to cross her will. He responds by saying that his will is his own, it will not be seduced (or corrupted).[44] Clytemnestra then begins a sequence of questions that intends precisely such a seduction. She succeeds by calling into question the context in which the significance of stepping on the tapestries is defined. If Agamemnon had vowed such an expensive offering to a god, would he trample on such luxury? He admits he would. If he were Priam, would he walk on the tapestry? Certainly, Priam would do so. Should he fear envy? Only if he rejects admiration as well. At this turn in the argument Agamemnon censures his wife for her desire for battle, a remark Clytemnestra turns to her advantage by flattering the king's sense of his own power: "Yet for the mighty even to give way is grace." Here, Clytemnestra inverts the reprimand by deflecting the imagery of battle away from herself and onto Agamemnon. Finally, Agamemnon asks if her victory is so important, and the queen

44. The word Agamemnon uses—*diaphtherounta*—can variously be translated as "corrupt," "seduce," "destroy," or "bribe"; see H. G. Liddell, Robert Scott, H. S. Jones, and Roderick McKenzie, *A Greek-English Lexicon* (Oxford: Clarendon Press, 1961), p. 418. Because of the sexual overtones of the exchange, I find "seduce" preferable, especially to Lattimore's rather tepid "make soft."

appropriately concludes the exchange with *pithou,* "be persuaded" (or "obey").

The triumph of Clytemnestra's persuasive power in this scene resides as much in her ability to redefine the context, and so the meaning, of Agamemnon's particular act, as in her exploitation of the ambiguity inherent in language. Under different circumstances or in another moral context, walking on rich carpets neither destroys wealth nor arouses the envy of men and gods. Clytemnestra again shows her ability, as she did with the beacon signals, to reencode meaning in a context chosen by her, and so achieve her persuasion. The queen's use of language is disturbing, and poses significant problems for the inauguration of a civic discourse, because it transgresses established definitions and boundaries, and so undermines the stability of the social order. With Clytemnestra, as with Thucydides' account of the stasis at Corcyra, words are liable to change their meanings.

But how is linguistic instability—the uncertainty involved in establishing a secure civic discourse—implicated in Clytemnestra's transgression of the male-ordered city? What does the difficult foundation of a democratic civic discourse have to do with the transgression and subsequent "repression" of the feminine other? How are gender and political discourse linked in this play? The *Eumenides* and the figure of Athena supply a more specific answer to that question (to which I return at greater length at the end of this chapter), but it is Clytemnestra herself who initially implicates the disruption of gender roles with the insecurity of language through her artful deception of Agamemnon. Clytemnestra swaps private for public, feminine for masculine, and so gains power, by her cunning manipulation of language. She gains access to the throne of Argos through deceit. Because civic discourse is gendered male in the trilogy's sexual code, Clytemnestra's assault through language is also an assault on the masculine prerogative of power.

Clytemnestra's trespasses against gender drive the action of the trilogy in an important sense, although the conflict and resultant suffering that follow cannot be reduced to the opposition between men and women. Other oppositions, most notably between generations (of gods and men) and between Greek and barbarian, overlay and overlap the sexual conflict, although the resolution of the trilogy cannot adequately be understood without reference to the contention and competition between men and women. So, for example, Orestes' opposition to Clytemnestra and Apollo's opposition to the Furies can be interpreted in generational terms:[45] Orestes returns to Argos to claim his patrimony as rightful heir of Agamemnon, while Apollo champions the enlightened views of a younger generation of gods. Yet Orestes also avenges the death of Agamemnon, a man and his father, by killing Clytemnestra, a woman and his mother. Apollo's entire defense of Orestes rests on the proclaimed superiority of the man, and Athena, a younger goddess (who does show respect for the elder Furies), bases her own decision in favor of acquittal on the priority of the male. However one looks at it, Aeschylus arrays the forces in his trilogy so that a confrontation between men and women and their respective values cannot be avoided.

The conflict between men and women does not begin with Clytemnestra's plot to murder Agamemnon and seize power in Argos, although that act (and the reciprocal act of revenge that follows it) is surely decisive for the way in which Aeschylus constructs the "problem" of the feminine other. Typically, the actions of Clytemnestra are overdetermined. First, there is the ancient curse on the house of Atreus: Thyestes seduced the wife of Atreus and then, having feasted on his own children in punishment, cursed the Atreidae. Aegisthus, the only surviving son of Thyestes, thus allies himself with Clytemnestra for reasons of his own private revenge. Then there is the abduction of Helen, a violation of guest friendship that sets in motion the disastrously costly Trojan War, the pursuit of which required Agamemnon's slaughter of Iphigeneia, perverse sacrifice to Artemis's anger at Zeus. Finally, there is Apollo's failed seduction of Cassandra and the Trojan prophetess's return to Argos with the conquering hero.

Here is a formidable list of reasons to explain Clytemnestra's act: ancient curse, revenge, longing turned to anger, jealousy. For R. P. Winnington-Ingram, however, these are all secondary to the central feature of Clytemnestra's anomalous personality: for Clytemnestra "hated Agamemnon not simply because he had killed her child, not because she loved Aegisthus, but out of a jealousy that was not jealousy of Chryseis or Cassandra, but of Agamemnon himself and his status as a man. For she herself is of manly temper, and the dominance of a man is abhorrent to her."[46] The blow struck against Agamemnon, then, is not merely a blow of vengeance, but also "a blow struck for her personal liberty."

45. As do the Furies themselves at *Eumenides* 778–79.

46. R. P. Winnington-Ingram, *Studies in Aeschylus* (Cambridge: Cambridge University Press, 1983), p. 105.

The watchman and chorus (the latter somewhat grudgingly) recognize Clytemnestra's formidable power. The former describes her as a woman with a man-counseling heart, and the ingenious signal light she devises and uses demonstrates her masculine control of resources to us and to the chorus. Both watchman and chorus praise her ability to speak like a man, and both mention her power (*kratei,* 10; *kratos,* 258). Finally, the word *kratei* marks the climax of her verbal dual with Agamemnon. Clytemnestra's anomalous character thus accounts for her anomalous actions. It is no coincidence that the queen enters on the word *nikē* (victory).

For Clytemnestra must not only gain a victory over Agamemnon, she must also prove herself stronger. This she does on her chosen field of battle, the purple tapestries. I have already examined this scene in terms of verbal deceit. Here I only want to comment briefly on the reversal of sexual roles and on the pervasive images of war, battle, and combat. Clytemnestra has already proved herself to be unnaturally knowledgeable about things martial in her description of Troy's defeat and the Greek plunder of the city (320–51). That account, however, is not wholly consistent with a role traditionally considered male. Michael Gagarin has noticed that while Clytemnestra plays a male role, she continues to represent a woman's point of view and feminine values. After announcing the Greek victory (320) she dwells upon the fate of the conquered, who are now enslaved (326–29), before she proceeds to describe the rather limited joys of the victors (330–37) and warn them against despoiling the altars of the city. Gagarin concludes that this view of the situation "with its concern for and understanding of the plight of the defeated survivors and its very limited sense of joy at the victory, can properly be called female."[47] Moreover, Clytemnestra's account contrasts markedly with that of the herald, who mentions the suffering of the army before Troy only to emphasize an unrestrained joy at the victory and the destruction of the holy places. So while Clytemnestra is well versed in the councils of men, she maintains what is traditionally considered a feminine sensibility.[48]

47. Gagarin, *Aeschylean Drama,* p. 93.

48. Two interesting points come to mind here: first, seeing the world from another's point of view, as Clytemnestra does, is tragedy's singular, although not unique, achievement. Second, Hannah Arendt defines political thinking as the ability to see the world from the point of view of somebody else; this she calls representative thinking (see Arendt, *Eichmann in Jerusalem: A Report on the Banality of Evil* [New York: Viking Press, 1964; repr., Penguin Books, 1977], p. 49). But like Agamemnon, Clytemnestra loses that capacity and sees only one side of a complex issue.

This conjunction of opposites is no less present in the carpet scene, where Clytemnestra joins battle with Agamemnon. The exchange between queen and king is littered with words of war: *machēs* (940), battle or combat; *to nikasthai* (941), the victor or the conqueror; *dēerios* (942), fight, battle, or contest; *katestrammai* (956), to be subdued, compelled, or subjected by another.[49] Clytemnestra will subdue Agamemnon as the conqueror subdued Troy. Yet here, too, something more complex occurs, because Clytemnestra first chooses to do battle with cunning words, not sharp swords, as the weapon of choice. She defeats Agamemnon in verbal contest so that she may all the more surely defeat him physically. Although Clytemnestra has a penchant for battle, she employs means the Greeks traditionally associated with women. Not the least of these is her final appeal to Agamemnon's masculine vanity, a danger of which the king is characteristically unaware.[50] The chorus will later complain of Agamemnon's ignominious death at the hands of a woman—and in the bath, not on the battlefield—a tacit acknowledgement that Clytemnestra, a woman, is more intelligent, and so stronger, than Agamemnon, a man.

Agamemnon portrays Clytemnestra as unnatural: it is not "normal" for the woman to best the man, much less kill him; it is not "natural" for the woman to want power (*kratos*) or to rule, although this is surely what motivates the queen, nor is it natural that a mother reject her children as Clytemnestra has Electra and Orestes. Aeschylus portrays the anomalous nature of Clytemnestra with a cluster of dragon, snake, and monster images, images reinforced by the chorus's allusion to the crimes of the Lemnian women.[51] But the perversion of the natural order is nowhere expressed in such terrifying terms as when Clytemnestra inverts the ritual language of fertility and death, life-giving rain and death-oozing blood. As she stands over the corpse of Agamemnon, she overturns not only the gendered order of the family and the city, but the order of the cosmos as well:

> Thus he went down, and the life struggled out of him;
> and as he died he spattered me with the dark red
> and violent driven rain of bitter savored blood
> to make me glad, as gardens stand among the showers
> of God in glory at the birthtime of the buds. (1388–92)

49. The list comes from J. Peter Euben, *The Tragedy of Political Theory: The Road Not Taken* (Princeton, N.J.: Princeton University Press, 1990), p. 74.

50. Winnington-Ingram, *Studies in Aeschylus,* p. 93.

51. Rabinowitz, "From Force to Persuasion," pp. 165–67.

Clytemnestra has transgressed the natural order so that blood and death bring rain and life in this unparalleled travesty of ritual language.[52]

I do not want to neglect the fact that much of what the queen does, she does in reaction to what Agamemnon has done to her and as part of her role in playing out the family's curse. Thus we must not forget that Agamemnon sacrificed Iphigeneia, was away at war for ten years, and then returned with Cassandra. Agamemnon surely insulted Clytemnestra in her status as a mother by killing Iphigeneia and in her status as a wife through his neglect of her and his infidelity.[53] I think a good case can be made in favor of Clytemnestra, although I am less interested in the extent of her "guilt" (as Vickers notes, she herself does not feel guilty) than in the *effects* her actions have on the linguistic and sexual order and on the way in which that order is (de)stabilized in the trilogy.

Significant for my analysis is that Clytemnestra gains power in Argos through her manipulative use of language, for her deliberate trespasses against the boundaries of both linguistic and sexual order. As Clytemnestra manipulates language to confound the male-ordered civic discourse, she joins those other transgressing women—Antigone, Medea, Agave—who pose a serious threat to the order of the patriarchal city. Clytemnestra challenges the hierarchies and rules of the public masculine world by leaving the interior space of the house for the exterior spaces of the city, by exchanging the powerlessness of a woman for the power of a man. Clytemnestra turns the linguistic and sexual order of the trilogy upside down.

III

My analysis of the previous scenes, like the trilogy itself, necessarily converges on the *Eumenides* and its promise of reconciliation. The final question I wish to consider concerns the extent to which the concluding play of the trilogy redeems this promise by solving the twin problems of establishing an effectively functioning civic discourse and integrating the feminine other into the democratic order of the polis. To do this, I shall comment on the trial itself, on the figure of Athena, and on Aeschylus's use of theatricality. I turn to these final scenes—to the trial of Orestes, the establishment of the Areopagus, Athena's persuasion of

52. See Vickers on the details of ritual parody, *Towards Greek Tragedy*, pp. 398–99.
53. Winnington-Ingram, *Studies in Aeschylus*, p. 111.

the Furies, the final procession—because how one reads the dynamics, outcome, and aftermath of the trial to a large degree determines how one understands the trilogy as a whole.

Critics have long noticed a double progression in the movement of the *Oresteia,* that action and imagery cohere.[54] The trilogy moves simultaneously toward the resolution of conflict and toward transparency in speech, twin aspects of the trilogy's composition that complement and mutually reinforce each other. On the level of action, legal justice replaces blood vengeance, Orestes is acquitted, the Furies are reconciled and take up their new duties in conjunction with the Areopagus, Argos and Athens are allied, sacrificial ritual is restored, men and women return to their proper places. The natural order of the world is set right. At the level of imagery and linguistic texture, Ann Lebeck has powerfully described how the *Oresteia* moves from enigmatic utterance to clear statement, from riddle to solution. Through its use of imagery and in the texture of its poetry, the trilogy transforms darkness into light, the blood-stained robes of *Agamemnon* into the festival garments of the final pageant, the dense poetry and claustrophobic atmosphere of the earlier plays into the comparatively straightforward and clear statements of the *Eumenides.*[55]

Yet a disturbing countermovement that keeps alive and intact the tensions and oppositions of the earlier plays, disappointing our hopes for a permanent resolution to the conflicts of the *Oresteia,* lies underneath, or perhaps alongside, the triumphant celebration of the well-ordered polis that crowns the trilogy. A number of ambiguities persist in the final scenes of the *Eumenides* that challenge our expectations of harmony, fulfillment, and reconciliation. First, of course, is the trial itself. Orestes is acquitted, but as Athena points out, this hardly constitutes an unalloyed victory for him or defeat and dishonor for the Furies (795). The oracle has come to pass, but this does not mean that Orestes is free of all guilt. Its wording is significantly negative: Orestes was to suffer no harm for what he did (799). An absence of punishment does not necessarily imply an absence of responsibility. The vote is also tied, and this in itself attests to the uncertainty of the case. But depending on

54. Ann Lebeck, *The Oresteia: A Study in Language and Structure* (Cambridge, Mass.: Harvard University Press, 1971), is the most complete, but see also Rabinowitz, "From Force to Persuasion" cited above.

55. One other way in which Aeschylus achieves this transformation is to revise the myth of the Delphic oracle's foundation in a way that anticipates the peaceful settlement that ends the trilogy.

how one interprets the voting procedure (another ambiguity), "the vote of Athena" means either that the jury of twelve citizens split equally, and Athena's was a casting vote in favor of Orestes, or else that the human jury numbered eleven, with Athena its twelfth, divine, member, who votes for Orestes and so achieves acquittal by a tie. The latter possibility means that a majority of the Athenian jurors voted *against* Orestes and Apollo and *for* Clytemnestra and the Furies.[56] Moreover, that Athena ultimately decides the case by either making or breaking a tie, and in so doing displaces the verdict from the human to the divine realm, indicates that human judgment and justice cannot decide the matter. It is Athena, not the legal process, that settles the conflict.

Although Athena ultimately decides the case based on grounds given by Apollo, there are a number of reasons why we ought to be skeptical of that god's authority and so of the triumph of the values for which he stands—those of polis, Greek, reason, progress, and the male—over the values of oikos, barbarian, passion, tradition, and the female. First, Apollo's dismissal of, and obvious contempt for, the Furies and their claims is counterproductive. For it is Athena, not Apollo, who actually fulfills the oracle. Moreover, Apollo is an essentially inconstant figure throughout the trilogy, and so his claim to partisan victory is suspect. Apollo sends the avenging Atreidae against Troy and a plague on the Greek avengers, destroys the Trojan Cassandra, and then sends Orestes to avenge her death and the death of Agamemnon.[57] Apollo is thus not always for the male, and on occasion he works with the Furies, rather than against them. Nor are the Furies always opposed to the younger gods or solely concerned with marriage: they have previously been linked with the will of Zeus, Orestes fears them if he neglects to avenge his father (*Choephoroi* 269–96), Cassandra associates the Furies

56. In *Form and Meaning,* pp. 65–6, Kitto makes an interesting and persuasive, although not conclusive, case for eleven jurors: he notices that between lines 711 and 733, Aeschylus has composed ten couplets and one triplet for a total of eleven verses. This would indicate eleven and not twelve jurors, a vote cast for each couplet, otherwise the playwright would have to send two voters to the urn at once, which makes no stage sense. The final triplet allows enough time for the eleventh juror to go to the urn and back to his seat, and then for Athena herself to approach the urn before beginning her speech. This makes onstage sense for Kitto, but it does not clarify the ambiguity in the language of the text, where, at 741, Athena says, in the optative, "victory is Orestes' even if the votes divide equally" (Lattimore's translation interpolates "other votes" to convey the sense that there are twelve jurors, but this is not what the text says), and again, at 752, where she says "equal is the number of ballots." Both phrases could include Athena's vote, so I am inclined to read the human vote as against Orestes.

57. Deborah Roberts, *Apollo and His Oracle in the Oresteia* (Göttingen: Vandenhoeck & Ruprecht, 1984), p. 70.

with the curse on the house of Atreus, and the Argive army is sent to Troy as an avenging Fury. The scope of the Furies' commitments is as wide as Apollo is ambiguous. Surely Aeschylus ends the trilogy in a way that partially vindicates Apollo by fulfilling his oracle. But through the ambiguous portrayal of the god, he also points to the tremendous human suffering along the way, suggesting the limits of such a vindication in a conclusion that is disturbing in that it both "resolves and leaves unresolved."[58]

Finally, there is evidence external to the trilogy indicating that an Athenian audience would suspect an Apollo who had previously gone over to the Persians and who has close associations with the Dorian (i.e., pro-Spartan) aristocracies.[59] A god who could be wrong about politics, Winnington-Ingram reasons, "is not necessarily right about men and women."[60] There is good reason, then, to be somewhat skeptical of Apollo's authority and arguments in his defense of Orestes.

Despite the momentous outcome in favor of Orestes, the trial is not the climax of the play. Even though Orestes is acquitted, the play is far from over. Almost a third of it, some 300 lines, still remains. Athena must persuade the Furies that they are not dishonored, that Orestes' acquittal does not mean their defeat, and that they should accept their new position as tutelary deities of the homicide court. Only when the Furies accede to Athena's combination of blandishments, threats, and respectful persuasion, does the reader (or the audience) feel secure.

Yet this feeling of security and release proves in no way permanent or conclusive. Even though Orestes is acquitted and the Furies are incorporated into the new order as the Eumenides (Kindly Ones), disturbing images and memories from the earlier plays continue to mar the joyous finale and provide both context for, and threat to, the trilogy's ultimate achievement. The whole citizenry of Athens participates in a pageant in which the luminous torchlight and the purple robes of the processional recall the sinister signal fires and the purple-stained carpet of *Agamemnon* as much as they joyously signify their transformation.

There is one other way in which the final scenes of the *Oresteia* recall both what has gone before and how precarious its accomplishments are. Later in this chapter I comment on the Furies' hymn to justice and the way in which Athena manipulates the ambiguities in the language

58. Ibid., p. 72.
59. Thomson, *Aeschylus and Athens*, p. 278.
60. Winnington-Ingram, *Studies in Aeschylus*, p. 121.

of *dikē* to establish the law court in the face of the goddesses' opposition. I do not want to discuss that scene any more than necessary here, except to note that when Athena echoes the Furies' sentiments in admonishing her citizens "never to cast fear utterly from the city," she, too, reminds the reader (and audience) of the conflict, perversion, and pollution that have gone before. Despite the "happy ending," as Brian Vickers remarks, "it is the violence and perversion that live on in the memory." The play thus creates a "remarkably powerful image of those threats against human being which are a corollary of our fragile existence." Vickers concludes, echoing Athena, that "reading the *Oresteia* makes one afraid for one's life."[61]

The founding of the democratic polis is a precarious achievement, however, not only because it rests on the outcome of an inconclusive trial, and because of the disturbing echoes in the *Eumenides,* but because the new order will not entirely do away with the conflict that arises when we find ourselves forced to choose between alternatives that equally claim our concern and commitment, like Agamemnon at Aulis and Orestes at Argos. Certainly, the collectivity of citizens, together with the newly instituted law court, will mitigate and mediate those tensions and oppositions that engender tragic experience, at least a little and for a while. But men and women will always be torn between conflicting commitments: to the oikos or the polis, to home, place, family, and friends on the one hand and to glory, honor, adventure, and immortal fame won at the expense of the former, on the other. Although fathers will not always be asked to choose between a daughter and their army, mothers and wives between a husband and a daughter, nor sons between a mother and a father, most of us will experience the difficulty of balancing career and family in a society that does not honor both equally. For nowhere does Aeschylus indicate that human beings can "structure their lives and commitments so that in the ordinary course of events they will be able to stay clear of serious conflict."[62] Nowhere does the *Oresteia* indicate that wisdom comes without suffering or that there is goodness without fragility. Wisdom must continually be rewon, while the goodness of the city depends on the unceasing and tireless efforts of its citizens. The trilogy does not let us forget that faith placed in finite solutions to complex human dilemmas is faith misplaced. The newly founded civic order, Aeschylus suggests, with its impartial and

61. *Towards Greek Tragedy,* p. 425.
62. Nussbaum, *Fragility of Goodness,* p. 51.

more comprehensive political and legal institutions, is not *the* solution to the problem of *dikē*, but it is perhaps *a* solution.

If it is true that from the opening lines of the *Agamemnon* to the final scenes of the *Eumenides,* the trilogy leads toward a resolution in the democratic polis, then it is equally true that the lines of that resolution converge on the figure of Athena. They do so in two ways.

I have already suggested that the *Oresteia* seeks a solution to the cycle of blood vengeance in the stability of civic discourse. As in Plato's *Republic,* the problem for Aeschylus lies in an ambiguous excess of meaning, a depth in signification that proliferates competing claims rather than reduces or resolves them. More often than not, characters use this ambiguity in language to set up barriers to communication rather than to establish it. The examples of linguistic transgression that occur throughout the trilogy thus challenge our ability to specify meaning in language, to control the power of speech, and so to rely on the stable categories that constitute the basis of the social order. In these terms, the foundation of the law court and the subsequent verdict in favor of acquittal aim to fix a meaning for *dikē,* to establish once and for all a secure civic discourse in which contending claims and competing interests might be adjudicated, if not reconciled. Yet, as we have seen, equal votes comprise that decision, an indication that the claims of each side weigh equally in the balance and that the newly formed legal institutions of the city cannot solve the problem of *dikē*. Aeschylus must displace the final decision to Athena's divine agency, a displacement that is crucial for a proper understanding of the trilogy's resolution. First, and most obviously, it is crucial because as a dramatic device, it heightens the tension in the scene. Moreover, such a displacement points once again to the failure of human communication and interpretation that persistently mars the trilogy. It is most important, however, because it places the burden of decision, hence of reconciliation, on Athena. For Athena is an interesting figure in Aeschylus's articulation of the discursive and sexual economy of the trilogy.[63]

Athena is important for the way in which she establishes linguistic order, and so justice, in the *Eumenides*. In the stasimon sung to justice (490–565), the Furies appeal to a sense of *dikē* familiar from the earlier plays of the trilogy. Theirs is a justice that relies on fear, respect, and reverence for the inherited bonds of obligation—without fear of just

63. The following discussion of Athena follows that of Goldhill, *Reading Greek Tragedy,* pp. 30–31.

retribution, parents would not feel themselves safe in the presence of their children. The result would be either anarchy or despotism. The Furies understand the social order to be coterminous with blood relations. They thus protect society by prosecuting crimes that violate the kinship structures of society, but in particular they are concerned with transgressions of the kind the matricide Orestes commits.[64] They understand justice to be identical with the reciprocal revenge of a *dikēphoron* (bringer of retribution).

Athena echoes the Furies' sentiment virtually word for word when she establishes the law court that will finally render justice and terminate the cycle of vengeance (681–710). She, too, urges the jurors and the audience "not to cast fear utterly from the city," nor to live in anarchy or despotism, but according to a middle way that is best. Yet Athena cannot mean what the Furies mean by *justice,* even though they use the same word. Why, then, do the Furies allow Athena to impanel a jury that will decide the case in other than their terms and so against them? Surely something more is happening here than merely the inclusion of the Furies in a wider understanding of justice.[65] Athena (or Aeschylus) plays upon the shifting and multivalent sense of justice at work in the trilogy. It is precisely this ambiguity in the meaning of *dikē* that enables Athena to establish the court against the better judgment of the Furies. Where the Furies demand *dikē* as reciprocal punishment, Athena offers *dikē* as law court, as legal judgment. She chastens the Furies with such shifting terms when she says "you wish to be called, not act, just" (430). That Athena and the Furies each appeal to *dikē* does not indicate, then, that they agree on its meaning.[66] In fact, given that the Furies violently oppose the decision for acquittal, we have to conclude that even in the end, they do not abandon their sense of *dikē* as reciprocal punishment. Athena establishes the law court and institutes a new legal order over the protests of the Furies by playing on the ambiguity of the term *dikē* itself. Athena here has recourse to the same strategy and tactics used by Clytemnestra.

Even though Athena founds the Areopagus and in so doing fixes a

64. Aeschylus downplays the fact that if Orestes did not avenge the murder of his father, the Furies would pursue him for his negligence.

65. This inclusionary thesis is the argument of H. D. F. Kitto, *Greek Tragedy: A Literary Study* (1961; 5th ed., London: Methuen, 1978): 94–5, Podlecki, *Political Background of Aeschylean Tragedy,* pp. 78–79, and Thomson, *Aeschylus and Athens,* p. 289.

66. Though this is the conclusion of Lloyd-Jones, in *Justice of Zeus,* 2d ed., pp. 94–95.

meaning for *dikē,* her work with respect to the Furies is far from over. Believing themselves dishonored by the younger generation of gods who favored Orestes' acquittal, the Furies now rage against Athens, threatening to poison and blight the land and its inhabitants. Through a combination of patient persuasion and discrete manipulation, threats backed by Zeus's thunderbolts and sincere promises, Athena charms the Furies into accepting the verdict and their new place as beneficent *metoikoi* of the city, as well as their transformed status as tutelary deities of the homicide court. Athena's is thus a victory of persuasive rhetoric:

> I admire the eyes
> of Persuasion, who guided the speech of my mouth
> toward these, when they were reluctant and wild.
> Zeus, who guides men's speech in councils, was too
> strong; and my ambition
> for good wins out in the whole issue. (970–75)

Just as the trilogy begins with Zeus Xenios (the god of guest friendship) and ends with Zeus Agoraios (the god of public meetings), it begins with the forceful persuasion of Clytemnestra and ends with the forceful persuasion of Athena.

The figure of Athena is also important to the resolution of the trilogy because she occupies an ambiguous space in Athens's sexual economy. A female goddess, Athena votes for Orestes on sexual grounds, for she is, as she says, "always for the male, with all my heart and strongly on my father's side" (737–38). Moreover, descended as she is solely from her father, Zeus, Athena has no mother and so has experienced none of the ties of commitment and continuity of place the *Oresteia* traditionally associates with the feminine. Here she seems to validate Apollo's argument for the primacy of the male as the "true" parent. Yet she is also a warrior and a virgin, and so doubly rejects the role of a woman in a patriarchal society. A trilogy that begins with Clytemnestra's usurpation of Agamemnon's power and prerogative ends with Athena's own transgression of the accepted boundaries of gender identification.

By now it should be clear that both in her ability to manipulate language and in her usurpation of what were traditionally considered male roles, Athena recalls Clytemnestra. But what are we to make of such a disturbing association? Does Athena allied with Clytemnestra undo all the work that Athena allied with Zeus has accomplished? The final play of the trilogy does conclude happily with the establishment of a civic discourse and the integration of the feminine other into the city's social order. Yet the play performed before the city it celebrates has depicted with immense force the internal tensions and oppositions of that discourse, not only in the clash of sexual and social interests but also in its challenge to the very possibility of the formulation of a civic language and sexual order grounded in rational legal procedure. Already so full of transgressions and manipulations, the *Oresteia* ends neither with the final restoration of a natural or "normal" order nor with the unambiguous achievement of clear and transparent communication. A reconciliation between men and women is achieved, but it is achieved by a figure who embodies all the transgressions of gender definition that the trilogy has sought to resolve. A civic discourse based on rational legal principles is established, but by a figure who transgresses its norms, and by means that partake of the persuasive rhetoric of manipulation the trilogy has fought to mitigate.

I therefore do not wholly agree with Brian Vickers when he argues, in reference to Clytemnestra, that "the final stages of the *Eumenides* complete Aeschylus' exorcism of her, a sustained concentration of moral disapproval rarely equalled in literature."[67] If Clytemnestra is exorcised, then, as we have seen, she is also resurrected in the figure of Athena. The man-woman Clytemnestra, who kills her husband, finds her counterpart in the god-goddess Athena, who similarly crosses the boundaries of gender definition.[68] Nor do I agree with H. D. F. Kitto that the *Eumenides* solves the problem of *dikē*.[69] If the achievement of the law court is to fix a meaning for *dikē* and so institute the shared civic language necessary to the polis, then the integrity of that language is violated at the very moment it is established. The figure that closes the trilogy cannot but remind us of the figure who opens it. Athena's association with Clytemnestra brings the *Oresteia* full circle, and so reopens all the negotiations the trilogy had hoped to settle.

There is one final way in which Athena recalls Clytemnestra and the uncertainty of *Agamemnon*, and so undermines the very order she, and by implication the *Oresteia*, strives to establish. Vernant has commented on the reflexive dimension of Aeschylus's trilogy. In particular, he has pointed out the manner in which the trial scene of the *Eumenides* invites the citizen-spectators to think of themselves as jurors (a role

67. Brian Vickers, *Towards Greek Tragedy*, p. 423.
68. On the importance of Clytemnestra for an understanding of Athena, see Winnington-Ingram, *Studies in Aeschylus*, 101–31.
69. Kitto, *Greek Tragedy* (1961), p. 95.

with which they would be intimately familiar) and judge the actors, the actions on stage, and the overall performance itself. Having witnessed a judgment on stage, the *Oresteia* asks its audience to reflect on the nature of judgment by rendering a judgment about the activity of judging. On another level, however, the trilogy reflects on its own activity in a decidedly more ambivalent fashion. I have been arguing that the text turns back and in upon itself in a movement that resists closure and so the hierarchical organization of values—the creation of a center—that the narrative establishes. It does so, in part, through its use of theatricality, by which I mean how the playwright calls attention to the performance itself as a theatrical spectacle.[70] Aeschylus employs this technique with surprising results in the *Oresteia,* most notably in the planning and execution of Agamemnon's murder. I have already discussed that sequence of scenes that culminate in the king's fateful step upon the crimson tapestries and analyzed them in terms of gender reversal and the manipulation of language. That interpretation portrayed Clytemnestra as something of a *strategos* in her own right, one who confronts and defeats her enemy in battle. I want to examine that scene afresh, this time in terms of its theatricality, and link it up with Athena and the trial of Orestes, in order to consider its significance for the trilogy as a whole.

Likening Clytemnestra to a general positioning and directing her troops as if for battle is certainly a plausible reading of that fatal encounter. Far more powerful, in this context, however, is to understand Clytemnestra in the role of a director, producer, or even playwright. She has prepared an elaborate scene, beginning with the system of signal fires, written a welcoming script for Agamemnon, assembled her deadly props, and even shown impatience when her maids miss their cue and fail to spread the tapestries in a timely fashion. In this play within a play, Clytemnestra writes, directs, acts, and produces the murder of her husband, and she has been many years in the plotting.

I have also noted how, through her persuasive rhetoric and her ambiguous sexuality, the figure of Athena recalls Clytemnestra. Here I want to point to a similarity between Clytemnestra's "staging" of Aga-

70. On theatricality, see Charles Segal, "Time, Theater, and Knowledge in the Tragedy of Oedipus," in *Edipo: Il teatro greco e la cultura europea,* ed. Bruno Gentili and Roberto Pretagostini (Rome: Edizioni dell'Ateneo, 1986), p. 463ff., and Froma I. Zeitlin, "Playing the Other: Theater, Theatricality and the Feminine in Greek Drama," in *Nothing to Do with Dionysus? Athenian Drama in Its Social Context,* ed. John A. Winkler and Froma I. Zeitlin, 63–95 (Princeton, N.J.: Princeton University Press, 1990).

memnon's murder and Athena's "staging" of Orestes' trial, a similarity that cuts across other aspects shared by these two figures. There are a number of ways in which the trial "staged" by Athena recalls the dramatic theater of Clytemnestra. First, a trial recalls the theater in its physical aspects, with a judge and jury seated on a raised platform or "stage," with testifying witnesses entering and exiting on cue, and with an audience of citizens, all potential jurors, in attendance. Second, the progress of a trial is similar to a "plot" (in the sense of both drama and intrigue), where identity and character are exposed, the truth about past or present actions revealed, and where a verdict or judgment is rendered on the protagonist. In establishing the Areopagus, calling the witnesses, selecting the jury and rendering the final decision, Athena writes the script, directs the "action" and determines the outcome of Orestes' trial much as a playwright or *chorēgos* would do a tragic performance. Athena's staging of Orestes' trial thus recalls Clytemnestra's own elaborate staging in *Agamemnon.*

But surely this pushes a point too far. After all, Clytemnestra commits a murder, Athena merely judges one. While I do not want to deny this important difference, I do want to emphasize once again the method of persuasion that Athena employs and the ambiguous space she occupies, disturbing characteristics she shares with Clytemnestra that *also* make it possible for her to end the bloodshed. But what does this mean for the play as a whole? The trilogy equates Clytemnestra, plotting, deceit, and verbal manipulation with being the playwright/producer/actress of one's own drama. Two points follow from this. First, we are forced to recall that theater itself relies on plots, plotting, illusion, deceit, and verbal ambiguity, in short, all of Clytemnestra's devices.[71] This alone should cast some doubt on the ability of the tragedy to render clear and secure meanings. But when we associate those same elements with Athena, then the law court, the justice it brings, and the *Oresteia* itself (and perhaps tragedy?) all share the same radical insecurities in regard to the stability of linguistic and sexual categories that Clytemnestra's theater so disturbingly conveys.

One reason the carpet scene is so powerful, and the trial of Orestes so awesome, is precisely because they, too, like a tragedy, are staged, and as such raise disturbing questions about the ability of the tragic performance itself to establish a reliable context for communication. If

71. See Zeitlin, "Playing the Other," pp. 81–83 on plots, deceit, and intrigue in Greek tragedy.

the theatricality of Clytemnestra and Athena so easily manipulates Agamemnon and the Furies, are not the spectators of the performance also susceptible to a similar manipulation by the playwright and his play? This further implies that as the *Oresteia* attempts to end the cycle of blood vengeance by fixing a clear and unambiguous meaning for *dikē,* it cannot escape or evade the ambiguities, uncertainties, and difficulties of speech dramatized by the play within the play. If I am right about Aeschylus's self-referential use of theatricality, then the *Oresteia* not only interrogates the "success" of Athena's founding, but also provides a powerful example of man's drive to circumscribe the world in intellectual and rational terms and a similarly powerful example of the limitations of that attempt.[72]

There is no final closure here, no unalloyed triumph of men over women, polis over oikos, new over old, what is chosen over what is inherited, reason over passion. Rather, the end of the trilogy introduces a series of new transgressions that forces the narrative to turn back upon itself in a destructuring movement that questions the very foundations of its own accomplishment. Through the figure of Athena, we have learned that the boundaries that constitute language and society are always already transgressed.[73] This final scene of ambiguous reconciliation, orchestrated by such a paradoxical and ambivalent figure, should draw us up short and force us to reflect on the violence concealed by constructed teleologies and hierarchies that appear "natural."

So much is true of the *Oresteia* itself: the trilogy also transgresses the "norms" of linguistic and sexual order in the very act, and in the very space, in which it establishes them. The *Oresteia* surely institutes and legitimates a democratically constituted hierarchy of values, establishes norms of inclusion and exclusion, and creates bonds of membership by drawing boundaries. But the trilogy also shows us how such boundaries are constituted, that they are ultimately political, and that such limits are transgressed the very moment they are established. The problem of *dikē* is not solved in the *Eumenides,* but the trilogy as a whole shows us that we cannot live without such (temporary) solutions. The *Oresteia* lays bare the construction of those solutions as enabling fictions, calling attention to their incomplete nature and revealing to the spectators how

72. Here I paraphrase Segal in "Time, Theater, and Knowledge," p. 463. Although Segal is describing the theater of Sophocles, I think his description applies equally well to the *Oresteia.*

73. This is part quotation and part paraphrase of Goldhill, *Language, Sexuality, Narrative,* p. 281.

a normal and normalizing order constructs the feminine as abject other, as the very constitutive outside of its own possibility, even when such an order harbors the most democratic of intentions. The trilogy thus as much reminds the audience of the violent exclusions and subordinations that constitute the democratic city in which they live as it validates that city.

In anticipation of all these reasons, this chapter began with the suggestion that no Greek tragedy could better illuminate the current controversy over democratic hopes and disciplinary reversals than Aeschylus's *Oresteia.* That suggestion framed a series of reflections on the dilemma—in contemporary theory—over the intentions and effects of a democratically achieved consensus. The present contest over the meaning of democracy vacillates between the quest to instantiate norms of consensus and the suspicion that such rationally achieved agreement is a regulative ideal, one more strategy that effectively masks the mechanism of power as it produces normalized and disciplined selves and citizens for the effective functioning of the order. That choice—between the regulative democratic ideal of critical theory and the endless genealogical subversion of democratic codes—was too narrowly construed and tended to resist any alternative path through the unstable terrain of contemporary democratic politics. Yet if we are to respect difference in our own increasingly heterogeneous and diverse society, and if we wish to preserve the preconditions of democratic governance as well, another route must be found. Aeschylus's treatment of the "feminine" as the constitutive other has been particularly helpful for illuminating a politics of identity and difference and in charting the dangerous territory of a democratic politics. The *Oresteia,* on this telling, can be made to yield a democratic politics of disturbance that maintains a commitment to the ideals of democratic consensus even as it disrupts democracy's normalizing effects. Such is Aeschylus's contribution to the contemporary contest over the meaning of democracy.

The central burden of this chapter has been to demonstrate that the *Oresteia* both celebrates the triumph of a democratic civic discourse and exposes the legacy of violence, exclusion, and subordination directed at the "feminine other" that accompanies that triumph. In a double movement, the trilogy articulates a positive vision of democratic life that seeks to disrupt and disturb the forces of normalization such a vision entails. This reading of Aeschylus has indicated that such forces of disturbance persist right through to the trilogy's very end (Athena as doubly ambiguous), enabling the *Oresteia* to help formulate a democratic sensibility that relentlessly politicizes the founding exclusions that constitute democratic practice (whether religious, cultural or sexual), while at the same time providing a democratic identity and order against which to struggle. That is one way in which the *Oresteia* negotiates the tension between a democratic critical theory and a genealogical critique of democracy.

The *Oresteia* achieves this, of course, not by dissolving that tension, but by deepening it. Democracy in the *Oresteia* requires the stable foundations of law grounded in rational legal procedure: justice as legal judgment replaces justice as reciprocal revenge. Yet as we have seen, genealogical critique uncovers a democratic reason embodied in the newly founded law court that is masculine in gender and founded squarely on women's exclusion from, and subordination to, the male-ordered polis.[74] Moreover, that foundation is itself traversed by its own fault lines, irregularities that portend further seismic disturbances in the bedrock of democracy. As a figure who already transgresses the very discursive and sexual norms of the democratic polis she aims to establish, Athena herself embodies the "paradox of founding" that Habermas's consensus theory of democracy seeks to evade.[75] Despite the celebratory and triumphant ending, the *Oresteia* constructs the meaning of the democratic founding, and so of democracy itself, as open to further contest, struggle, and renegotiation. Read this way, Aeschylus's trilogy alerts us to the antidemocratic preconditions and practices of democratic rule *and* to the positive role played by a "democratic politics of disturbance," a politics that, like the disturbing transgressions of Clytemnestra and Athena, "projects new challenges to old relations of identity and difference, disrupts the dogmatism of settled understandings and exposes violences and exclusions in fixed arrangements of democratic rule."[76] Such a reading of the *Oresteia* indicates one way in which a democratic critical theory and a genealogical critique of democracy, if properly understood, might contribute to the formidable task of democratizing difference.

It might even be the case that what I have said about Athena and the

74. Thomson, *Aeschylus and Athens,* p. 288, goes so far as to say that "Aeschylus regarded the subordination of women (quite correctly) as an indispensable condition of democracy."

75. On the place of gender in Habermas's work, see Nancy Fraser, "What's Critical about Critical Theory? The Case of Habermas and Gender," in *Feminism as Critique,* ed. Drucilla Cornell and Seyla Benhabib (New York: Routledge, 1990), pp. 31–56.

76. Connolly, "Democracy and Territoriality," p. 473.

Oresteia applies to tragedy as well. In the theater of Dionysus, the citizen-spectators come to learn that the categories of society are never as stable as they appear. During a civic ritual that celebrates the city and its democratic traditions, a play like Aeschylus's *Oresteia* both participates in that celebration *and* radically disrupts the "normalized" order it constructs.

Let me end this chapter and preface the next with Zeitlin's characterization of Dionysus, the god of tragedy, as a transgressor, a description that applies equally well to the figure of Athena: "This mixture . . . is one of the emblems of his paradoxical role as a disrupter of the normal social categories; in his own person he attests to the *coincidentia oppositorum* that challenges the hierarchies and rules of the public masculine world, reintroducing into it confusions, conflicts, tensions and ambiguities, insisting always on the more complex nature of life than masculine aspirations would allow."[77]

As much may be said about Max Horkheimer's and Theodor Adorno's *Dialectic of Enlightenment.*

77. Zeitlin, "Playing the Other," p. 66.

6

Conclusion

The Tragedy of Critical Theory

There is no document of civilization which is not at the same time a document of barbarism.

—Walter Benjamin, in *Illuminations*

The unexamined life is not worth living.

—Socrates, in *Apology* 38

A book that takes the tale of Oedipus's tragic fate as a paradigmatic expression of the ambiguous relationship between human intelligence and power that characterizes ages of enlightenment appropriately concludes by looking at Max Horkheimer and Theodor Adorno's *Dialectic of Enlightenment.* Yet the images of light and darkness, sight and blindness that pervade the two texts, Sophocles' *Oedipus Tyrannos* and Horkheimer and Adorno's *Dialectic,* only partially justify my pairing of a Greek tragedy with a near-contemporary work of critical theory. Since Greek tragedy (and theory) seems otherwise helplessly unrelated to critical social theory, I should say something more about the reasons, internal both to *Dialectic* and to my own project, that invite, if not compel, such a favorable comparison. I have already mentioned *Dialectic*'s tragic sensibility, the tragic history of its authors, and the way in which it establishes a dialogue between Greek tragedy and the modern enlightenment. But there are other strategic, structural, and thematic reasons for pairing a work of critical theory with Greek tragedy.[1]

1. I largely pass over the Marxist background of Horkheimer and Adorno's *Dialectic of Enlightenment* (trans. John Cumming [New York: Continuum Books, 1972]), first, because I assume it to be unproblematic; second, because I have little to add to the voluminous scholarship on the critical theorists' place in the tradition of Western Marxism; and third, because I am deliberately reading *Dialectic* out of its traditional context in order to generate new insights. Putting it in the context of Foucault, Nietzsche, and trag-

This book ends with a chapter on Horkheimer and Adorno in order to redeem a promise made at its start. Chapter 1 framed the subsequent readings of Greek tragedy and philosophy in the context of a recent and ongoing contest over the meaning and legacy of the Enlightenment. It deliberately juxtaposed classical and contemporary texts in an effort to initiate a dialogue between the two that would chart an alternative route through the shifting terrain of (post)modernity and so encourage reflection on submerged or neglected theoretical and practical possibilities of the moment. That juxtaposition sought to reappropriate the way in which Greek tragedy brought its past on stage in order to illuminate and redefine the contours of its present. Yet that juxtaposition has been as much a prolegomenon to a dialogue between classical and contemporary theory as the conducting of one. Because *Dialectic* embodies direct similarities—both substantive and structural—with Greek drama and theory, it makes explicit what has thus far remained implicit in my argument and thereby achieves the dialogue between tragedy and enlightenment that I seek.

Another reason for ending this book with a chapter on Horkheimer and Adorno's *Dialectic* has to do with my claim that contemporary theory ought to become more like Greek tragedy and classical political theory. The collaborative work of the critical theorists is paradigmatic in its distinctive ability to hold the contradictions of modernity in productive tension—to think with those contradictions in order to think through them. That ability derives, of course, from *Dialectic*'s appropriation of the style, structure, and textual strategies of Greek tragedy and political theory. Like the best works of Athenian literature and philosophy, Horkheimer and Adorno's book negotiates the dilemmas, perplexities, and ambiguities present within enlightened thought, the construction of theoretical discourses, and the search for ultimate foundations in a way that deepens, rather than dissolves, the riddles it seeks to comprehend. For these reasons (further elaborated below) I find this early work by Horkheimer and Adorno—if read in terms supplied by Greek tragedy and classical political theory—to be superior to Habermas's reconstructed critical theory and Foucault's genealogical critique, models of criticism that tend to polarize, dissolve, then dismiss the very contradictions Horkheimer and Adorno regard as fundamental to thinking

edy is meant, not only to revitalize a book fallen into disuse, but also to demonstrate the ability of classical thought to address the important issues of postmodernity.

through (in both senses) modernity. This concluding chapter thus takes Horkheimer and Adorno's collaborative work as exemplary, a paradigm for contemporary critical theorists to emulate and imitate.[2]

Although I treat *Dialectic* as exemplary for thinking a (post)modernity in tension with itself, the book is not without its own limitations, blindnesses, and evasions. Notorious for their rigidly dismissive criticisms of popular culture (culture as industry), Horkheimer and Adorno countenance only a high modernist culture and art that in its form and content resists and destabilizes the commodification and homogenization that pervades late capitalist culture. Yet critical theory's rejection of the popular surely forecloses one of the more promising avenues of political practice opened up by the politics of cultural difference and popular resistance currently available today. One way to reestablish closer relations between theory and practice might be through just such a politics of everyday life, at the level of the production and consumption of cultural commodities. Through an appeal to the ambivalent boundaries apparent in Greek tragedy between high and low culture, cultural production and cultural consumption (a tension that Horkheimer and Adorno fail to exploit), I turn their rejection of popular culture against the critical theorists themselves. That exclusion then becomes instructive for a democratic politics of resistance that seeks to confront and contest an all-too-pervasive system of commodified culture. In spite of Horkheimer's and Adorno's insistence on the seamless functioning of the culture industry—and their wholesale dismissal of the popular—*Dialectic* contains within itself the resources to retheorize the political possibilities of popular culture, in which the commodities that constitute it are, not merely the congealed residues of domination, but sites of contest and fields for struggle over cultural meanings. Horkheimer and Adorno would no doubt resist such an illicit appropriation

2. My reading of *Dialectic* is a sympathetic one. I am not overly concerned to defend some of its more contentious claims, for instance, that German fascism is to be deduced from the logic of the dominant ratio itself, or that capitalism, fascism, and totalitarianism share the same fundamental logic. I am highly critical of Horkheimer and Adorno's views on the culture industry and the abolition of the individual, although I also believe their position has merit. After all, in the face of the integrative powers of the administrative state and the capitalist economy, the forces of popular culture have not yet brought the revolution. I am most concerned here that the collaborative work of Horkheimer and Adorno be taken seriously again; that it be read in the context of Greek tragedy, and that Greek tragedy and classical thought in general be recognized as valuable sources for thinking about contemporary political and theoretical problems. The value of *Dialectic of Enlightenment* lies in its ability to teach us *how to think* about the world of people and things, which, like Greek tragedy, it does by both precept and example.

of their work, but I am convinced that as an attempt to seek out locations and practices of resistance to, and disruption of, the system of administered pleasures, it remains true to the radical impulse of the critical theorists. Although I shall have some critical things to say about Horkheimer and Adorno's book, its sense of the tragic, its ability to encompass the contradictions, dilemmas, and perplexities of enlightenment, its uncompromising commitment to critical thought, and its openness to critical revision all lend it paradigmatic status as a book that is particularly good to think with, and through, while negotiating the unstable terrain of postmodernity.

I

As an indication of *Dialectic*'s ability to think the dilemmas of postmodernity in tension, let me return to a few of the themes raised by Habermas and Foucault and subsequently elaborated in the plays and dialogues, and so bring the book back to its beginnings. Horkheimer and Adorno share Habermas's concern with communication and the community it makes possible. They are in search of a language adequate to a world indelibly marked by the advent of concentration camps, a language that has not been thoroughly devalued, debased, or replaced by the methodistic logic of a wholly instrumentalized reason fit only to serve blind domination. Exiles themselves, the authors of *Dialectic* experienced both the literal and metaphysical homelessness of modern society their book describes. Horkheimer and Adorno thus remind us of the tremendous and irreparable damage wrought by modernity, which Habermas recognizes but too often forgets. *Dialectic* continually invokes the lives that have been damaged, lost, or destroyed, the experiences that have been repressed, subjugated, or smoothed over by the functionalist coherence of a system that must either expand or perish. Like watching Greek tragedy, reading *Dialectic* is an experience in remembering.[3]

Yet in spite of their radically critical stance and heroic intransigence in the face of "damaged life," Horkheimer and Adorno do not so much offer solutions to cure our ills as they raise new problems and pose new questions. Where Habermas would solve the paradox of enlightenment,

3. Karen Hermassi, *Polity and Theatre in Historical Perspective* (Berkeley: University of California Press, 1977), pp. 3–24, offers a fine discussion of the tragic theater as an act of collective recollection.

Horkheimer and Adorno deepen it; where Habermas seeks a method that would clarify all that is mysterious, ambiguous, and opaque about our lives and the world, Horkheimer and Adorno search out mystery, discontinuity, and the irruption of the unexpected as so many examples and acts of resistance against increasing systematization. Nor is this merely a matter of substance: it involves rhetorical style as well. Although wary of instrumentalization, Habermas nonetheless favors a technically streamlined language that reflects his preference for transparent analysis and discursive knowledge. Horkheimer and Adorno, on the other hand, embody and honor the poetic image as well as the theoretical concept. In this regard, *Dialectic* echoes the philosophical poetics of Aeschylus and Sophocles and the poetical philosophy of Plato as much as it anticipates the critical theory of Habermas. Horkheimer and Adorno understand all too well that surface clarity is often purchased at the expense of the richness, diversity, and depth of human experience. The ironic inversions, tragic reversals, and playful juxtapositions that mark *Dialectic* contrast all too sharply with the prose of a reconstructed critical theory that threatens to bring about the overly administered world the theorist seems to fear.[4]

Horkheimer and Adorno also share Foucault's concern with the disciplinary effects of "total" or "global" theory. They equally suspect the rhetoric of "enlightenment" and "liberation" as masks that conceal the workings of power. The authors of *Dialectic of Enlightenment* fear the advance of systemic thinking, a will to know the whole that contravenes thought's humane impulse and leads to an administered world. Motivated by fear of the unknown, enlightened thought marginalizes and suppresses all experience that falls outside the charmed circle of its discourse. What it cannot quantify, it writes off as mere literature.[5] Totalitarian as any system, enlightened thought imagines itself to have mastered nature and men. Yet the concepts of total theory issue in so many "false idols and defective ideas of the absolute" that they help bring about the slavery they intended to abolish. In ascribing truth to the whole, enlightened thought affirms the present, abandons its critical capacity, and seals its fate ever more surely. Horkheimer and Adorno thus suspect theoretical concepts that promise enlightenment, libera-

4. "As much as Habermas places communication and language in the center of his theory, they almost always remain objects of theory, as though theory were a language beyond speech," Rainer Nägele observes in "Freud, Habermas and the Dialectic of Enlightenment: On Real and Ideal Discourse," *New German Critique* 22 (1981): 42–43.

5. Horkheimer and Adorno, *Dialectic,* p. 7.

tion, and progress. Yet they are also convinced that "social freedom is inseparable from enlightened thought." *Dialectic* thus pursues a relentless critique of reason that nonetheless refuses to give up the ideas of justice and freedom to further functionalization by the general systems analysts and their managers. Enlightenment may well be fatal, or it may have in it the resources necessary to divert its seemingly inexorable course. *Dialectic* is in either case an attempt to alter the course of a progressive flood now rushing out of control.

Dialectic's ability to hold in tension the contradictions of modernity (prose and poetry, system and individual, reason and revelation, and so on) lies, in part, in the distinctive form of immanent criticism it shares with Greek tragedy and political theory. In the case of tragedy, this meant first that the playwright expressed a positive debt to the largely effaced mythic tradition that nourished him, even as he distanced himself from that tradition. Second, it meant that tragedy celebrated the city's cultural, religious, and political accomplishments with a dramatic performance that radically questioned those accomplishments. For Socratic philosophy, it meant adopting much of the structure and many of the themes of tragedy to philosophy, although Socratic elenchus, unlike its tragic counterpart, repudiated the political institutions that occasioned it and brought the practice of critical inquiry to each individual Athenian citizen. In the *Republic,* Plato expressed a philosophical debt to Socrates while distancing himself from Socratic philosophy. *Dialectic* stands in a similar relation to enlightenment: it forwards a radical and uncompromising critique of enlightenment, yet acknowledges a positive debt to enlightened thought. As they formulate it, Horkheimer and Adorno's critique of enlightenment "is intended to prepare the way for a positive notion of enlightenment which will release it from entanglement in blind domination."[6] As a critique of philosophy, critical theory refuses to abandon philosophy. It pursues this task by seeking out the reflective components in the Western philosophical tradition and encouraging that tradition to consider itself. *Dialectic* thus locates itself squarely within an intellectual tradition and uses its resources to recall that tradition to its forgotten, suppressed, or ignored principles in a way that seeks to go beyond them.

There are also good thematic reasons for concluding a book about ancient tragedy and philosophical dialogue with a chapter on this seminal work of critical theory. *Dialectic* resumes key themes developed in

6. Ibid., xvi.

the discussions on Sophocles, Socrates, Plato, and Aeschylus and transposes them to a modern register in which the powers of an administrative state, global capitalism, and an increasingly commodified culture replace (and replicate) the archaic powers of fate, nature, and the gods. For instance, the discussion in chapter 2 of Sophocles' Ode to Man introduced a basic antinomy between knowledge and power, between the seemingly unlimited capacity of our shaping intelligence and our inability fully to control nature, other men and women, and ourselves. The Ode describes man as *deinos:* as both wonderful, mighty, clever, and skillful *and* awful, terrible, dangerous, and savage. Horkheimer and Adorno recognize the similarly ambiguous nature of human skill and intelligence and the inherent connection between civilization and savagery. *Dialectic* dramatizes the tragic fate of enlightened thought, from its genesis in archaic myth through the successive stages of philosophy and science to its final reversion to barbarism. Although enlightenment had always aimed at liberating men from fear and establishing their sovereignty, Horkheimer and Adorno find that "the fully enlightened earth radiates disaster triumphant." The authors of *Dialectic* had set themselves no less a task than the "discovery of why mankind, instead of entering into a truly human condition, is sinking into a new kind of barbarism."[7] An Athenian audience, watching Sophocles' *Oedipus* for the first time, might similarly have asked, "How could such an intelligent and noble man commit such blind acts of bestiality?"

Dialectic shares even more striking parallels with Sophocles' *Oedipus.* In its choice of themes, its sensibility, and its aims, *Dialectic* invites a sustained comparison with Sophocles' play. The dialectic between identity and difference, Horkheimer's and Adorno's analysis of systems thinking, and the reversion of civilization into savagery all recall themes familiar from *Oedipus:* the metaphor of incest that dominates the play; Oedipus's peculiar ability to solve riddles, save for those that pertain to himself; and the reversal of his status from highest to lowest in the city, from king to scapegoat. Since I discuss these themes at length in the present chapter, I do not want to say any more than necessary here, save to observe that Horkheimer and Adorno are appropriately compared to Sophocles because their work complexly embodies a heroic steadfastness, coupled with respect and honor for an infinitely complex world.

Insofar as *Dialectic* urges enlightened thought to reflect on its own

7. Ibid., 3, xi.

contradictions and consider its recidivist element, Horkheimer and Adorno emulate Socrates' philosophical practice. Socrates persistently admonished his fellow citizens to think about what they were doing both in and to Athens. *Dialectic* shares this commitment to thought and aims to nourish the "theoretical faculty," a faculty threatened with extinction. The problem with enlightenment is that it gives itself over to a method that is inimical to thought as such. If, as the authors say, in the correct application of method, the answer is already decided from the start, then there is no mystery and no desire to reveal mystery. Enlightenment ruthlessly extinguishes the awe and wonder that accompanies multifaceted experience and prompts a Socrates to become philosophical in the first place. *Dialectic* is thus Socratic, not only in its admonishment to self-reflection, but also in its surprise at, and interest in, the multiplicity and multivocity of the world.

Since Horkheimer and Adorno warn against reason's imperialism—its desire both to know all and command all—they implicitly adopt the Delphic injunctions "Know thyself" and "Nothing in excess." Like the poets, politicians, and craftsmen examined by Socrates, enlightened thought deceives itself into thinking it possesses a knowledge of the whole that in fact it does not. Horkheimer and Adorno warn against mistaking partial for complete knowledge and thus excluding from view what falls outside of a "system." They encourage their readers to reflect on the course of enlightenment as both intellectual operation and historical actuality. They are convinced that salvation lies only in our ability to reflect on the implicit patterns, structures, and assumptions that inform what we are doing to ourselves and to the world. Yet even as Horkheimer and Adorno ask enlightened thought to "enlighten" itself about its own identity, methods, motives, and intentions, they remain aware that "enlightenment" can be as dangerous as the mythic forces it seeks to dispel. When they insist that "false clarity is only another name for myth; and myth has always been obscure and enlightening at the same time,"[8] the authors of the *Dialectic* share the Socratic insight that all communication necessarily involves deception and self-deception as the condition of its possibility and the motivation for its activity. Nor do Horkheimer and Adorno confuse thought with enlightenment; rather, they try to redefine the meaning of enlightenment and rescue it from self-destruction, much as Socrates attempted to redefine the meanings of citizenship, piety, and wisdom throughout his life.

8. Ibid., xiv.

Lastly, a tone of deep political and theoretical pessimism pervades *Dialectic,* recalling Socrates' own heroic, yet pessimistic, allegiance to, and defiance of, Athens. World events had forced Horkheimer and Adorno to abandon hope in revolutionary theory and praxis.[9] In response to a contemporary crisis, *Dialectic* rejected the proletariat's transformative mission and the theory that elaborated it. Henceforth, Horkheimer and Adorno would address themselves to "an imaginary witness." Moreover, recent developments had revealed, not the revolutionizing potential of scientific and technological advances, but the integrative and repressive power of a reason that too readily became the obverse side of domination. Horkheimer and Adorno concluded that "in the present collapse of bourgeois civilization not only the pursuit but the meaning of science has become problematical."[10] In the face of totalitarianism on the left as well as the right, the authors of *Dialectic* nonetheless remained steadfastly committed to the tradition of enlightened thought by means of their critique of enlightenment. *Dialectic* heroically attempts to incite thinking and preserve those qualities in things and people that make distinctions, and hence judgments, possible in an era that would liquidate all thought and thinking individuals alike. Like the condemned Socrates before his judges, the authors of *Dialectic* stood before the tribunal of history, condemned as anachronisms that could only impede "progress." Later, Adorno would reflect on just such a "failure" of philosophy: "Philosophy, which once seemed obsolete, lives on because the moment to realize it was missed."[11] The heroic steadfastness of Horkheimer and Adorno in the face of defeat by the seemingly anonymous administration of men and things made their philosophy tragic philosophy.

In Plato's *Republic,* Socrates holds out the hope of a reconciliation between knowledge and power, an epistemological and practical unity in which either philosophers become kings or kings philosophize (473d). Horkheimer and Adorno project a similar desire for a utopian moment of reconciliation between reason and reality. That moment they found present as unfulfilled longing in the fundamental document of Western

9. This is truer of Horkheimer than of Adorno, who as early as 1931 had criticized the Marxian concept of totality, as well as the assumptions implicit in Marx's "Theses on Feuerbach," in his lecture "The Actuality of Philosophy" (reprinted in *Telos* 31 (Spring 1977): 120–33. For the influence of contemporary historical events on the theoretical development of Horkheimer and Adorno, see Helmut Dubiel, *Theory and Practice* (Cambridge, Mass.: MIT Press, 1985).

10. Horkheimer and Adorno, *Dialectic,* p. xi.

11. Theodor W. Adorno, *Negative Dialectics* (New York: Continuum Books, 1973), p. 3.

civilization, Homer's *Odyssey,* and symbolized in the lure of the Sirens' song. The need for freedom and home, however, proved stronger than the desire for eternal happiness, a desire Odysseus fulfilled by renouncing it. Nevertheless, the authors suggest that freedom from domination requires universal reconciliation with nature: "By virtue of the remembrance of nature in the subject, in whose fulfillment the unacknowledged truth of all culture lies hidden, enlightenment is universally opposed to domination." The reconciliation of reason and nature that eradicates domination is no less fleeting and offers no more of a final resting point, respite, or closure than the momentary reconciliation between politics and philosophy projected in the *Republic.* Moreover, a final reconciliation would signify a unity no less totalitarian than the social and cultural uniformity enlightenment itself aims to bring about. Suspecting its own desire for a reconciled totality, *Dialectic* "issued no reassuring proclamation that Ithaca had been sighted," Christian Lenhardt observes. In a time when thought can dissolve domination, Horkheimer and Adorno say, "enlightenment becomes wholesale deception of the masses."[12]

To the extent that Horkheimer and Adorno occupy themselves with the suffering of the individual in what they call the "system" (understood both conceptually and socially), *Dialectic of Enlightenment* reintroduces Aeschylus's concern with the fate of the other in a putatively democratic society. Rooted in a radical fear of the unknown, systems thinking turns difference into hierarchy, while simultaneously excluding whatever does not conform to its own ideal.[13] Horkheimer and Adorno thus wrestle with the problem of the individual as social other, who, in the midst of the uniform collectivity, suffers from the false identity of society and individual. It is the task of critical theory (at least as that is understood in the *Dialectic*) to permit this "other" to speak, to lend a voice to suffering, and so to truth. To be sure, ancient playwright and critical theorists place their accents differently: where Aeschylus's

12. Horkheimer and Adorno, *Dialectic,* p. 40; Christian Lenhardt, "The Wanderings of Enlightenment," in *On Critical Theory,* ed. John O'Neill, pp. 52–53 (New York: Seabury Press, 1976); *Dialectic,* p. 42. Joel Whitebrook's attempt in "The Politics of Redemption," *Telos* 63 (Spring 1985), to distance himself from the so-called "politics of redemption" that he claims flows from Horkheimer's and Adorno's totalizing critique of reason is misguided in my view.

13. Horkheimer and Adorno see this logic at work in the structure of scientific thinking, in the development of philosophical systems, and in the phenomenon of culture as industry. Since I develop these themes at length below, I shall restrict my comments here to the dialectic between democracy and normalization.

legendary heroes and heroines challenge the norms of the democratic order from the center of the city and during its most important religious festival, Horkheimer and Adorno give voice to the other from a place of "permanent exile,"[14] disrupting the hegemonic system from its boundaries and margins. And where the heroine of Aeschylus's *Agamemnon* remains a liminal figure, paradoxically defining the norms of her society even as she defies them, modern mass democracy attempts to banish the other (and tragedy) by integrating it into the architecture of its own uniformity (although Horkheimer and Adorno themselves stand apart from, even as they are a part of, the tradition they criticize). Finally, where Greek tragedy had ultimate and assuring recourse to the bounded world of stage, orchestra, and theater, the critical theorists pursue a dialectical high-wire act in their attempt to maintain the tension between an increasingly uniform collectivity and "the development of autonomous, independent individuals who judge and decide consciously for themselves," these being the "precondition for a democratic society."[15]

Horkheimer and Adorno never tire of insisting that social freedom is inseparable from enlightened thought, but they consistently resist the "temptation to transparency" that characterizes all enlightenment, especially in its modern, positivistic incarnation. We must render modern relations of domination visible and legible, for the workings of power must not, and—given the available technologies of surveillance, discipline, and control—cannot, remain impenetrably obscure. Yet the zealous quest for complete transparency as a response to fear of the unknown other becomes a further means for reducing the complexity of the world and the irony of action in it, elements that democratic politics cannot do without. That is one reason why, in the *Eumenides,* although Apollo's arguments apparently "win" the case for Orestes, the Olympians, and the male, Aeschylus leaves no doubt that the "solution" is achieved arbitrarily and not without a measure of violence, and that the newly won order is a fragile and precarious achievement, susceptible to pressures that will irreparably fracture it. This temptation to transparency is also why Horkheimer and Adorno refused to theorize (and so objectify) a concept of rationality. In their refusal, however, they suc-

14. To borrow the title of Martin Jay's collection of essays on the Frankfurt School, *Permanent Exiles: Essays on the Intellectual Migration from Germany to America* (New York: Columbia University Press, 1986).

15. Theodor W. Adorno, "The Culture Industry Reconsidered" (1964), *New German Critique* 6 (Fall 1975).

ceed quite well in articulating the ambiguity, irony, and complexity of language that lends a civic discourse its life in the first place. If there is such a thing as a poetics for a democratic politics, *Dialectic,* despite its almost willful obscurity, approaches that goal somewhat like Aeschylus's *Oresteia.*

Finally, Horkheimer and Adorno's deployment of "effective history," their "untimely" use of the past, recapitulates the way in which Greek tragedy used its own archaic past to illuminate and redefine the contours of the present. Critical theory can teach us how we might similarly "use" the classical texts of tragedy and philosophy to do the same. The authors of *Dialectic* appropriate the style and sensibility of classical literature and philosophy in order to make the unprecedented aspects of modernity intelligible, yet in so doing they retain their distinctively modern concerns and purposes. By juxtaposing the mythical past with the enlightened present, archaic barbarism with the most recent phenomena, *Dialectic* embodies and imitates all the tensions and ambiguities that characterize a tragic performance, a philosophical dialogue, and a modernity at odds with itself. When Horkheimer and Adorno insist upon the necessity of moral language and responsible action in the face of linguistic devaluation and the anonymous administration of men and women as things, they appeal to a fundamental teaching of the tragic theater that still informs political thinking today:[16] we are forced to speak and act in a world we never made, and to bear responsibility for our words and deeds.

All this suggests that Horkheimer and Adorno's *Dialectic* exemplifies how the themes, style, and language of Greek tragedy can provide a point of reference and a source of inspiration for theorizing in and about the present. As I have indicated, this means reading a work of contemporary theory in terms provided by Greek tragedy, and as a modern tragedy, a tragedy of enlightenment. To do so, I shall elaborate a number of affinities, first in structure, then in content, and finally in aim, between Greek tragedy (as represented by Sophocles' *Oedipus*) and *Dialectic,* seeking to give substance to my claim that the thought of the classical polis can nourish the contemporary theoretical imagination in a way that will help us think with and through the perplexities and contradictions of postmodernity.

16. I am thinking of Hannah Arendt's *Eichmann in Jerusalem: A Report on the Banality of Evil* (New York: Viking Press, 1964; repr., Penguin Books, 1977); see esp. pp. 286–87.

II

By *structure* I mean not only the obvious characteristics of a work's form—whether it be a play, a dialogue, a novel, or a treatise—but also its style, sensibility, and tone; the kinds of images it uses and evokes; the texture of its language and the architecture of its composition; the rhetorical strategies it employs to persuade its readers (or audience) and the way in which these form-al elements work with or against a text's explicit or surface argument.

Dialectic of Enlightenment recalls the structure, style, and sensibility of Greek tragedy in a number of different ways.[17] First, unlike a philosophical or theoretical treatise, but like tragedy, it embodies the form of a drama or dramatic dialogue. *Dialectic*'s vital principle, Horkheimer and Adorno assert, is "the tension between the two intellectual temperaments conjoined in it."[18] The two different voices united in the book achieve the plurality of positions, viewpoints, and arguments that define tragedy's concern with moral communication and debate. Multiple voices lend *Dialectic* a certain multidimensionality, which contributes to an open-ended and ongoing, rather than a declamatory, authoritative, or monologic, model of communication. By presenting multiple positions, and so multiple points of engagement, Horkheimer and Adorno encourage the reader to "enter critically and actively into the give and take of debate much as a spectator of a tragedy is invited to reflect about the meaning of events on stage."[19] *Dialectic* thus asks the reader to take sides and make judgments, just as tragedy encouraged its spectators to judge the action of the characters in a drama. Horkheimer and Adorno, of course, ask us to reflect on the meaning and consequences of enlightenment and judge them for ourselves.

In tragedy, great and heroic deeds or terrible suffering are called forth as responses to real life events and crises.[20] Theoretical reflection in *Dialectic* is likewise a response to a lived crisis of fundamental importance. As a response to the rise of fascism in Europe, the Stalinization of the revolution in Russia, and the commodification of everyday life in the United States, *Dialectic* attains an immediacy and urgency usually lacking in "objective" theoretical texts, yet present in Greek tragedy. Trag-

17. Martha C. Nussbaum, *The Fragility of Goodness: Luck and Ethics in Greek Tragedy and Philosophy* (Cambridge: Cambridge University Press, 1986), pp. 122 ff., argues a relationship between Greek tragedy and Plato's dialogues.
18. Horkheimer and Adorno, *Dialectic,* ix.
19. Nussbaum, *Fragility of Goodness,* p. 126.
20. Ibid., p. 130.

edy also makes plain the stakes involved in human action and debate, providing a set of motivations for entering into debate or pursuing a course of action by revealing how and why characters undertake a discussion and what sorts of problems call forth reflection.[21] *Dialectic* similarly shows us the stakes involved in theoretical reflection.

Third, like tragedy, Horkheimer and Adorno suspect any attempt to construct a single, unitary, or comprehensive account of the world.[22] *Dialectic* is concerned to "display to us the irreducible richness of human value"[23] against social forces that would reduce both humans and their values to problems of economic exchange and bureaucratic administration. Tragedy sought to present the "complexity and indeterminacy of the lived practical situation,"[24] and *Dialectic* likewise honors the particular, the individual, and the concrete in all its complexity and suspects overly general, abstract, determinate, and reductionist accounts that simplify the world. The ancient playwrights and the authors of *Dialectic* share Michel Foucault's suspicion of total or global theory.

The architecture of the book further reflects this concern with concrete particulars and the suspicion of unitary, hierarchical, and functionalizing knowledge. Comprised of a number of mutually referential essays and subtitled "Philosophical Fragments," *Dialectic* breaks off inconclusively in a series of notes and drafts. The aphoristic structure of the work thus reiterates its concern with the particular fragment and individual detail and further reinforces its warning against succumbing to the tyranny of the kind of knowledge that would unify all experience. But a fragmentary style is not necessarily fragmented, and neither does it signify a lack of theoretical coherence. Like the best Greek tragedy, which simultaneously denies and presents the world as possessing an intelligible meaning, the philosophical fragments of *Dialectic* are mediated by a thematic unity that make it an excellent example of the very order it supposedly rejects.[25] Horkheimer and Adorno have managed to create a theoretical form that achieves the diversity within unity that has always eluded enlightenment itself.

Fourthly, *Dialectic* shares with Greek tragedy the form of an elen-

21. Ibid., p. 127.
22. Ibid., p. 130.
23. Ibid., p. 134.
24. Ibid.
25. Timothy J. Reiss reads Greek tragedy this way in *Tragedy and Truth: Studies in the Development of a Renaissance and Neoclassical Discourse* (New Haven, Conn.: Yale University Press 1980), p. 21.

chus, or cross-examination.[26] As in a play that charts the course of a character's most confidently asserted claims about himself and the world around him, claims that further developments subsequently prove wrong, Horkheimer and Adorno show us how enlightened thinking blinds itself to the meanings and consequences of its own achievements and how its grasp of, and control over, practical problems is irreversibly deflated. In their narrative, enlightenment follows the course of a tragic reversal: its unreflected assumptions about its own truth and value are undermined. Reason may once have promised the subject control and mastery, but now it ruthlessly controls and masters the subject itself.

Lastly, and perhaps most important, Horkheimer and Adorno work as much through theoretical argument as through poetic images, associations, tones, textures, and sensibilities that evoke the "passional knowledge" of Greek tragedy. Like tragedy, *Dialectic* engages not only our wits but our passions, appealing as much to the power of our emotions as to the power of our reason. To read *Dialectic* as a tragedy means to read it as lament at the tremendous destruction wrought by modernity. If, as Aeschylus realized, the passional knowledge of tragedy is the kind that comes through suffering, then the wisdom contained in *Dialectic* is truly tragic.

III

Not only do the ubiquitous images of light and darkness, sight and blindness that pervade Sophocles' *Oedipus* invite sustained comparison with Horkheimer's and Adorno's *Dialectic,* there are other, more systematic and substantive reasons as well why no classical text better illuminates a contemporary one. Both *Dialectic* and *Oedipus* focus on the ambiguity of man's power to control his world and manage his life by intelligence, and both consider that issue through the themes of civilization and savagery and identity and difference.

As we saw in chapter 2, one dominant theme in Sophocles' *Oedipus* is the fine line that separates civilization from savagery, the city from the wild, enlightenment from myth. Oedipus is the paradigmatic civilizing hero, a man who uses the powers of intellect and reason to vanquish the threat of undifferentiated chaos. By solving the riddle of the Sphinx, Oedipus triumphs over untamed nature; with his solution, he

26. Nussbaum, *Fragility of Goodness,* p. 129.

enthrones "man" as the measure of all things, and himself as master of Thebes. When Oedipus boasts that he destroyed the death-dealing Sphinx alone and with unaided intellect, he asserts that rational mastery of the world upon which all the greatest achievements of Greek civilization were thought to rest. Yet Oedipus transgresses the very boundaries he seeks to establish. For all his civilizing power, Oedipus remains a creature of the wild, unable to banish the "nature" within himself. Rescued from the mountain fastness of Cithaeron, he becomes a beast himself, killing his father in the wild, committing incest at the very hearth of the city, finally banished from the human community that nurtured him. Oedipus is himself a savage, a destroyer of civilized values and the city that embodies them, his will and intellect mortal threats to the hard-won human order of the polis.

By dramatizing the dialectic of civilization and savagery, Sophocles suggests that civilization is a precarious achievement and its reversion to savagery a persistent and imminent possibility, if not an inescapable reality. Human intellect and reason possess the power to lift us out of nature *and* return us to barbarity. In the case of Oedipus, the assiduous and unwavering application of reason reveals not only human progress but bestial regression as well. Every step Oedipus takes in his search for the murderer proves the power of his intellectual progress to be the progress of a tyrannical power. Reason and the mastery it brings constitute the obverse side of a savage tyranny. All the achievements of human civilization centered on Oedipus "come to reflect the ambiguity of man's power to control his world and manage his life by intelligence."[27] Oscillating between intellectual mastery and ignorance, between godlike omniscience and fateful resignation, Oedipus lacks an appropriately political kind of knowledge. In terms of the play as a whole, this means a collective and deliberative, rather than a singular and analytic, knowledge; one that is simultaneously active and shaping *and* passive and receptive, a knowledge that reflects on the conditions of its own possibility and heeds its mortal limits. Oedipus and Thebes, however, lack the kind of knowledge tragedy itself inculcates in its citizen audience.[28] As long as they do, they are bound to repeat an endless pattern

27. Charles P. Segal, *Tragedy and Civilization: An Interpretation of Sophocles* (Cambridge, Mass.: Harvard University Press, 1981), p. 232.

28. On the educative function of tragedy, see J. Peter Euben, ed., *Greek Tragedy and Political Theory* (Berkeley: University of California Press, 1986), esp. introduction and Stephen Salkever, "Tragedy and the Education of the Demos."

of incest, trapped within the inexorable dialectic of civilization and savagery.[29]

Horkheimer's and Adorno's book also concerns the dialectic between civilization and savagery, reason and tyranny, enlightenment and myth. The authors of *Dialectic of Enlightenment* sought "nothing less than the discovery of why mankind, instead of entering into a truly human condition, is sinking into a new kind of barbarism."[30] They confronted the simultaneity of material progress and social regression: what the authors characterized as the indefatigable self-destructiveness of enlightenment. Kant had laid the philosophical foundations of a purely formalistic reason; Sade and Nietzsche, the "black writers of the bourgeoisie,"[31] mercilessly elicited the implications of enlightenment by insisting that formalistic reason is no more closely allied to morality than immorality and by denying the possibility of deriving from reason any fundamental argument against murder; but it was Hitler and the fascists who brought enlightenment to its logical conclusion in a return to outright barbarism.

Consistent with the central thesis of their book, Horkheimer and Adorno interpret the Holocaust as a deadly combination of myth (anti-Semitism) and enlightenment (bureaucratically and rationally organized mass murder), the savage reversion of civilization into barbarism. That rationalism should culminate in collectively legitimated mass murder was not an isolated anachronistic irruption of savagery into modern civilization but the crystallization of its organizing principle. The "irrationalism" of anti-Semitism proceeds from the "nature of the dominant *ratio* itself, and the world which corresponds to its image."[32] The thesis that civilization and savagery are inextricably linked finds tragic testimony in the methodically administered destruction of whole nations.[33]

29. On the eternal return of the same in the Oedipus plays, see Froma I. Zeitlin, "Thebes: Theater of Self and Society in Athenian Drama," in Euben, ed., *Greek Tragedy and Political Theory,* pp. 101–41.

30. Horkheimer and Adorno, *Dialectic,* xi.

31. Ibid., 17.

32. Ibid., xvii.

33. Cf. Walter Benjamin's "Every document of civilization is also a document of barbarism" (*Illuminations,* trans. Harry Zohn, ed. Hannah Arendt [New York: Schocken Books, 1969; repr., 1986], p. 256). Adorno elsewhere characterizes modernity's psychological principle as "frigidity"—that is, as the capacity to see one's fellows devoured without experiencing guilt or physical pain. Arendt comes to a similar conclusion, but calls it thoughtlessness: the inability to think from the standpoint of somebody else made it possible for Eichmann to efficiently organize mass murder (*Eichmann in Jerusalem* [1977], p. 49).

Unlike György Lukács, on the left, and Karl Popper and Friedrich von Hayek, on the right, Horkheimer and Adorno sought the cause for the destruction of all civilized values—for barbarism on a hitherto unprecedented scale—in the triumph of scientific method and its extension into, and domination over, all spheres of life.[34]

Where Lukács argued that the commodity form and the reification it necessarily brings are specific to capitalist economic organization, both Popper and Hayek blamed socialism and the labor movement: Popper because Marxism had replaced the "piecemeal social engineering" of liberalism with historicism and utopianism; Hayek because socialism had introduced the ideas of planning and state intervention into the successful functioning of competitive capitalism. But fascism does not only become possible as a result of the wholesale reification of society, through either the market or centralized planning. Nor is it merely the truth of a liberalism stripped bare to reveal the naked inequalities and oppression inherent in the apparently free exchange of the market. Rather, fascism paradoxically embodies elements of both myth and enlightenment. In its attempt to free men from the imperatives of nature, it enslaves them to a second nature. The fault lies as much with the methods of the natural sciences (the practice of systematization) and their counterpart in epistemology (logical positivism) as with the market and capitalist relations of production (although domination certainly intensifies under these latter historical conditions). Horkheimer and Adorno radically question the pursuit of both unreflective science and systematic logic and attempt to expose the structure of formal reason as a structure of domination and so understand the entwinement of enlightenment and myth, of reason and madness, that accompanied German fascism.

They pursue one aspect of this dialectic between enlightenment and myth by suggesting a connection between the intellectual mastery of nature and tyranny over men and women. Reason, which once worked

34. Although Horkheimer and Adorno's *Dialectic* interprets the reversal of enlightenment by means of Lukács's concept of rationalization as reification, Lukács does not deal with fascism directly; see György Lukács, *History and Class Consciousness: Studies in Marxist Dialectics*, trans. Rodney Livingstone (Cambridge, Mass.: MIT Press, 1971), esp. "Reification and the Consciousness of the Proletariat," pp. 83–222. And see Friedrich August von Hayek, *The Road to Serfdom* (Chicago: University of Chicago Press, 1944), and Karl Popper, *The Open Society and Its Enemies* (1949; Princeton: Princeton University Press, 1966).

by concepts and images, now refers to method alone. Indifferent to the qualitatively and individually unique, insensitive to multiplicity and particularity,[35] impatient with tradition and history, as well as with religion, metaphysics, and philosophy, the domination of discursive logic in the conceptual sphere tends to domination in actuality. The aim of enlightenment is the subsumption of all particulars under the general, "the substitution of formula for concept, rule and probability for cause and motive."[36] But all systems of knowledge obscure as much as they reveal, exclude as they include, foreclose human possibilities as they disclose the secrets of nature and enslave the subjects they originally intended to liberate. Blind to the course of its own progress, enlightenment pays for each and every advance in material production with the increased impotence and pliability of the masses. The unprecedented increase in economic productivity of all kinds promises greater social justice, yet the technical apparatus and the groups that administer it "assume a superiority disproportionate to the rest of the population. Even though the individual disappears before the apparatus which serves him, that apparatus provides for him as never before."[37] Promising the subject control and mastery, enlightenment ruthlessly controls and masters the subject. If enlightenment aimed originally at freeing man from fear of mythic powers, it has replaced those archaic forces with a new myth of things as they actually are in order to justify a correspondingly new kind of terror. Fear of departing from the charmed circle of facts—terror of the unknown and hatred of the unknowable—identifies the modern self with its archaic counterpart. Enlightenment behaves like Sophocles' Oedipus: it liberates the species from the aweful power of nature, but it also brings with it a new plague. Both remedy and poison, savior and destroyer, civilized and savage, farsighted in its commanding vision yet blind to the ambiguity of its own identity, actions, and consequences, enlightenment is not only *deinon* (awesome, terrifying), but *pharmakon* (remedy, poison) as well.

To the extent that *Dialectic* is concerned with the self-destruction of enlightenment's emancipatory intent *and* with the precarious divisions

35. Horkheimer and Adorno, *Dialectic,* p. 7.
36. Ibid., p. 5.
37. Ibid., p. xiv.

that separate civilization from savagery, it recalls the moral judgment of Sophocles' *Oedipus*. In their attempt to make Auschwitz intelligible, Horkheimer and Adorno evoke the moral sensibility of tragedy, where the poverty of current linguistic expression proves inadequate to the unprecedented nature of the new barbarism. Adorno used to speak of a "universal context of guilt," a phrase that alludes to the impossibility of completing anything in the spirit in which it was conceived. No matter how generous or radical the intent, our best plans go wrong. We act in order to extricate ourselves from the ravages of enlightenment in its capitalist and fascist phases, only to entangle ourselves in them ever more deeply. Like Oedipus, we continually reinforce the power of a fate whose hold we seek to break. Even when the traditional theories of virtue have collapsed under the weight of rationalist skepticism, when we ought to, but cannot, do anything right, we still must act and be judged for our actions. *Dialectic* refuses to abandon the moral language of guilt and responsibility at a time when the force of fate, congealed in the logic and power of immense economic and bureaucratic systems, seems unassailable. Horkheimer and Adorno anticipate another German émigré, Hannah Arendt, who looked to the moral language of Greek tragedy in order to understand the unprecedented nature of the Holocaust. Insisting that Eichmann be tried for his specific deeds and not his motives, Arendt reiterates the tragic self-judgment of Oedipus: we are responsible for our particular deeds, no matter how generously, nobly, or—as in the case of Eichmann—how indifferently they are conceived.[38] The authors of *Dialectic* and Arendt agree with Greek tragedy that we must decide and act in a world we never made, and that such decisions and actions are tragic.

Chapter 2 also considered in detail Oedipus's problem-solving mentality. His answer to the Sphinx's riddle, "It is man," reveals a unique ability to apprehend unity amid the multiplicity of forms, to organize the data of experience rationally. Oedipus reduces all "problems" of difference to their lowest common denominators, the better to solve them. Impatient with multiple meanings, diverse or contradictory voices and plural points of view, he imposes his unitary vision on the world to the exclusion of varied and variegated possibilities. The unity he achieves is, however, attained at the expense of the plurality that makes a polis possible in the first place. By insisting that words and the

38. Arendt, *Eichmann in Jerusalem* (1977), p. 278.

world have only one meaning; by reducing the complexity and flexibility of language; by diluting the richness and harmonizing the differences within Thebes itself, Oedipus threatens to liquidate the distinctions that constitute the city he sets out to save.

Horkheimer and Adorno's book also wrestles with the dialectic between identity and difference, uniformity and individuality, the one and the many. They explore that dialectic through a consideration of enlightenment's will to unity, the production of a uniform and characterless "mass" culture, and through the problem of "system" in both theory and practice.

The Enlightenment's tendency to reduce the many-faceted and contradictory nature of experience to a singular unity apprehensible under the laws of formal reason already finds its expression in the ancient enlightenment. Just as Xenophanes derided the multiplicity of deities as so many false projections of man himself, Horkheimer and Adorno said, the most recent school of logic denounced the words of language as false coin better replaced by neutral counters.[39] "On the road to modern science men renounce any claim to meaning": there is no difference between the totemic animal, the dreams of the ghost-seer, and the absolute Idea. The rich multiplicity of forms is reduced to position and arrangement, history to fact, things to matter. Science, guided by method, "makes the dissimilar comparable by reducing it to abstract quantities. To the enlightenment, that which does not reduce to numbers, and ultimately to the one, becomes illusion; modern positivism writes it off as literature."[40] From Parmenides to Bertrand Russell, unity is the slogan: "The destruction of gods and qualities alike is insisted upon."[41] The modern Enlightenment, replete with experimental science, formal logic and advanced method—all of which provided a schema for the calculability of the world—brought to fruition the extirpation of distinctions that the disenchantment of nature had always sought.

Enlightenment, however, is as democratic as the logic it employs. Not only are qualities dissolved in thought, but "men are brought to actual conformity as well."[42] Those who are not find their way into

39. Horkheimer and Adorno, *Dialectic,* p. 5.
40. Ibid., p. 7.
41. Ibid., p. 8.
42. Ibid., p. 12.

"total" institutions that increasingly resemble society itself.[43] Whether through the market or the state apparatus that protects its clients from the dislocations caused by the former, our society is ruled by equivalence. "We were given our individuality as unique in each case, different to all others, so that it might all the more surely be made the same as any other."[44] Equivalence, exchange, abstraction—all tools of enlightenment—treat individuals as did fate, the notion of which they reject: they liquidate them. The false unity of the individual and the collectivity nevertheless shows through. The more homogeneous society becomes, the more its members are subjected to the repetition, standarization, and uniformity of productive and administrative processes at all levels and in all spheres of existence, the more that society disintegrates. "Men are once again made to be mere species beings, exactly like one another through *isolation* in the forcibly united collectivity."[45] Paradoxically, Horkheimer and Adorno might argue, we are a community of isolates.

The regression of enlightenment to ideology (myth) evident in the products of mass culture gives Horkheimer and Adorno occasion for reflecting on the demise of autonomous art (tragedy included) and on the corresponding abolition of the individual.[46] The late modern counterpart to the tragic world of the Greek theater is the "culture industry."[47] Unlike Greek tragedy, however, that industry aims, not to encourage moral reflection, invigorate substantive debate, or elucidate the distinctions that make judgment possible, but rather to stultify, stupefy, and create a "culture" of unthinking, pliable masses. The products of the culture industry have lost any power to contradict the audiences' expectations, question their norms of thought, or challenge their standards of intelligibility. Culture industry commodities have little or no critical function. Television, music, and film all encourage an attentive, but essentially passive, passionless, and uncritical reception, which they induce through patterned and predigested products: programs watch

43. Here Horkheimer and Adorno anticipate, e.g., Michel Foucault's *Madness and Civilization: A History of Insanity in the Age of Reason,* trans. Richard Howard (New York: Pantheon Books, 1965); *Discipline and Punish: The Birth of the Prison,* trans. Alan Sheridan (New York: Pantheon Books, 1977); and *The Birth of the Clinic: An Archeology of Medical Perception,* trans. A. M. Sheridan Smith (New York: Pantheon Books, 1973).

44. Horkheimer and Adorno, *Dialectic,* p. 13.

45. Ibid., p. 36.

46. Ibid., p. 154.

47. The phrase "culture industry" was first used by Horkheimer and Adorno, who preferred it to "mass culture" because of the latter phrase's populist connotations. They oppose "mass culture" not because it is democratic but precisely because it is not.

for their audiences as popular music hears *for* those who listen.[48] Mass-mediated cultural products thus reproduce and strengthen, rather than question, existing social and cultural boundaries. The result is not an image of society rent by contradiction, but the false identity of society and individual that urges the smooth integration of the latter into the former. If any passion is evinced, it is a passion for identification. In the context of culture as industry, tragedy, which once meant protest, now means consolation.

Where Greek tragedy valued and displayed the irreducible richness and complexity of human life, enlightenment treats culture as the ancient tyrant treated Thebes: science disproves the old oracles of religion, metaphysics, and philosophy daily; increasing social differentiation and technological specialization produce chaos, while the culture industry "now impresses the same stamp on everything . . . Films, radio and magazines make up a system which is uniform as a whole and in every part."[49] The culture industry obliterates distinctions and refuses to produce or sanction anything that in any way differs from its own rules, its own ideas about consumers, and above all itself. It makes everyone the same, collapsing plurality and individuality into unity, uniformity, and anonymity, thereby destroying rather than sustaining the distinctions and differences that Greek tragedy (and a democratic politics) necessarily presuppose. The culture industry promotes that reduction in thought and society against which Sophocles warned: the incestuous repetition of the same that forever turns back and in upon itself, a repetition and standardization devoid of the exogamous relations and energy necessary to revitalize a people or a culture.

Yet the authors of *Dialectic* are quick to point out that mass culture does not shrink from suffering: "Tragedy made into a carefully calculated and accepted aspect of the world is a blessing."[50] If "tragic" suffering is to be shown, it must be integrated in such a way that the system can profitably use it. Tragedy thus becomes an institution for moral improvement, just as suffering justifies the world that made it necessary. Tragedy has to resemble fate and is reduced to the threat to destroy anyone who does not cooperate with the higher powers: "Tragic fate becomes just punishment for those who resist becoming whatever the sys-

48. Theodor W. Adorno and George Simpson, "On Popular Music," *Studies in Philosophy and Social Science* 9, 1 (special issue, 1941): 48.
49. Horkheimer and Adorno, *Dialectic,* p. 120.
50. Ibid., p. 151.

tem wants."[51] The culture industry discards tragedy by integrating both it and the individual. The substance of Greek tragedy is the opposition of its heroes to society. The need to identify, to fit in, to find refuge in the collectivity remain unfulfilled in ancient tragedy, and the tension between hero and society is unresolved. Oedipus and Antigone both defy the conventional codes of their communities and suffer for it. Today, the "miracle of integration" has brought such would-be heroes into line: the individual must find refuge in society by identifying with it and renouncing his or her individuality. The tension in tragedy dissipates into the false identity of society and individual. Where Greek tragedy refuses final narrative closure and keeps the "individual" alive, the productions of the pleasure industry affirm reconciliation and refuge and thereby defeat tragedy. For Horkheimer and Adorno, such a "liquidation of tragedy confirms the abolition of the individual."[52]

While I certainly do not want to deny the integrative power of administered enjoyment in late capitalism, I do want to suggest that *Dialectic* only tells half the story of the culture industry, that this evasion flows from currents deep within the book (if not within the authors themselves), and that the resources for theorizing forms of popular resistance to commodified culture reside within the spaces between tragedy and enlightenment marked out by *Dialectic* itself.

Irredeemable elitists, cultural mandarins, bourgeois intellectuals, insufferable high modernists—these are a few of the more and less pejorative epithets deployed by students of popular, democratic culture and practice against Horkheimer and Adorno. These critics rightly sense the critical theorists' hostility to virtually all forms of the popular, but mistakenly interpret that sentiment as simply antidemocratic or elitist. Reflecting on the eclipse of the critical, thinking public, which was unable to resist the advances of mass culture, Adorno summed up the effects of the culture industry as, in fact, antidemocratic: "It impedes the development of autonomous, independent individuals who judge and decide consciously for themselves. These, however, would be the precondition for a democratic society which needs adults who have come of age in order to sustain itself and develop."[53] Ever fearful of fascism, Horkheimer and Adorno criticized the culture industry precisely for its undemocratic aspects. In *Dialectic,* they looked to Greek tragedy

51. Ibid., p. 153.
52. Ibid., p. 154.
53. Adorno, "Culture Industry Reconsidered," p. 135.

as an example of the kind of cultural production able to provide the thoughtful, critical citizens that contemporary democracy requires. Yet the forms, sites, and subjects of popular resistance to the commodity system that produces those subjects have proliferated in recent years (no doubt in ignorance of the accomplishments of Greek tragedy), opening the *Dialectic*'s antidemocratic interpretation of the pleasure industry to radical, populist revision.

But how are we to explain Horkheimer and Adorno's hostility to the popular forms of enjoyment of the time (Hollywood movies, musicals, jazz, radio, magazines), and their barely concealed contempt for those who enjoy them? I want to suggest that the prejudices of (especially) Adorno's social and cultural milieu—European bourgeois intellectual and high modernist aesthetic sensibility—fail to explain the central position cultural criticism occupies in *Dialectic* and other works of critical theory. Enforced exile in a city as apparently barbaric as Los Angeles (whither Adorno had followed Horkheimer, who had left New York for health reasons) might account for much of Adorno's personal hostility to popular culture, but his criticisms are rooted more deeply, and more systematically, in the theory's conceptual apparatus. The concept of reification is Adorno's central interpretive category for decoding the presence of congealed power in cultural productions and so in society. Adorno deploys that concept in order to expose those structures of a cultural product as homologous to structures of social domination. Hence the following contemptuous denunciation of jazz: "Rebelling feebly, they are always ready to duck, following the lead of jazz, which integrates stumbling and coming-too-soon into the collective march lock-step."[54]

In this example, Adorno's decoding of culture as commodity unproblematically maps the meaning of the reified product (song, movie, advertisement) onto the social structure itself: identical, indistinguishable mass-produced and fetishized products must also signify identical, indistinguishable, mass-produced "individuals" subject to the power of the fetish they themselves have created. Commodities stamp their falsely individualized imprint on their consumers, who nonetheless see through the deception. This critique of the culture industry, a critique that proceeds from the concept of reification, focuses exclusively on the meaning of cultural *production*, ignoring the equally important mean-

54. Theodor W. Adorno, *Prisms*, trans. Samuel and Shierry Weber (Boston: MIT Press, 1981), p. 128.

ing of cultural *consumption.* While this productivist bias in the analysis of cultural commodities does lead to a supple disclosure of the integrative power of late capitalist commodity production, it simultaneously occludes from view the proliferation of possible sites and spaces where the cultural meanings of these commodities might be (re)appropriated in order to resist, contest, or subvert the imperatives of the commodity system. While it is certainly true that culture as commodity possesses integrative force, like any artifact of culture, the products of the culture industry are objects whose meaning exceeds—surpasses—the intention of the producer. The products of the pleasure industry take on meanings of their own once they reach the street. That surplus meaning—the meaning produced by the subcultures who appropriate it—only becomes visible with a shift of focus (which Adorno refused) away from production and toward the many and varied uses to which cultural commodities are subjected by those who purchase them.

From this perspective, the commodities of the culture industry lose some of their integrative, repressive power, and the unexpected uses to which subcultural or countercultural groups put them appear as sites and examples of resistant and rebellious subjectivity. Without romanticizing this form of cultural power, we must be alert to the ways in which the commodities of the culture industry constitute a site of struggle over meanings, out of which new selves, new subjectivities, and sometimes new political possibilities are (re)fashioned. Shopping malls, video arcades, bebop, hip-hop, MTV, and Madonna all have their subversive, countercultural uses, which often resist the seemingly irreversible transition to fully administered enjoyment. Pleasures, bodies, and desires are the central elements in this struggle over meanings, elements not so different from those already found in the Sirens episode analyzed by Horkheimer and Adorno. In that scene from Homer, the pleasure-consuming Odysseus (allegory for the later bourgeois enjoyment of art) must tie himself to the mast, renounce his freedom, his enjoyment, and himself as he impotently listens to the Sirens' song. Contemporary consumers of culture are infinitely more imaginative than their archaic and bourgeois counterparts in contesting the predetermined meanings of the culture system: they give up the rational *strategy* of an Odysseus for the *tactical* raids of the (sub)urban guerrilla in order to bend received cultural meanings, contest structures of domination, and resist the inertia of cultural commodification from deep within enemy territory.

But how can *Dialectic* be made more responsive (and more responsible) to the possibilities of cultural resistance that reside in the surplus meanings generated by the users of cultural commodities? That possibility lies in loosening its dependence on a theory of cultural production by teasing out the strands of Greek tragedy that undermine the critical theorists' valorization of "high" culture. The ambivalent cultural dynamics of Greek tragedy—tragic drama as popular entertainment as well as autonomous art form—provide an instructive and ironic parallel to the popular culture Horkheimer and Adorno reject. Such a reappropriation of Greek tragedy by the forces of the popular constitutes a subversive undertaking that is no less an abandonment of a rational strategy for a tactical raid than that performed by a host of today's resistant and (re)fashioned selves. It amounts to reading *Dialectic* against itself and against its conclusions, to searching out meaning and possibilities in the text that eluded the authors.

Greek tragedy, as we have seen, provides the authors of *Dialectic* with a model of critical political education: by portraying heroes and heroines who refuse assimilation into the system or the system's categories, by representing a society rent and fissured by contradictions, Greek tragedy constitutes for the critical theorists an exemplary form of cultural resistance to the integrative powers of a mass democratic society that is one step away from fascism. What Horkheimer and Adorno's account of tragedy elides, however, is the radically popular nature of ancient dramatic festivals and performances and the ambivalent position of the playwrights in regard to cultural transmission.

First, the plays were subject to audience approval in the form of a competition and so were required to negotiate the distance between providing cultural critique and popular entertainment. Plays were successful largely to the extent that they combined both these elements. The performances, themselves, then, were sites of popular struggle over cultural meanings. The playwrights engaged, not only in an agon among themselves for first prize, but in a contest whose parameters were bounded by the requirements of the art form and popular tastes—an agon constituted by their relationship to the popular audience.

Second, the productivist paradigm of cultural commodification describes Greek tragedy no better than it describes contemporary popular culture. The tragedians stood in a decidedly ambivalent structural relation to their culture: they were never merely producers of a critical discourse that could be directly mapped onto an Athenian society that did not measure up to its standards. The playwrights were also cultural "consumers" of a sort, of the ancient myths and legends that constituted (and reconstituted) the popular cultural traditions of the city. Like the consumers of contemporary popular culture, the tragedians purposefully remade and refashioned the cultural products available to them. Those reappropriations of the myths and their reworking in tragedy must be seen as acts that contest and transform received cultural accommodations and meanings, that resist and destabilize potentially homogenizing cultural constructions. Aeschylus, for example, not only problematized such binary categories as male/female, Greek/barbarian, reason/passion, and new/old, but also rewrote the ancient myths to bring previously elided questions of gender and public power on stage. From this perspective, a Greek tragedy like the *Oresteia* appears as a site of struggle over social and cultural meanings, as a product of culture that, in the hands of the playwright, exemplifies the ongoing process of making and remaking cultural meanings, much as the products of the culture industry are refashioned by the rebellious and resistant selves who appropriate them in a myriad of ways never intended by the producer.

In turning *Dialectic* against itself, in forcing it against its intent to yield a (grudging) valorization of (some aspects of) popular culture, my reading nonetheless remains true to its vocation of resistance. What makes the book such a powerful work is its tenacious subversion of all theoretical, political, and narrative closures, its resistance to integrative systems and concepts that attempt to order reality without remainder. Horkheimer and Adorno would no doubt resist my own tactical raids on the boundaries they draw between high and low culture, on the distinction they make between the productions of the pleasure industry and the pleasure experienced in consuming those products in ways that surely were never meant. Even so, the political possibilities that emerge from the newfound sites and practices of resistance, contest, and renegotiation that accompany the contemporary refashioning of the postmodern popular and democratic subject are true to the deepest impulses of a critical theory dedicated to empowering forms of difference and resisting the power of conceptual and social conformity.[55]

55. This account and appropriation of popular democratic culture and practice draws on Paul Gilroy, *The Black Atlantic: Modernity and Double Consciousness* (Cambridge, Mass.: Harvard University Press, 1993), esp. ch. 3, "Jewels Brought from Bondage: Black Music and the Politics of Authenticity," and *Small Acts: Thoughts on the Politics of Black Cultures* (London: Serpent's Tail Press, 1993); Michel de Certeau, *The Practice of Everyday Life* (Berkeley: University of California Press, 1984); John Fiske, *Reading the Popular* (Boston: Unwin Hyman, 1989); Jean Baudrillard, *Fatal Strategies* (New York: Semiotext(e), 1990); Dick Hebdige, *Subculture: The Meaning of Style* (London: Methuen,

Horkheimer and Adorno further elaborate the dialectic between identity and difference, uniformity and individuality, with reference to what they call the system. In the tradition of the Western Enlightenment, from Descartes and Leibniz to Kant, *reason* refers to the unified organization of data: rationality requires the consistent and coherent construction of concepts. This unity, consistency, and coherence is the system. Unity resides in agreement: "The resolution of contradiction is the system *in nuce*."[56] Since there is to be complete harmony, uniformity, and homogeneity among the elements of the system, thought as such is reduced to the creation of unified, scientific order and the derivation of factual knowledge from principles. Thinking must make system and perception accord by reconciling the antagonism between the general and the particular, the concept and the facts. Just as the facts are predicted from the system, so must they also confirm it. All systems are closed and exclusionary.

Horkheimer and Adorno regard Hegel's philosophy as an example of a closed system, despite his dialectical critique of Kant. In the anticipatory identification of history and philosophy—totality in system and society—Hegel contravenes his own prohibition against making the conscious result of the whole process of negation into an absolute.[57] Nonetheless, systems interpret the world and in that regard are necessary components of our lives. They call for an orderly organization and presentation of experience, without which we could not survive. But more often than not, systems claim their concepts to be adequate to their object. They claim to have identified it fully. In systems thinking, there is a kind of paranoia to embrace the whole: a system tolerates nothing outside of itself. Fear of the unknown, of departing from the rigid organization of facts, proves to be the psychological principle behind the Enlightenment penchant for system.[58] But reality does not go into its concept without remainder. Systems inevitably enter into conflict with the "objects" they purport to grasp. The multiplicity of qualities disappears in the system, only to return later to contradict it. History defies systems, as the fate of Hegel's philosophy demonstrates

---

1979); Roland Barthes, *Mythologies* (London: Paladin, 1973); Pierre Bourdieu, *Distinction: A Social Critique of the Judgement of Taste* (Cambridge, Mass.: Harvard University Press, 1984); and Umberto Eco, *Travels in Hyperreality: Essays,* trans. William Weaver (London: Picador; New York: Harcourt, Brace, Jovanovich, 1986).

56. Horkheimer and Adorno, *Dialectic,* p. 82.

57. Ibid., p. 24.

58. Ibid., p. xiv.

and the dialectic of enlightenment attests. If history does have any unity, it is not given by any systematic construction but by suffering.[59]

Conceptual systems find their homologue in society. The tendency in contemporary social institutions toward total organization is the historical counterpart to systemic thinking; the particular is subsumed under the general concept as the individual is subsumed under the "plan." "Being is apprehended under the aspect of manufacture and administration. Everything—even the human individual, not to speak of the animal—is converted into the repeatable, replaceable process, into a mere example for the conceptual models of the system."[60] Individuals are interchangeable parts in an economic and bureaucratic apparatus bent solely on self-preservation. The difficulty is to make sense of the world of people and things while doing it the least violence, a task Sophocles' *Oedipus* dramatized in all its tragic dimensions. Horkheimer and Adorno similarly both construe and deny the kind of thinking that allowed Oedipus initially to save Thebes and subsequently to threaten it with ruin. Their alternative to systems thinking resembles what Arendt called representative thinking, the capacity to think from the standpoint of somebody else.[61] This capacity is precisely what conceptual (and social) systems deny, since they treat their constituent elements as objects rather than as subjects: "To be an object also is part of the meaning of subjectivity; but it is not equally part of the meaning of objectivity to be a subject."[62]

Systems are thus theoretical *and* political problems, which helps explain why *Dialectic* is so difficult to read, and why it has been so ruthlessly criticized as both a theoretical and political "failure." If the point is somehow to avoid the chaos that the complete absence of system induces *and* the collapse into unity and uniformity that a total system requires, then *Dialectic* pursues a number of strategies to this end. I have already mentioned how *Dialectic* consciously avoids a language that would too easily accommodate itself to current linguistic and conceptual conventions as an act of resistance against the system; how the two voices conjoined in the text practice the dialogue it recommends; how the emphasis it places on specific qualities, individual characteristics, and unique distinctions rejects the tendencies toward systematic unity

59. David Held, *Introduction to Critical Theory* (Berkeley: University of California Press, 1984), p. 216.
60. Horkheimer and Adorno, *Dialectic,* p. 84.
61. Arendt, *Eichmann in Jerusalem* (1977), p. 49.
62. Adorno, *Negative Dialectics* p. 183.

in theory and society; how the structure of the book, a whole composed of fragments, reiterates and performs the authors' concern to achieve a plurality within unity; and, finally, how, by looking to the archaic sensibility and language of tragedy, *Dialectic* finds there a source of energy to reinvigorate our theoretical and political language. In these various ways, Horkheimer and Adorno attempt to mediate the distance between two poles of an irreconcilable dialectic, between too much unity and too much diversity.

There is another way, however, in which *Dialectic* mediates between the poles of identity and difference. Earlier, I argued that the disintegrating structure of *Dialectic* reiterated its theoretical claim concerning the transition to the world of the administered life. On another level of articulation, the structural armature of the work deliberately checks its theoretical direction. *Dialectic* seems to offer a systematic or "total" critique of rationalization. Yet if rationalization, as actuality and ideology, is total, how can the authors know it? Have they not effectively conceded defeat by relinquishing the ground on which to base their claims? What critics see as a contradiction or impassable aporia in theory construction,[63] I see as a deliberate textual strategy to undermine the book's own impulse toward total critique and so avoid precisely the premature closure its critics fear. *Dialectic* offers a comprehensive critique of reason and at the same time deliberately dismantles the very theoretical totality it forwards. It is precisely the structure of the book, its disintegration into fragments, that questions its own substantive claims and opposes the impulse toward totalized critique.[64] The structure of *Dialectic* reverses the direction of its theoretical intentions by joining in opposition two ways of pursuing social critique. The disintegrating structure of the book thus reverses its theoretical claims in order to reverse the reversal of enlightenment itself.

IV

My final reason for reading the *Dialectic* in terms of Greek tragedy has to do with a set of intentions and strategies they share. I am referring

63. Jürgen Habermas, *The Theory of Communicative Action: Reason and the Rationalization of Society*, trans. Thomas McCarthy (Boston: Beacon Press, 1984); Seyla Beno habib, "Modernity and the Aporias of Critical Theory," *New German Critique* 49 (Fall 1981), and *Critique, Norm and Utopia: A Study of the Foundations of Critical Theory* (New York: Columbia University Press, 1986), pp. 147–85.

64. It is also this structure that the critics ignore when interpreting *Dialectic*.

here to the way in which both use the past in an "untimely" fashion in order to raise timely questions about the cultural and political regimes they respectively inhabit. Greek tragedy performed this critical task in at least two ways. First, it juxtaposed dramatic content to ritual context. As part of a religious festival, a tragic performance was an occasion for the city as a whole to "reconsecrate, remember and rededicate itself to sustaining its traditions of collective life."[65] Yet the content of the dramatic performances radically challenged the accepted traditions in which the ritual was embedded. Tragedy presented a world torn by conflict and contradiction. In the language of structural anthropology, all the codes—ritual, religious, sexual, familial, and political—are either inverted or violated. The acceptable relationships between parents and children, men and women, rulers and ruled, public and private, citizen and foreigner are all strained to the breaking point. Tragedy suspends the normal intelligibility of the world and so calls forth reflective questioning concerning the order that is given us and that we create.

Secondly, tragedy expressed an ambivalent and critical attitude to the city's presently constituted order through the formal structure of the performance itself, through the tension between the two elements that occupied the tragic stage. On one hand, there was the chorus, representing the collectivity of democratic citizens; on the other, opposite it, there was a legendary warrior king like Oedipus, representing the heroic and mythical past.[66] The juxtaposition of present democratic citizenship, represented by the chorus of trained citizens, and past heroic kingship, embodied in the aristocratic Oedipus, questioned present democratic achievements and past dynastic beginnings alike. A second set of oppositions also cut across the first. Where the citizen chorus chanted its songs in the archaic lyric of a past heroic age, a legendary warrior king like Oedipus spoke his lines in the contemporary idiom of Athens. Projected into the mythic past, Oedipus embodied the character and performed the deeds of a legendary king, while seeming to speak and act in the immediate present. Through such juxtaposition in the formal structure of the play, Sophocles refused to glorify the past,

65. Euben, ed., *Greek Tragedy and Political Theory,* introduction.

66. Jean-Pierre Vernant, "Tensions and Ambiguities in Greek Tragedy," in id. and Pierre Vidal-Naquet, *Myth and Tragedy in Ancient Greece,* trans. Janet Loyd (New York: Zone Books, 1980), pp. 32–33.

even as the play turned the present into a problem that the past could illuminate from within the tradition of a public festival.

Dialectic likewise suspends its readers between past and present in a way that neither glorifies the former nor reifies the latter, even as it positions itself within the tradition it criticizes. Horkheimer and Adorno juxtapose past and present, myth and enlightenment, by reading Homer's *Odyssey* as a disposition of modernity and the most recent historical developments as a return to archaic barbarism. The authors of *Dialectic* thus parallel the way in which Greek tragedy brought mythic past and enlightened present together in an uneasy unity of opposites on stage.

Horkheimer and Adorno's reading of the *Odyssey* sets out to assess the social and psychic costs of modern rationalism against the background of reason's prehistory in archaic myth: "No literary work testifies more eloquently to the interconnectedness of enlightenment and myth than Homer's which is the fundamental text of European civilization."[67] It reveals that, contrary to enlightened thinking, the opposition between myth and enlightenment is not absolute. On one hand, the epic poem is already rationalized: it bears Francis Bacon's "right mark." On the other hand, when enlightenment posits itself as the absolute other of myth, it enthrones itself as a new myth. By juxtaposing the archaic past of Homer's epic with our own modern present, *Dialectic* undermines the opposition between reason and myth and so questions our confidence in the progress of reason and the superiority of modern cultural accomplishments it brings.

In doing so, it recalls Sophocles' play and Oedipus, that other civilizing hero: on one level, the *Odyssey* is about the triumph of human skill and intellect over the dark, powerful, mythic forces that populate a hostile world. Odysseus, alone and unaided, relies solely on his native intelligence and cunning to overcome the dreadful obstacles that bar his way home, while his less enlightened companions perish. On another level, Horkheimer and Adorno read the *Odyssey* as a reflection on the highly ambivalent nature of human intellect and power. In Homer, the authors of *Dialectic* already find the entwinement of reason and myth that marks the modern structures of economic and political domination. Odysseus rules the ship on the return voyage not solely because of his superior skill but also because of his aristocratic standing. In Odys-

67. Horkheimer and Adorno, *Dialectic*, pp. 45–46.

seus, the man of reason and the king, two strands of a theory of legitimacy emerge. He grounds his rule in both unaided intellectual achievement and hereditary entitlement, in both enlightenment and myth.[68] Under pressure of circumstance, Odysseus abdicates as king in order to take the helm as a bureaucratic expert exerting political domination in the name of a rationality whose goal is self-preservation. By reason of this victory over myth, both Odysseus and modern political systems enthrone the myth of reason.[69]

The dialectic of the Homeric enlightenment reveals more than the entanglement of myth and reason. Horkheimer and Adorno read the *Odyssey* as a prehistoric portrait of modernity: the epic appears as the "historico-philosophic counterpart to the novel," and Odysseus as the "prototype of the bourgeois individual."[70] Individuation of the autonomous self and regression to undifferentiated chaos form the poles of an unreconciled dialectic. In his encounter with the Cyclopes, Odysseus must deny his identity in order to preserve it. He tricks Polyphemus by giving his name as Oudeis (Nobody), which sounds enough like Odysseus to delight the listener with a pun and simultaneously conceal and reveal the identity of the hero, who barely escapes the rocks hurled at his boat. Risk-taking, renunciation, and the sublimation of the instincts into art are further elements of bourgeois life prefigured in Odysseus's encounter with the mythic forces of nature. The principle of risk in the encounter with the Sirens allows Odysseus to listen to their deadly sweet song while his crew members close their ears. Had he not hazarded to listen, the voyage would have been safe and uneventful. But the risk Odysseus takes is a calculated one, in which he may be sure of a favorable return (in both senses of that word). The ropes that bind him to the mast also save him from the danger of mortal pleasure. The counterpart to bourgeois risk-taking is either renunciation or sublimation: renunciation because Odysseus may listen to the Sirens' song, yet as soon as pleasure appears within his grasp, the crew members secure his fetters ever more tightly, "just as later the bourgeois foregoes happiness the more tenaciously the more he realizes that his increasing power

68. Here is another instance in which a theme from *Oedipus Tyrannos* resonates with Horkheimer and Adorno's reading of Homer: we find the same confusing juxtaposition of hereditary entitlement (myth) and superior intellect (enlightenment) as grounds for political rule in Sophocles' play.

69. Lenhardt, "Wanderings of Enlightenment," p. 41.

70. Horkheimer and Adorno, *Dialectic*, p. 43.

has put it within his reach";[71] sublimation because Odysseus mediates the bodily felt tension between his desire for emancipation from the forces of nature and the urge to regress to prerational pleasure in the same way that the modern bourgeois will reconcile the antagonism between work and pleasure; that is, through the contemplation of art.[72] The episode with the Sirens gives mute testimony to the dialectic of power and impotence.

Thus far Horkheimer and Adorno have exposed self-denial, repression, and sublimation as the archaic elements in modern ego formation and individuation. They have been concerned, up to this point in the text, to analyze similarities between modern bourgeois and premodern aristocratic structures of ideology and consciousness. But that analysis makes only half their argument and tells only half their story. Despite the purging of Marxist language and categories from the final edition of *Dialectic,* the book does not wholly abandon the key categories of Marx's critical political economy. The authors understood well enough the importance of economic domination in a society organized by capitalism (whether in its liberal, monopoly, or statist phases). In fact, most of Adorno's *cultural* criticism (his musicology, for instance) aimed at decoding structures of social and economic domination congealed in various aesthetic productions. His analyses, however, did not seek to establish a causal mechanism between economy and culture. Rather, his process of decoding sought to illuminate both the content and the form of a cultural work as *homologous* to a structure of domination in society. The key concept of reification—no less operative in the present context—was Adorno's central interpretive category for understanding modern society in both its capitalist and fascist stages. It is to reification, exchange, and the commodity form to which *Dialectic* now turns in order to complete the critical juxtaposition of archaic to modern society.

At the midpoint of the excursus on Homer, therefore, lie the concepts of equivalence and commodity exchange nascent in the archaic practice of sacrifice: "While economic exchange may be viewed as a secularization of sacrifice, it is equally true that sacrifice is the magical prototype of rational exchange."[73] *Dialectic* here juxtaposes the commod-

71. Ibid., p. 34.
72. Lenhardt, "Wanderings of Enlightenment," p. 44.
73. Horkheimer and Adorno, *Dialectic,* p. 49.

ity system of present-day capitalism to the archaic practice of sacrifice in order to reveal the irrationality of the former. Odysseus proves himself capable not only of deceiving the gods about what he owes but also of intelligent bargaining to reduce his liability. "The benevolence of the deities is expected to have something to do with the *specific magnitude* of hecatombs": sacrificial offerings are not wholly exchangeable. Odysseus cunningly explores the elasticity of that magnitude, thereby releasing the price system of mythical sacrifice from its rigid structure and subjecting the mythical contract to the "forces of the market." The bourgeois principles of exploitation through substitution (equivalence) are thus already well entrenched in the mythical world of the epic. Odysseus merely enlarges the scope of those principles through deceit and enlightened bargaining, thereby "exposing the relativism inherent in the notion of equivalence" and demystifying the "natural" mechanism of exchange.[74]

The Homeric epic also enacts the transformation of sacrifice into self-sacrifice and so provides a presentient allegory of bourgeois renunciation. The sacrifice to which Odysseus subjects himself in the Sirens episode, "the denial of nature in man for the sake of domination over non-human nature and over other men,"[75] already points to the loss of freedom men and women will experience in an excessively technicized and rationalized world. Odysseus's encounter presents the paradox of triumphant reason familiar from *Oedipus:* "Man's domination over himself, which grounds his selfhood, is almost always the destruction of the subject in whose service it is undertaken; for the substance which is dominated, suppressed and dissolved by virtue of self-preservation is none other than that very life as functions of which the achievements of self-preservation find their sole definition and determination: it is, in fact, what is to be preserved."[76] Enlightenment, whether archaic or modern, turns back and in on itself in a paradoxical process of loss: the practice of self-renunciation gives away more of life than it gives back. The mastery of nature is paid for in self-repression and the repression of others: just as Oedipus virtually destroys the city he set out to liberate, and Odysseus both saves and wastes his life and the lives of his crew, so too does enlightenment threaten with destruction that which it set out to preserve.

74. Lenhardt, "Wanderings of Enlightenment," p. 47.
75. Horkheimer and Adorno, *Dialectic,* p. 54.
76. Ibid., pp. 54–55.

Throughout the first "Excursus" on the *Odyssey,* Horkheimer and Adorno juxtapose archaic elements to modern phenomena. The discovery of self-denial, repression, the sublimation of instincts, and renunciation through self-sacrifice in Homer evoke in us a highly ambivalent attitude. We cannot denounce them without denouncing ourselves, yet we surely want to disassociate ourselves from the cruelty and barbarism of the archaic past. But that is precisely what Horkheimer and Adorno will not allow. When we consider our own present, it appears as wholly barbaric and irrational as the remote past of the epic. *Dialectic* juxtaposes the archaic past to the most recent historical developments in order to show that "the social situation of modern man is strikingly dissimilar yet reminiscent of the first attempt to survive by establishing an order based on reason."[77] Their strategy thus works in two directions at once: it aims to free us from a reified present in which political and economic structures appear natural *and* it works against any nostalgic return to a falsely idealized past. Horkheimer and Adorno criticized contemporary reason as myth while they simultaneously presented historical progress as the return of the "ever-identical," as a new disposition of myth. They pointed to the most recent history (anti-Semitism, fascism, monopoly capitalism) as a regression to archaic barbarism, and interpreted the epic of the *Odyssey* as an expression of the most modern, with Odysseus as the "prototype of the bourgeois individual."

The juxtaposition of the archaic past to the events of the present is no undialectical attempt "to follow the (largely effaced) path that leads back to the origins of instrumental reason, so as to *outdo* the concept of objective reason."[78] Nor is it an attempt to construe the process of rationalization as a negative philosophy of history. Rather, Horkheimer and Adorno seek to "read an archaic image as a configuration of modernity"[79] in a way that would open up the present to critical assessment. They make the archaic appear meaningful in the light of the present, while the very newness and modernity of the present they reveal as significant in light of the archaic. Like Greek tragedy, *Dialectic* juxtaposes the moments of a seemingly overcome past to the most barbaric, most irrational phenomena of the present in order to demythologize the pres-

77. Lenhardt, "Wanderings of Enlightenment," p. 48.

78. Habermas, *Theory of Communicative Action,* 1: 382.

79. Susan Buck-Morss, *The Origins of Negative Dialectics: Theodor Adorno, Walter Benjamin and the Frankfurt Institute* (New York: Free Press, 1977), p. 59.

ent and the past's hold over it. Their juxtaposition of the archaic to the modern thus worked not to establish a historical origin for a noninstrumentalized reason, but to criticize the present through the deployment of a critical history and so undermine belief in the myth of history as progress.

V

If my presentation has been persuasive, Horkheimer and Adorno's *Dialectic of Enlightenment* exemplifies what a dialogue between Greek tragedy (and by extension the thought of the classical polis) and contemporary theory can accomplish. The authors of *Dialectic* sought "a form of linguistic expression"[80] that would resist assimilation to the systems of bureaucratic domination and economic production of late capitalism. The themes, style, and language of Greek tragedy provide the necessary point of reference for revitalizing a theoretical and political language all but completely degraded and devalued by the proliferation of method, technique, and calculative reason. *Dialectic* looks to the archaic sensibility of the tragic consciousness in its relation to myth, fate, and morality in order to locate an outside point of leverage from which to comprehend and resist the ever more tightly sealed "systems" of mass deception (the culture industry) and outright barbarism (the Holocaust). *Dialectic* thus stands to the present as Greek tragedy stood to the ancient city. It "uses" the past, Greek tragedy included, to provide us with a critical view of ourselves, much as Greek tragedy used its own past to provide the polis with a critical consideration of its own public and private life. Since Horkheimer and Adorno learn how to "use" the past from Greek tragedy, they reject the easy nostalgia of conservative cultural criticism together with its wholesale assimilation of the past to the present as a negation of the past's critical potential. Greek tragedy (and theory) can surely help to loosen the hold modern forms of life exert on us, but a return to the past is neither possible nor desirable. Like tragedy, Horkheimer's and Adorno's narrative account of atrocity offers no consolation for the entanglement of history, savagery, and civilization save the hard-won wisdom that comes through suffering. *Dialectic* heeds its own admonition that it is the duty of thinking men and women to cultivate such wisdom.

80. Horkheimer and Adorno, *Dialectic,* p. xii.

Works Cited

Adorno, Theodor W. "The Actuality of Philosophy." *Telos* 31 (Spring 1977): 120–33.

———. "The Culture Industry Reconsidered." 1964. *New German Critique* 6 (Fall 1975): 12–19.

———. *Negative Dialectics*. New York: Continuum Books, 1973.

———. *Prisms*. Translated by Samuel and Shierry Weber. Boston: MIT Press, 1981.

Adorno, Theodor W., and George Simpson. "On Popular Music." *Studies in Philosophy and Social Science* 9, 1 (special issue, 1941).

Aeschylus. *Agamemnon*. Edited by J. D. Denniston and D. L. Page. Oxford: Oxford University Press, 1957.

———. *Eumenides*. Edited by Anthony J. Podlecki. Warminster, Eng.: Aris & Phillips, 1989.

———. *Oresteia*. Edited by Denys Page. Oxford: Clarendon Press, 1972.

———. *Oresteia*. Edited by George Thomson. 2 vols. Cambridge: Cambridge University Press, 1938. Rev. ed., Amsterdam and Prague, 1966.

———. *Oresteia*. Translated by Richmond Lattimore. Vol. 1 of *The Complete Greek Tragedies*, ed. David Grene and Richmond Lattimore. Chicago: University of Chicago Press, 1953.

Andrewes, A. *The Greek Tyrants*. 1956. 4th ed. New York: Harper & Row, 1962.

Annas, Julia. *An Introduction to Plato's Republic*. Oxford: Clarendon Press, 1981.

Appadurai, Arjun. "Disjuncture and Difference in the Global Cultural Economy." In *The Phantom Public Sphere*, ed. Bruce Robbins, 269–95. Minneapolis: University of Minnesota Press, 1993.

Arendt, Hannah. *Between Past and Future*. New York: Viking Press, 1958.

———. *Eichmann in Jerusalem: A Report on the Banality of Evil.* New York: Viking Press, 1964. Reprint, Penguin Books, 1977.
———. *The Human Condition.* Chicago: University of Chicago Press, 1958.
Bamberger, L. "The Myth of Matriarchy: Why Men Rule in Primitive Society." In *Women, Culture and Society,* ed. Michelle Rosaldo and Louise Lamphere. Stanford: Stanford University Press, 1974.
Barthes, Roland. *Mythologies.* London: Paladin, 1973.
Baudrillard, Jean. *Fatal Strategies.* New York: Semiotext(e), 1990.
———. *In the Shadow of the Silent Majority.* New York: Semiotext(e), 1983.
———. "The Precession of Simulacra." In *Simulations,* pp. 1–79. New York: Semiotext(e), 1983.
Benardete, Seth. "A Reading of Sophocles' *Antigone* I." *Interpretation* 4, 3 (Spring 1975): 148–96.
———. "Sophocles' *Oedipus Tyrannos.*" In *Sophocles: A Collection of Critical Essays,* ed. Thomas Woodward. Englewood Cliffs, N.J.: Prentice-Hall, 1966.
Benhabib, Seyla. *Critique, Norm and Utopia: A Study of the Foundations of Critical Theory.* New York: Columbia University Press, 1986.
———. "Models of Public Space: Hannah Arendt, the Liberal Tradition and Jürgen Habermas." In *Habermas and the Public Sphere,* ed. Craig Calhoun, pp. 73–98. Cambridge, Mass.: MIT Press, 1992.
———. "Modernity and the Aporias of Critical Theory." *Telos* 21 (Fall 1981): 47–74.
Benjamin, Walter. *Illuminations.* Translated by Harry Zohn. Edited with an introduction by Hannah Arendt. New York: Schocken Books, 1969. Reprint, 1986.
———. *The Origin of German Tragic Drama.* Translated by John Osborne. London: NLB, 1977.
Bernal, Martin. *Black Athena: The Afroasiatic Roots of Classical Civilization.* Vol. 1. New Brunswick, N.J.: Rutgers University Press, 1987.
Bernstein, Richard, ed. *Habermas and Modernity.* Oxford: Blackwell, 1985.
Betensky, Aya. "Aeschylus' *Oresteia:* The Power of Clytemnestra." *Ramus* 7, 1 (1978): 11–25.
Blanchot, Maurice. *L'Entretien infini.* Paris: Gallimard, 1969.
Bloom, Allan. *The Republic of Plato.* New York: Basic Books, 1968.
Bluck, R. S. "Is Plato's *Republic* a Theocracy?" *Philosophical Quarterly* 5, 18 (Jan. 1955): 69–73.
Bourdieu, Pierre. *Distinction: A Social Critique of the Judgement of Taste.* Cambridge, Mass.: Harvard University Press, 1984.
Bowra, C. M. *Sophoclean Tragedy.* Oxford: Clarendon Press, 1944.
Brown, Wendy L. *Manhood and Politics: A Feminist Reading in Political Theory.* Totowa, N.J.: Rowman & Littlefield, 1988.
Buck-Morss, Susan. *The Origins of Negative Dialectics: Theodor Adorno, Walter Benjamin and the Frankfurt Institute.* New York: Free Press, 1977.
Burton, R. W. B. *The Chorus in Sophocles' Tragedies.* Oxford: Clarendon Press, 1980.

Butler, Judith. *Bodies That Matter: On the Discursive Limits of "Sex."* New York: Routledge, 1993.

Buxton, R. G. A. "Blindness and Limits: Sophokles and the Logic of Myth." *Journal of Hellenic Studies* 100 (1980): 22–37.

Cameron, Alister. *The Identity of Oedipus the King.* New York: New York University Press, 1968.

Chantraine, Pierre. *Dictionnaire etymologique de la langue grecque.* Paris: Editions Klincksieck, 1970.

Clay, Diskin. "On Reading the *Republic.*" In *Platonic Writings / Platonic Readings,* ed. Charles L. Griswold. Routledge: New York, 1988.

Connerton, Paul. *The Tragedy of Enlightenment: An Essay on the Frankfurt School.* London: Cambridge University Press, 1980.

Connolly, William. "Democracy and Territoriality." *Millenium: Journal of International Studies* 20, 3 (Winter 1991).

———. *Identity/Difference.* Ithaca, N.Y.: Cornell University Press, 1991.

———. *Politics and Ambiguity.* Madison: University of Wisconson Press, 1987.

———. *The Terms of Political Discourse.* 2d ed. Princeton, N.J.: Princeton University Press, 1983.

———. "Tocqueville, Territory and Violence." *Theory, Culture and Society* 11, 1 Feb. 1994): 19–41.

Cook, Albert. *Enactment: Greek Tragedy.* Chicago: Swallow Press, 1971.

Cornford, F. M. *The Unwritten Philosophy and Other Essays.* Cambridge: Cambridge University Press, 1950.

Cross, R. C., and A. D. Woozley. *Plato's* Republic: *A Philosophical Commentary.* New York: St. Martin's Press, 1964.

Dahl, Robert A. *Democracy and Its Critics.* New Haven, Conn.: Yale University Press, 1989.

Dawson, Michael. "A Black Counterpublic? Economic Earthquakes, Racial Agenda(s), and Black Politics." *Public Culture* 7 (1994): 195–223.

De Certeau, Michel. *The Practice of Everyday Life.* Berkeley: University of California Press, 1984.

De Magalhaes-Vilhena, V. *Socrate et la legende platonicienne.* Paris: Presses universitaires de France, 1952.

Derrida, Jacques. "Plato's Pharmacy." In *Dissemination,* trans. Barbara Johnson. Chicago: University of Chicago Press, 1981.

Dodds, E. R. "Morals and Politics in the *Oresteia.*" *Proceedings of the Cambridge Philological Society* 186, 6 (1960): 19–31.

———. "On Misunderstanding the *Oedipus Rex.*" In *Greek Tragedy: Modern Essays in Criticism,* ed. Erich Segal, pp. 177–209. New York: Harper & Row, 1983.

Dover, K. J. "The Political Aspect of Aeschylus's *Eumenides.*" *Journal of Hellenic Studies* 77, 1 (1957): 230–37.

Dubiel, Helmut. *Theory and Practice.* Cambridge, Mass.: MIT Press, 1985.

Eco, Umberto. *Travels in Hyperreality: Essays.* Translated by William Weaver. London: Picador; New York: Harcourt, Brace, Jovanovich, 1986.

Ehrenberg, Victor. *Sophocles and Pericles.* Oxford: Oxford University Press, 1954.
Eley, Geoff. "Nations, Publics and Political Cultures: Placing Habermas in the Nineteenth Century." In *Habermas and the Public Sphere,* ed. Craig Calhoun, pp. 289–339. Cambridge, Mass.: MIT Press, 1992.
Elshtain, Jean Bethke. *Public Man, Private Woman.* Princeton, N.J.: Princeton University Press, 1981.
Euben, J. Peter. "Creatures of a Day: Thought and Action in Thucydides." In *Political Theory and Praxis: New Perspectives,* ed. Terence Ball, pp. 28–56. Minneapolis: University of Minnesota Press, 1977.
———. *The Tragedy of Political Theory: The Road Not Taken.* Princeton, N.J.: Princeton University Press, 1990.
Euben, J. Peter, ed. *Greek Tragedy and Political Theory.* Berkeley: University of California Press, 1986.
Euben, J. Peter, Josiah Ober, and John Wallach, eds. *Athenian Political Thought and the Reconstruction of American Democracy.* Ithaca, N.Y.: Cornell University Press, 1994.
Ferrari, Giovanni. *Listening to the Cicadas: A Study of Plato's Phaedrus.* Cambridge: Cambridge University Press, 1987.
Festugiere, André. *Contemplation et vie contemplative selon Platon.* Paris: J. Vrin, 1936.
Finley, John H., Jr. *Pindar and Aeschylus.* Cambridge, Mass.: Harvard University Press, 1966.
Fiske, John. *Reading the Popular.* Boston: Unwin Hyman, 1989.
Foucault, Michel. *The Birth of the Clinic: An Archeology of Medical Perception.* Translated by A. M. Sheridan Smith. New York: Pantheon Books, 1973.
———. *Discipline and Punish: The Birth of the Prison.* Translated by Alan Sheridan. New York: Pantheon Books, 1977. Reprint, New York: Vintage Books, 1979.
———. "The Ethic of Care for the Self." In *The Final Foucault,* ed. James Bernauer and David Rasmussen. Cambridge, Mass.: MIT Press, 1988.
———. *The History of Sexuality.* Translated by Robert Hurley. Vol. 1. New York: Pantheon Books, 1978.
———. *Madness and Civilization: A History of Insanity in the Age of Reason.* Translated by Richard Howard. New York: Pantheon Books, 1965.
———. "Nietzsche, Genealogy, History." In *The Foucault Reader,* ed. Paul Rabinow. New York: Pantheon Books, 1984.
———. *Power/Knowledge: Selected Interviews and Other Writings, 1972–77.* Edited by Colin Gordon. New York: Pantheon Books, 1980.
———. "The Subject and Power." In *Michel Foucault: Beyond Structuralism and Hermeneutics,* ed. Hubert Dreyfus and Paul Rabinow. Chicago: University of Chicago Press, 1982.
———. *L'Usage des plaisirs.* Paris: Gallimard, 1984.
———. *The Use of Pleasure.* Translated by Robert Hurley. Vol. 2 of *The History of Sexuality.* New York: Vintage Books, 1986.
Fraser, Nancy. "Foucault on Modern Power: Empirical Insights and Normative Confusions." *Praxis International* 1 (1981).

———. "Rethinking the Public Sphere: A Contribution to the Critique of Actually Existing Democracy." *Social Text* 8, 9 (1990): 56–80.

———. "What's Critical about Critical Theory? The Case of Habermas and Gender." In *Feminism as Critique,* ed. Drucilla Cornell and Seyla Benhabib, pp. 31–56. New York: Routledge, 1990.

Friedländer, Paul. *Plato.* 3 vols. 1928–30. Translated by Hans Meyerhoff. New York: Pantheon Books, 1958. Bollingen Series, 59.

Friedman, George. *The Political Philosophy of the Frankfurt School.* Ithaca, N.Y.: Cornell University Press, 1981.

Frisk, Hjalmar. *Griechisches Etymologisches Wörterbuch.* Heidelberg: C. Winter, 1960.

Gadamer, Hans-Georg. *Dialogue and Dialectic: Eight Hermeneutical Studies on Plato.* Translated by Christopher P. Smith. New Haven, Conn.: Yale University Press, 1980.

Gagarin, Michael. *Aeschylean Drama.* Berkeley: University of California Press, 1976.

Gaisford, Thomas, ed. *Etymologicum Magnum.* 1848. Amsterdam: Adolf M. Hakkert, 1967.

Gandesha, Samir. "The Theatre of the 'Other': Adorno, Poststructuralism and the Critique of Identity." In *Philosophy and Social Criticism* 17, 3 (1991): 243–63.

Gardiner, C. P. *The Sophoclean Chorus.* Iowa City: University of Iowa Press, 1987.

Gilroy, Paul. *The Black Atlantic: Modernity and Double Consciousness.* Cambridge, Mass.: Harvard University Press, 1993.

———. *Small Acts: Thoughts on the Politics of Black Cultures.* London: Serpent's Tail Press, 1993.

Goheen, R. F. *The Imagery of Sophocles' Antigone: A Study of Poetic Language and Structure.* Princeton, N.J.: Princeton University Press, 1951.

Goldhill, Simon. *Aeschylus: The Oresteia.* Cambridge: Cambridge University Press, 1992.

———. *Language, Sexuality, Narrative: The Oresteia.* Cambridge: Cambridge University Press, 1984.

———. *Reading Greek Tragedy.* Cambridge: Cambridge University Press, 1986.

Grene, David, and Richmond Lattimore, eds. *The Complete Greek Tragedies,* vol. 1: *Sophocles.* Chicago: University of Chicago Press, 1991.

Griswold, Charles L., ed. *Platonic Writings / Platonic Readings.* New York: Routledge, 1988.

Guthrie, W. K. C. *Plato: The Man and His Dialogues.* Vol. 4 of *A History of Greek Philosophy.* Cambridge: Cambridge University Press, 1975.

Habermas, Jürgen. *Communication and the Evolution of Society.* Translated by Thomas McCarthy. Boston: Beacon Press, 1979.

———. "The Entwinement of Myth and Enlightenment: Rereading *Dialectic of Enlightenment.*" *New German Critique* 26 (Spring/Summer 1982). Republished in *The Philosophical Discourse of Modernity: Twelve Lectures,* trans. Frederick G. Lawrence. Cambridge, Mass.: MIT Press, 1987.

———. "Geschichte und Evolution." In *Zur Rekonstruktion des Historischen Materialismus*. Frankfurt: Suhrkamp, 1976.

———. *Knowledge and Human Interests*. Translated by Jeremy J. Shapiro. Boston: Beacon Press, 1971.

———. "Modernity vs. Postmodernity." *New German Critique* 22 (Winter 1981): 3–14.

———. *Moral Consciousness and Communicative Action*. Translated by C. Lenhardt and S. Nicholsen. Cambridge, Mass.: MIT Press, 1990.

———. "On Leveling the Genre Distinction between Philosophy and Rhetoric." In *The Philosophical Discourse of Modernity: Twelve Lectures*, trans. Frederick G. Lawrence, pp. 185–210. Cambridge, Mass.: MIT Press, 1987.

———. *The Philosophical Discourse of Modernity: Twelve Lectures*. Translated by Frederick G. Lawrence. Cambridge, Mass.: MIT Press, 1987.

———. *Theory and Practice*. Translated by John Viertel. Boston: Beacon Press, 1973.

———. *The Theory of Communicative Action: Reason and the Rationalization of Society*. Vol. 2, *Lifeworld and System: A Critique of Functionalist Reason*. Translated by Thomas McCarthy. Boston: Beacon Press, 1984, 1987.

———. *Toward a Rational Society: Student Protest, Science, and Politics*. Translated by Jeremy J. Shapiro. Boston: Beacon Press, 1970.

Hall, Dale. "The Republic and the Limits of Politics." *Political Theory* 5, 3 (Aug. 1977).

Hartsock, Nancy C. M. *Money, Sex, and Power: Toward a Feminist Historical Materialism*. New York: Longman, 1983.

Hayek, Friedrich August von. *The Road to Serfdom*. Chicago: University of Chicago Press, 1944.

Hebdige, Dick. *Subculture: The Meaning of Style*. London: Methuen, 1979.

Heidegger, Martin. *Being and Time*. Translated by John Macquarrie and Edward Robinson. New York: Harper, 1962.

Held, David. *Introduction to Critical Theory*. Berkeley: University of California Press, 1984.

Helmbold, W. C. "The Paradox of Oedipus" *American Journal of Philology* 72, 3 (1951): 293–300.

Hermassi, Karen. *Polity and Theatre in Historical Perspective*. Berkeley: University of California Press, 1977.

Holmes, Stephen T. "Aristippus in and out of Athens." *American Political Science Review* 73, 1 (Mar. 1979): 113–27.

Honig, Bonnie. "Arendt, Identity and Difference." *Political Theory* 16, no 1 (Feb. 1988): 77–98.

———. *Political Theory and the Displacement of Politics*. Ithaca, N.Y.: Cornell University Press, 1993.

———. "Toward an Agonistic Feminism." In *Feminists Theorize the Political*, ed. Judith Butler and Joan Scott, pp. 215–35. New York: Routledge, 1992.

Horkheimer, Max. *Critical Theory: Selected Essays*. Translated by Matthew J. O'Connell et al. New York: Herder and Herder, 1972.

Horkheimer, Max, and Theodor W. Adorno. *Dialectic of Enlightenment*. Translated by John Cumming. New York: Continuum Books, 1969.

Hoy, David C. "Foucault: Modern or Postmodern?" In *After Foucault: Humanistic Knowledge, Postmodern Challenges,* ed. Jonathan Arac, 12–41. New Brunswick, N.J.: Rutgers University Press, 1988.

Hoy, David C., and Thomas McCarthy. *Critical Theory.* Cambridge, Mass.: Blackwell, 1994.

Ignatieff, Michael. *The Needs of Strangers.* New York: Viking Press, 1984.

Irwin, T. H. *Plato's Moral Theory.* Oxford: Oxford University Press, 1977.

Jacques, J. H. *Plato's "Republic": A Beginner's Guide.* Derby, Eng.: Citadel Press; London: Tom Stacey, 1971.

Jaeger, Werner. *Paideia: The Ideals of Greek Culture.* Vol. 2. New York: Oxford University Press, 1943.

Jameson, Fredric. "Postmodernism, or, The Cultural Logic of Late Capitalism." *New Left Review* 146 (July/Aug. 1984): 53–92.

Jay, Martin. "Habermas and Modernism." *Praxis International* 4 (1984)

———. *Marxism and Totality: The Adventures of a Concept from Lukács to Habermas.* Berkeley: University of California Press, 1984.

———. *Permanent Exiles: Essays on the Intellectual Migration from Germany to America.* New York: Columbia University Press, 1986.

Jones, John. *On Aristotle and Greek Tragedy.* London: Chatto & Windus, 1962.

Jones, Leslie Ann. "The Role of Ephialtes in the Rise of Athenian Democracy." *Classical Antiquity* 6, 1 (Apr. 1987): 53–76.

Kahn, Charles. "Dialogue and Dialectic in Plato's Gorgias." In *Oxford Studies in Ancient Philosophy,* vol. 1, ed. Julia Annas. Oxford: Clarendon Press, 1983.

———. "Did Plato Write Socratic Dialogues?" In *Essays on the Philosophy of Socrates,* ed. Hugh H. Benson. New York: Oxford University Press, 1992.

Kellner, Douglas. "Critical Theory Today: Revisiting the Classics." *Theory, Culture and Society* 10, 2 (May 1993): 43–60.

Kirkwood, G. M. *Sophoclean Drama.* Ithaca, N.Y.: Cornell University Press, 1957.

Kitto, H. D. F. *Form and Meaning in Greek Drama.* London: Methuen, 1956.

———. *Greek Tragedy: A Literary Study.* 1961. 5th ed. London: Methuen, 1978.

———. *Sophocles, Dramatist and Philosopher.* Westport, Conn.: Greenwood Press, 1981.

Klein, Jacob. *A Commentary on Plato's Meno.* Chapel Hill: University of North Carolina Press, 1965.

Knox, Bernard. *The Heroic Temper: Studies in Sophoclean Tragedy.* Berkeley: University of California Press, 1964.

———. *Oedipus at Thebes.* New Haven, Conn.: Yale University Press, 1957.

Landes, Joan. *Women and the Public Sphere in the Age of the French Revolution.* Ithaca, N.Y.: Cornell University Press, 1988.

Lane, Warren, and Ann Lane. "Athenian Political Thought and the Feminist Politics of Poiesis and Praxis." In *Athenian Political Thought and the Reconstruction of American Democracy,* ed. J. Peter Euben, Josiah Ober, and John Wallach, pp. 265–88. Ithaca, N.Y.: Cornell University Press, 1994.

Lash, Scott, and John Urry. *The End of Organized Capitalism.* Madison, University of Wisconsin Press, 1987.

Lebeck, Anne. *The Oresteia: A Study in Language and Structure.* Cambridge, Mass.: Harvard University Press, 1971.

Lefort, Claude. *Democracy and Political Theory.* Translated by David Marcy. Minneapolis: University of Minnesota Pess, 1988.

Lenhardt, Christian. "The Wanderings of Enlightenment." In *On Critical Theory,* ed. John O'Neill, pp. 52–53. New York: Seabury Press, 1976.

Lesky, A. *Greek Tragic Poetry.* Translated by M. Dillon. New Haven, Conn.: Yale University Press, 1983.

Liddell, H. G., Robert Scott, H. S. Jones, and Roderick McKenzie. *A Greek-English Lexicon.* Oxford: Clarendon Press, 1961.

Lloyd-Jones, Hugh. *The Justice of Zeus.* 1971. 2d ed. Berkeley: University of California Press, 1983.

Love, Nancy S. "Epistemology and Exchange: Marx, Nietzsche and Critical Theory." *New German Critique* 41 (Spring/Summer 1987).

———. *Marx, Nietzsche and Modernity.* New York: Columbia University Press, 1986.

Lukács, György. *History and Class Consciousness: Studies in Marxist Dialectics.* Translated by Rodney Livingstone. Cambridge, Mass.: MIT Press, 1971.

Lyotard, Jean-François, and Jean-Loup Thébaud. *Just Gaming.* Translated by Wlad Godzich. Minneapolis: University of Minnesota Press, 1985.

———. *The Postmodern Condition: A Report on Knowledge.* Translated by Geoff Bennington and Brian Massumi. Minneapolis: University of Minnesota Press, 1984.

Macleod, C. W. "Politics and the *Oresteia.*" *Journal of Hellenic Studies* 102 (1982): 124–44.

Marx, Karl, and Friedrich Engels. *The Marx-Engels Reader.* Edited by Robert C. Tucker. 2d ed. New York: Norton, 1978.

McKim, Richard. "Shame and Truth in Plato's *Gorgias.*" In *Platonic Writings / Platonic Readings,* ed. Charles L. Griswold, pp. 34–48. New York: Routledge, 1988.

Meier, Christian. *The Greek Discovery of Politics.* Cambridge, Mass: Harvard University Press, 1990.

Miller, James. "Some Implications of Nietzsche's Thought for Marxism." *Telos* 37 (Fall 1978): 22–41.

Millett, Kate. *Sexual Politics.* Garden City, N.Y.: Doubleday, 1971.

Mouffe, Chantal. "Democratic Citizenship and the Political Community." In *Feminists Theorize the Political,* ed. Judith Butler and Joan Scott. New York: Routledge, 1992.

———. ed. *Dimensions of Radical Democracy.* New York: Verso, 1992.

Nägele, Rainer. "Freud, Habermas and the Dialectic of Enlightenment: On Real and Ideal Discourse." *New German Critique* 22 (Winter 1981): 41–62.

Nichols, Mary P. "The *Republic*'s Two Alternatives: Philosopher-Kings and Socrates." *Political Theory* 12, 2 (May 1984): 252–74.

———. *Socrates and the Political Community: An Ancient Debate.* Albany, N.Y.: State University of New York Press, 1987.
Nietzsche, Friedrich. *The Genealogy of Morals.* 1887. New York: Modern Library, 1918.
———. "On the Uses and Disadvantages of History for Life." 1874. In *Untimely Meditations,* trans. R. J. Hollingdale. Cambridge: Routledge & Kegan Paul, 1983.
———. *The Twilight of the Idols.* 1889. Translated by R. J. Hollingdale. New York: Penguin Books, 1969.
———. *The Will to Power.* 1906. Translated by Walter Kaufmann and R. J. Hollingdale. New York: Vintage Books, 1968.
Nightingale, Andrea. "Plato's *Gorgias* and Euripides' *Antiope:* A Study in Generic Transformation." *Classical Antiquity* 11, 1 (Apr. 1992): 121–41.
Norton, Anne. *Republic of Signs: Liberal Theory and American Popular Culture.* Chicago: University of Chicago Press, 1993.
Nussbaum, Martha. *The Fragility of Goodness: Luck and Ethics in Greek Literature and Philosophy.* Cambridge: University of Cambridge Press, 1986.
O'Brien, Mary. *The Politics of Reproduction.* Boston: Routledge & Kegan Paul, 1981.
Okin, Susan. *Women in Western Political Thought.* Princeton, N.J.: Princeton University Press, 1979.
Ostwald, Martin. *From Popular Sovereignty to the Sovereignty of Law: Law, Society and Politics in Fifth-Century Athens.* Berkeley: University of California Press, 1986.
Patterson, Orlando. *Freedom,* vol 1: *Freedom in the Making of Western Culture.* New York: Basic Books, 1991.
Peradotto, John. *Man in the Middle Voice: Name and Narration in the Odyssey.* Princeton, N.J.: Princeton University Press, 1990.
Peterson Richard. *Democratic Philosophy and the Politics of Knowledge.* University Park: Pennsylvania State University Press, 1996.
Pickard-Cambridge, A. *The Dramatic Festivals of Athens.* 2d ed. Oxford: Oxford University Press, 1968.
Pitkin, Hanna. "Justice: On Relating Public and Private." *Political Theory* 9, 3 (Aug. 1981): 303–26.
Plass, Paul. "Philosophical Anonymity and Irony in the Platonic Dialogues." *American Journal of Philology* 85, 3 (1964): 254–78.
Plato. *Gorgias: A Revised Text with Introduction and Commentary.* Translated and edited by E. R. Dodds. Oxford: Clarendon Press, 1959.
———. *Gorgias.* Translated by Terence Irwin. Oxford: Clarendon Press, 1979.
———. *Platonis Opera.* Edited by John Burnet. 1902. Oxford: Clarendon Press, 1962.
Podlecki, Anthony J. *The Political Background of Aeschylean Tragedy.* Ann Arbor: University of Michigan Press, 1966.
Pohlenz, Max. *Aus Platos Werdezeit: Philologische Untersuchungen.* Berlin: Weidmann, 1913.

Pomeroy, Sarah B. *Goddesses, Whores, Wives, and Slaves: Women in Classical Antiquity.* New York: Schocken Books, 1975.
Popper, Karl. *The Open Society and Its Enemies,* vol 1: *The Spell of Plato.* 1949. 5th ed. Princeton, N.J.: Princeton University Press, 1966.
Poster, Mark. *Critical Theory and Poststructuralism.* Ithaca, N.Y.: Cornell University Press, 1989.
Pütz, Peter. "Nietzsche and Critical Theory." *Telos* 50 (Winter 1981–82).
Rabinowitz, Nancy. "From Force to Persuasion: Aeschylus' *Oresteia* as Cosmogonic Myth." *Ramus* 10, 2 (1981): 159–91.
Randall, J. H. *Plato: Dramatist of the Life of Reason.* New York: Columbia University Press, 1970.
Reinhardt, Mark. *The Art of Being Free.* Ithaca, N.Y.: Cornell University Press, 1997.
Reiss, Timothy J. *Tragedy and Truth: Studies in the Development of a Renaissance and Neoclassical Discourse.* New Haven, Conn.: Yale University Press, 1980.
Robbins, Bruce, ed. *The Phantom Public Sphere.* Minneapolis: University of Minnesota Press, 1993.
Roberts, Deborah. *Apollo and His Oracle in the Oresteia.* Göttingen: Vandenhoeck & Ruprecht, 1984.
Rocco, Christopher. "Between Modernity and Postmodernity." *Political Theory* 22, 1 (Feb. 1994): 71–97.
Rose, Gillian. *The Melancholy Science: An Introduction to the Thought of Theodor Adorno.* New York: Columbia University Press, 1978.
Ryan, Mary P. *Women in Public: Between Banners and Ballots, 1825–1880.* Baltimore: Johns Hopkins University Press, 1990.
Sallis, John. *Being and Logos: The Way of the Platonic Dialogue.* Pittsburgh, Pa.: Duquesne University Press, 1975.
Saxonhouse, Arlene. "The Philosophy of the Particular and the Universality of the City: Socrates' Education of Euthyphro." *Political Theory* 16, 2 (May 1988).
———. "The Tyranny of Reason in the World of the Polis." *American Political Science Review* 82, 4 (Dec. 1988): 1261–75.
———. "An Unspoken Theme in Plato's *Gorgias:* War." *Interpretation* 11, 2 (May 1983): 142–44.
Scodel, Ruth. *Sophocles.* Boston: Twayne, 1984.
Seale, David. *Vision and Stagecraft in Sophocles.* Chicago: University of Chicago Press, 1982.
Segal, Charles P. "Greek Tragedy and Society: A Structuralist Perspective." In id., *Interpreting Greek Tragedy: Myth, Poetry, Text.* Ithaca, N.Y.: Cornell University Press, 1986.
———. "The Music of the Sphinx." In *Contemporary Literary Hermeneutics and Interpretation of Classical Texts,* ed. Stephanus Kresic. Ottawa: Ottawa University Press, 1981.
———. "Sophocles' Praise of Man and the Conflicts of the *Antigone.*" *Arion* 3, 2 (Summer 1964): 46–66.

———. "Sophocles." In *Ancient Writers: Greece and Rome.* New York: Charles Scribner's Sons, 1982.

———. "Time, Theater, and Knowledge in the Tragedy of Oedipus." In *Edipo: Il teatro greco e la cultura europea,* ed. Bruno Gentili and Roberto Pretagostini. Quaderni urbinati di cultura classica: Atti del convegno internazionale, 3. Rome: Edizioni dell'Ateneo, 1986.

———. *Tragedy and Civilization: An Interpretation of Sophocles.* Cambridge, Mass.: Harvard University Press, 1981.

Sesonske, Alexander. *Plato's Republic: Interpretation and Criticism.* Belmont Calif.: Wadsworth Publishing, 1966.

Sheppard, J. T. *The Wisdom of Sophocles.* London: G. Allen & Unwin, 1947.

Shorey, Paul. *What Plato Said.* Chicago: University of Chicago Press, 1933.

Slater, P. E. *The Glory of Hera: Greek Mythology and the Greek Family.* Boston: Beacon Press, 1968.

Snell, Bruno. *The Discovery of the Mind: The Greek Origins of European Thought.* Translated by T. G. Rosenmeyer. 1953. New York: Dover, 1982.

Sophocles. *The Oedipus Tyrannus.* Edited by M. L. Earle. New York: American Book Co., 1901.

———. *The Oedipus Tyrannus.* Edited by R. C. Jebb. Cambridge: Cambridge University Press, 1897.

Springborg, Patricia. "Hannah Arendt and the Classical Republican Tradition." In *Thinking, Judging, Freedom,* ed. G. T. Kaplan and C. S. Kessler, pp. 9–17. Sydney: G. Allen & Unwin, 1989.

Strauss, Leo. *The City and Man.* New York: Rand McNally, 1964.

Taplin, Oliver. "Emotion and Meaning in Greek Tragedy." In *Greek Tragedy: Modern Essays in Criticism,* ed. Erich Segal. New York: Harper & Row, 1983.

Taylor, A. E. *Plato: The Man and His Work.* 1926. 3d ed. New York: Dial Press, 1929.

Thomson, George. *Aeschylus and Athens.* New York: International Publishers, 1950.

Tonelli, Franco. *Sophocles' Oedipus and the Tale of the Theatre.* Ravenna: Longo Editore, 1983.

Vernant, Jean-Pierre. "Greek Tragedy: Problems of Interpretation." In *Language of Criticism and the Sciences of Man,* ed. Richard Macksey and Eugene Donato. Baltimore: Johns Hopkins Press, 1970.

———. "Tensions and Ambiguities in Greek Tragedy." In J.-P. Vernant and Pierre Vidal-Naquet, *Myth and Tragedy in Ancient Greece,* trans. Janet Lloyd. New York: Zone Books, 1980.

Vernant, Jean-Pierre, and Pierre Vidal-Naquet. *Myth and Tragedy in Ancient Greece.* Translated by Janet Lloyd. New York: Zone Books, 1980.

Versenyi, Laszlo. *Man's Measure: A Study of the Greek Image of Man from Homer to Sophocles.* Albany: State University of New York Press, 1974.

Vickers, Brian. *Towards Greek Tragedy: Drama, Myth, Society.* 1973. New York: Longman, 1979.

Villa, Dana. "Postmodernism and the Public Sphere." *American Political Science Review* 86, 3 (Sept. 1992): 712–21.
Virilio, Paul. *The Lost Dimension.* New York: Semiotext(e), 1991.
Voegelin, Eric. *Plato and Aristotle,* vol. 2: *Order and History.* Baton Rouge: Louisiana State University Press, 1957.
Waldock, A. J. A. *Sophocles the Dramatist.* Cambridge: Cambridge University Press, 1951.
Warner, Michael. "The Mass Public and the Mass Subject." In *The Phantom Public Sphere,* ed. Bruce Robbins, pp, 234–56. Minneapolis: University of Minnesota Press, 1993.
Whitebrook, Joel. "The Politics of Redemption." *Telos* 63 (Spring 1985).
Whitehead, Alfred North. *Process and Reality: An Essay in Cosmology.* Edited by D. R. Griffin and D. W. Sherburne. New York: Free Press, 1978.
Whitman, Cedric. *The Heroic Paradox: Essays on Homer, Sophocles and Aristophanes.* Ithaca, N.Y.: Cornell University Press, 1980.
Wilamowitz-Moellendorf, Ulrich von. *Platon: Sein Leben und seine Werke.* 2 vols. 1919. 3d ed., Berlin: Weidmann, 1959–62.
Williams, Bernard. *Shame and Necessity.* Berkeley: University of California Press, 1993.
Winnington-Ingram, R. P. *Sophocles: An Interpretation.* Cambridge: Cambridge University Press, 1980.
———. *Studies in Aeschylus.* Cambridge: Cambridge University Press, 1983.
Wiser, James L. "The Force of Reason: On Reading Plato's *Gorgias.*" In *The Ethical Dimension of Political Life: Essays in Honor of John H. Hallowell,* ed. Francis Canavan. Durham, N.C.: Duke University Press, 1983.
Wolin, Sheldon. "Democracy and the Welfare State: Theoretical Connections between *Staatsräson* and *Wohlfahrtstaaträson.*" In *The Presence of the Past: Essays on the State and the Constitution,* pp. 151–79. Baltimore: Johns Hopkins University Press, 1989.
———. "Democracy in the Discourse of Postmodernism." *Social Research* 57, 1 (1990): 5–30.
———. "Political Theory as a Vocation." *American Political Science Review* 63, 4 (Dec. 1969): 1062–82.
———. *Politics and Vision: Continuity and Innovation in Western Political Thought.* Boston: Little, Brown, 1961.
Yeatman, Anna. "Beyond Natural Right: The Conditions for Universal Citizenship." *Social Concept* 4, 2 (June 1988): 3–32.
Zeitlin, Froma I. "The Dynamics of Misogyny: Myth and Mythmaking in the *Oresteia.*" *Arethusa* 11, 1–2 (Spring/Fall 1978): 149–81.
———. "Playing the Other: Theater, Theatricality and the Feminine in Greek Drama." In *Nothing to Do with Dionysus? Athenian Drama in Its Social Context,* ed. John A. Winkler and Froma I. Zeitlin, pp. 63–95. Princeton, N.J.: Princeton University Press, 1990.
———. "Thebes: Theater of Self and Society in Athenian Drama." In *Greek*

Tragedy and Political Theory, ed. J. Peter Euben, pp. 101–41. Berkeley: University of California Press, 1986.

———. "Thebes: Theater of Self and Society in Athenian Drama." In *Nothing to Do with Dionysus? Athenian Drama in Its Social Context,* ed. John A. Winkler and Froma I. Zeitlin, pp. 130–67. Princeton, N.J.: Princeton University Press: 1990.

Index

Designer: Ina Clausen
Compositor: J. Jarrett Engineering, Inc.
Text: 10/13 Sabon
Display: Sabon
Printer: Thomson-Shore, Inc.
Binder: Thomson-Shore, Inc.